Ocean Resources and U.S. Intergovernmental Relations in the 1980s

About the Book and Editor

This book examines the U.S. system of intergovernmental relations as they pertain to ocean resources. The exploitation of the oceans, with regard to fisheries, marine mammals, hydrocarbons and economic minerals, waste disposal, and coastal zone management, is analyzed in the context of the Reagan Administration's New Federalism. The contributors document the relationships between the various levels of government (federal, state, and local) that are involved in ocean resource management and explore the problems associated with the use of specific resources. They suggest reasons as to why no single pattern of governmental guidelines for dealing with the oceans has emerged during the Reagan years and discuss how existing federal systems might be altered to improve the management and conservation of ocean resources.

Maynard Silva is a research specialist with the Marine Policy and Ocean Management Center, Woods Hole Oceanographic Institution.

Ocean Resources and U.S. Intergovernmental Relations in the 1980s

edited by Maynard Silva

Routledge
Taylor & Francis Group

NEW YORK AND LONDON

First published 1986 by Westview Press, Inc.

Published 2021 by Routledge
605 Third Avenue, New York, NY 10017
2 Park Square, Milton Park, Abingdon, Oxon OX14 4RN

Routledge is an imprint of the Taylor & Francis Group, an informa business

Library of Congress Catalog Card Number: 86-51019

ISBN 13: 978-0-3670-0876-5 (hbk)
ISBN 13: 978-0-3671-5863-7 (pbk)

Printed in the United Kingdom
by Henry Ling Limited

Contents

viii

Preface

The chapters in this volume represent revised
versions of papers presented at a workshop, "Ocean
Resources and Intergovernmental Relations in the 1980s,"
held in September of 1985. Specifically, they examine the
roles of the federal, state, and local governments of the
United States in the management of ocean and coastal
resources. The workshop was sponsored by the Marine
Policy and Ocean Management Center of the Woods Hole
Oceanographic Institution with funding from the J. N. Pew,
Jr., Charitable Trust.

The impetus for the workshop came from two
presentations at very different fora. The first was a
1982 conference sponsored by the University of Rhode
Island's Center for Ocean Management Studies. The general
consensus of that workshop was that the Reagan
Administration was fulfilling his campaign promise to
replace the existing system of intergovernmental
relations, or federalism, with a "new federalism." This
new federalism would include the curbing of federal
government expansion, returning powers and substantial
responsibilities to the states and redirecting government
revenues from the federal to the state level.
Additionally, it was felt that these systemic changes
would necessarily effect the intergovernmental management
of coastal and ocean resources.

The second forum was a roundtable on the "Reagan
Federalism" conducted at the 1984 annual meeting of the
American Political Science Association. Political
scientists being a contentious lot, it would be difficult
to say that a consensus emerged. However, the position of
the plurality seemed to be that, yes, there had been some
changes in the U.S. system of intergovernmental relations

(IGR). <u>But</u> those changes could not be claimed to indicate
a metamorphosis. In fact, much of the IGR system in place
on Reagan's 1981 inauguration was still in place and
functioning much as it had under Carter and other recent
presidents.

These somewhat opposed views (i.e., much had
changed vs. not much had changed), suggested to this
writer that it was perhaps an appropriate time for a
thorough appraisal of the system of intergovernmental
relations in place for the management of U.S. ocean and
coastal resources and activities. To this end, the above-
mentioned workshop was organized and the papers which now
comprise this volume were commissioned. Each of the
authors was asked to consider questions such as: Has the
Reagan Administration affected the system of IGR for ocean
and coastal resources? For all, or only for some of those
resources? Where they exist, what are the differences?
Can we say that a new system of ocean federalism has
emerged during the Reagan years?

The first three chapters are provided as background
to help in the appraisal of the Reagan Administration's
influence. Anton reviews the variety of models that have
been suggested for the U.S. system generally. Bradley and
Ingram analyze the intergovernmental arrangements that
exist for other natural resources. Silva and King provide
a record of intergovernmental relations and ocean
resources through 1980.

The next five chapters look at specific examples of
intergovernmental arrangements for the management of ocean
resources. Rieser examines marine fisheries. Kellert's
chapter addresses the issue of marine mammals. The system
of intergovernmental relations for outer continental shelf
oil and gas resources (and by extension hard minerals) is
explored by Hildreth. Lester and Hamilton review the
related cases of ocean dumping and at-sea incineration of
hazardous waste. Hershman broadly considers the activity
of coastal zone management.

The final two chapters are offered both as summary
statements and as indications of what can be expected
in the future. Cicin-Sain provides an explanation of why
each ocean and coastal resource or activity has a
different pattern of intergovernmental relations. Knecht
concludes the volume with thoughts on how the roles of
local, state, and federal government can be changed to
improve the management of U.S. resources in the 1980s and
into the future.

In addition to the authors , I would like to thank the other participants of the workshop. Their comments and observations made the workshop and this volume qualitatively better. They were Robert Bowen, Gary Brewer, Charles F. Broches, Paul M. Fye, Timothy Hennessey, Patricia Hughes, William Lahey, Kem Lowry, Richard Schaefer, and Whitney Tilt.

Gratitude should also be expressed to Ellen Gately, Judy Fenwick, Rosamund Ladner, and Ethel Le Fave for their behind-the-scenes efforts at the workshop. This volume could not have been completed without the editorial assistance of Judy Fenwick and the word processing skills of Ellen Gately.

Final thanks must be given to the past and current directors of the Marine Policy and Ocean Management Center, David A. Ross and James Broadus, respectively.

Maynard Silva

1

Models of American Intergovernmental Relations

Thomas J. Anton

For many years, students of American federalism have
struggled to develop parsimonious explanations for the
joint activities of local, state, and national
governments. To say that the struggle has been successful
would be far too generous; our efforts continue to be
confounded by the enormous variety and complexity of
American politics. Nonetheless, I think it fair to say
that we mave made significant progress. Although a
dominant conceptual paradigm has not emerged, nor is a
single paradigm likely to become dominant, we have begun
to clarify major alternative approaches, and we are doing
a great deal more systematic work designed to clarify
these approaches. In this chapter I attempt to document
these assertions by reviewing several important conceptual
models of American federalism now in use. These models, I
will suggest, reflect the legal and cultural context
within which the political issue of federalism is
debated. I will also suggest that they reflect
considerable improvement in our ability to move beyond
confusion to an appreciation of intergovernmental
political behavior.

The Federal Context

Federalism may be thought of as a system of rules for
the division of public policy responsibility among a
number of autonomous governmental agencies. These rules
define the scope of authority available to the autonomous
agencies--who can do what--and they provide a framework to
govern relationships between agencies. The agencies

1

remain autonomous, but they are also linked together by rules that govern their common activities.[1]

Since all modern states include a large number of government agencies, it is perfectly legitimate to ask what differentiates federal systems from others. Even highly centralized governing systems, officially controlled by a single executive or a tiny committee, find it necessary to diffuse some authority to other agencies, particularly if public responsibility extends over a large physical territory. Once diffused, the pieces of authority available to other, noncentral, agencies allow them to act autonomously in many situations, regardless of the formal degree of system centralization.[2] Similarly, states referred to as "unitary" typically operate with rules that assign formal responsibilities to a variety of subnational governments, as well as the central state agencies.[3] How is federalism different?

The formal answer lies in the degree of autonomy available to the constituent units. In principle, federal systems allocate broad powers to all units, each of which can act in these broad areas without gaining approval from any other unit. All constituent units, furthermore, have a guarantee of continued existence so long as the system exists because they are the system. Neither of these conditions prevails in unitary or centralized states. The pieces of authority available to subnational units in such systems typically are very carefully and narrowly constrained, rather than broadly defined, and even these constrained responsibilities are subject to change or even elimination by the central government. Central government actions in unitary systems can often be quite remarkable. In Sweden, for example, legislation initiated by the governing political party led to elimination of 90% of all local governments between 1952 and 1975, despite a thousand-year tradition of strong local governance.[4] A change of that magnitude, initiated by national officials, would be simply unthinkable in the American context.

A more behavioral answer is that federal systems define a broader base of political participation than unitary states. The distribution of authority among multiple units provides multiple arenas for the exercise of responsibility and thus multiple opportunities for political participation. Broad definition of responsibilities, furthermore, implies that large numbers of individuals will be motivated to participate, since they will have some real interest in government action. When constituent units enjoy substantial autonomy, no

central action is required to initiate the agitation and
resolution of issues within the domain of each unit.
Instead, unit members are free to pursue those issues with
as much energy as they can muster. Providing arenas for
political action within, as well as among, constituent
units, in short, structures a federal bias in favor of
more rather than less political participation.

The participatory bias of federalism is certainly
evident in the United States, where federalism has helped
to produce the most "governed" nation in the world--at
last count more than 82,000 separate units of government
were in existence (Bureau of the Census 1985). Fifty
states, whose autonomy and continued existence are
guaranteed by the Constitution, are active in a broad
range of policy areas, and continue to expand their areas
of responsibility through innovative actions in highway
safety (seatbelt laws), environmental protection (bottle
bills), or jobs (economic development programs).[5] Each
state has created its own legal and administrative system,
giving the nation as a whole some 41,000 local and county
governments, another 26,000 special districts, and more
than 15,000 school districts. Except for 12,000 special
districts, each of these units has taxing power, its own
officials, and authority to act on behalf of some defined
public. More importantly, nearly 500,000 elected
officials work with more than 13 million appointed
officials in performing these state and local
responsibilities (Bureau of the Census 1985). When the
President and Vice President, members of Congress, and the
2,800,000 civilian employees of the national government
are added to this list, it becomes even more apparent that
federal government in the United States is an important
participatory sport.

No sport could be quite so popular unless it reflected
widely shared values. One supportive value in the
American context is that citizen participation in public
affairs is a major personal and civic virtue.
Demonstrating that virtue requires opportunities to define
and debate matters of "public" concern--hence the large
number of governments whose presence guarantees that
opportunities for participation will be regular and
plentiful. It is also important to remember that the
historic American fear of centralized authority remains
alive and well, sustained by generations of politicians
and civic leaders who have repeatedly preached the virtues
of small government, carefully controlled by an informed
and participating citizenry. From this point of view, the

existence of many governments is a guarantee against
excessive power exercised by a single agency. Americans,
in short, believe in the value of participation but they
do not want too much government. The paradoxical result
is a system with a great deal of government, cut up into
so many small pieces that no one piece can easily achieve
any objective other than providing opportunities for
citizen participation.[6]

Apart from its emphasis on participation, perhaps the
most distinctive aspect of American federalism is its
structural ambiguity. As suggested earlier, federalism
can be defined as a system of rules for allocating public
responsibilities among autonomous governmental units. In
the United States the most important of these rules are
set forth in the U.S. Constitution which, at first glance,
appears to be clear. A national government created by
agreement of the autonomous states is granted authority
over a series of governmental functions that are
"enumerated" in the Constitutional document itself. All
functions not mentioned in the Constitution are, in the
famous tenth amendment, "reserved" to the states or to the
people.[7] The formula seems simple, but two centuries of
dispute and tinkering have made plain that the original
division of authority among autonomous units was wholly
imprecise.

The enumeration of Congressional powers in Article I,
Section 8 is straightforward enough, but the last sentence
of the same article authorizes Congress "To make all Laws
which shall be necessary and proper for carrying into
Execution the foregoing Powers, and all other Powers
vested by this Constitution in the Government of the
United States, or in any Department or Officer thereof."
Extending Congressional authority beyond enumerated powers
to any powers required to carry out the enumerated powers
largely destroyed the significance of enumeration. Taken
together with an essentially unlimited grant of power to
levy and collect taxes for the "general welfare of the
United States," (Article I, Section 8) the implied powers
written into the Constitution give the national government
free rein to undertake whatever policies, in whatever
areas, it deems worthy of national attention. The
enumeration contained in the Constitution expresses powers
thought to be essential by the framers, but the document
itself makes plain that a broad and open-ended grant of
additional authority was also envisioned by its authors.

From the state point of view the tenth amendment that
reserves all non-enumerated powers to the states fails to

indicate just what those "reserved" powers might be.
Although there are a few powers the states are expressly
prohibited from exercising--for example, states may not
make treaties, coin money, or grant any title of
nobility--these prohibitions are few in number, leaving
the states free to define the scope of authority available
to them as "reserved" powers. Not surprisingly, the
states have made use of this undefined authority to ·
undertake activities in areas already occupied by national
government policies, just as the national government has
invaded many areas already occupied by a number of state
policies. Instead of a clear demarcation of
responsibilities, then, the U.S. Constitution offers vague
boundaries, virtually inviting the national and state
governments to occupy jointly whatever policy space they
prefer.

A major consequence of Constitutional ambiguity is
that rules for the division of power among governments
must be continuously renegotiated through political
processes that are inherently dynamic. The essential
federalist question is, which government should undertake
what activity on whose budget? Because answers to that
question cannot be derived from the Constitution,
politicians carry the burden of formulating acceptable
answers. Acceptable answers vary widely, reflecting
social change and divergent political philosophies. Among
the varied conceptualizations that have shaped acceptable
answers to the question, however, are two that recur with
great frequency. One, reflecting both rationality and
public distaste for government excess, is the framework of
efficiency. The other, reflecting the flexibility
guaranteed by Constitutional ambiguity, is the framework
of national purpose. These frameworks are occasionally
intertwined, but they more often are used independently to
organize political debate on different components of the
American policy process: the evaluation of current
programs and the initiation of new programs.

The efficiency framework is commonly found at all
levels of government but is probably used more frequently,
with greater success, among state and local governments.
Its use is often triggered by public reports of official
corruption, misuse of tax funds, or candidates for public
office who find it effective as both a campaign device and
a program for action if the office is achieved. When
triggered by reports of corruption or misuse of funds, the
framework commonly focuses attention on the alleged
wrongdoers, insisting that they be brought to justice and

that their wrongs be corrected, usually through some kind
of internal reform such as new reporting requirements or
new qualifications for employment. When used as an
electoral or government program, the efficiency framework
typically focuses on the waste caused by program
duplication or slothful governmental behavior, and leads
to proposals for either greater coordination among
governments or government consolidation, or both. With
impressive frequency, such proposals are produced by
"blue-ribbon" committees of business notables, whose
knowledge of business is presumed to justify the
recommendations made to public officials (Downs and Larkey
1985).

Whether based on corruption or perceptions of waste,
the efficiency framework carries the same normative
message: government should do its job at the least
possible cost to taxpayers, producing the maximum possible
product per tax dollar spent. The popularity of this
message is apparent in the quite dramatic reduction in the
number of school districts in the United States, from
108,579 as recently as 1942 to little more than 15,000
today, as well as in the constant tinkering with
government structure that occurs in all states, all the
time (Anton 1985). But the message is heard in Washington
as well, causing periodic efforts to reduce waste or
eliminate overlapping agency responsibilities within the
national government. The well-publicized efforts of
President Reagan's Private Sector Survey on Cost
Control--the so-called Grace Commission--are the most
recent example of a national interest that typically
follows a well-worn script: a committee of prominent
businessmen is appointed, they "contribute" a good deal of
time to deliberations over wasteful spending, a largely
undocumented report is issued, claiming the possibility of
very large expenditure savings if waste is eliminated.
Such reports seldom have substantial impact, but they
serve to dramatize the national government's commitment to
efficiency. Since so many of the programs discussed in
such reports are jointly operated by the national, state
and local governments, the federal sources of waste are
also dramatized.

Just as "efficiency" frames many federal debates over
existing operations of government, "national purpose"
provides a conceptual frame commonly used to debate
proposals for new government activities. Although less
effective in resolving issues than the efficiency
framework, national purpose typically generates far more

attention, primarily because its opposite is "states' rights." Thus, proponents of new national government programs typically must counter arguments that such programs are properly the business of the states, rather than the national government. Among state and local governments, proponents of new programs often face opposition from those who argue that the activities proposed should be national rather than state or local, responsibilities. At issue in all such debates is the fundamental question of national purpose, What government actions properly should be regarded as national responsibilities and what actions properly should be undertaken by the states and their localities? Constitutional ambiguity on this question prohibits any "final" resolution. Instead we debate the matter endlessly, using every proposal for some new public responsibility as an occasion to redefine the federal balance. In this sense, American federal politics resemble a permanent Constitutional Convention.

Politicians involved in these debates often find it useful to argue that the Constitution provides clear guidance on the division of responsibilities among governments. President Reagan's proposals for a "New Federalism," for example, seem obviously motivated by his belief that "The Constitution provides clear distinctions between the roles of the Federal Government and of the States and localities," and that these clear distinctions " . . . have become a confused mess" during the past twenty years (Executive Office of the President 1983). Although this image of Constitutional clarity, reflected in the legal doctrine of "Dual Federalism," was used for many years by the Supreme Court to prohibit national government action on a variety of social problems, it is no longer regarded as a serious barrier to federal action. Reflecting an earlier but still vital tradition of Constitutional scholarship (Wechsler 1954; Davis 1967), recent scholars emphasize the political character of the Constitution, hence the ambiguity of Constitutional language, and reject the notion that such language can determine the substance of state or federal authority. In this political view, the Constitution provides a procedural framework for allocating responsibilities rather than any particular allocation. Were it otherwise, Constitutional adjustments to take account of social change would have been impossible in the past and would be impossible now.

A good example of Constitutional pragmatism is the recent decision of the U.S. Supreme Court to abandon its effort to find a definition of "traditional" that could be used consistently to bar federal action at the local level. After years of federal program growth, supported by a permissive Supreme Court, the Court issued a ruling in 1976 that seemed to place new limits on the reach of national power. In <u>National League of Cities v. Usery</u> (426 U.S. 833), the Court held that the Commerce Clause of the Constitution did not empower Congress to enforce the minimum wage and overtime provisions of the National Fair Labor Standards Act (FLSA) against the states " . . . in areas of traditional governmental functions." The case had been initiated by the National League of Cities and a number of other state and local governments in reaction against 1974 amendments to the FLSA that extended provisions of that act to employees of virtually all state and local governments. According to the League of Cities, the 1974 amendments trespassed on the powers reserved to the states by the Tenth Amendment. The Court agreed, holding that " . . . insofar as the challenged amendments operate to directly displace the States' freedom to structure integral operations in areas of traditional governmental functions, they are not within the authority granted Congress by the Commerce Clause." Although Mr. Justice Rehnquist, who wrote the majority opinion, did not attempt to define the phrase "traditional governmental functions," he did list a few activities he believed clearly fell within its ambit: fire protection, police protection, sanitation, public health, and parks and recreation. Depending on what other activities might be defined as "traditional," the Usery decision was a potentially major limitation on federal power.

Finding a definition of "traditional" that could be applied consistently to individual cases, however, proved to be extraordinarily difficult. Litigation of the issue after the Usery decision produced a series of confused and inconsistent results. Regulating ambulance services, licensing automobile drivers, operating a municipal airport, or operating a highway authority were held to be "traditional" functions protected by Usery, while regulation of traffic on public roads, regulation of air transportation, operation of a mental health center, or provision of domestic services for the aged and handicapped were judged to be nontraditional functions. An opportunity to consider what distinguished one group of services from the other was presented when Joe G. Garcia

and other employees of the San Antonio Metropolitan
Transit Authority filed suit to force the Authority to pay
them overtime wages in accordance with the FLSA. Was this
transit authority a "traditional" governmental function
and thus exempt from FLSA rules on overtime pay? Or was
it a nontraditional activity and thus required to follow
those national rules? Could Joe Garcia get his overtime
pay or not?

In Garcia v. San Antonio Metropolitan Transit
Authority (105 S.Ct. 1005, 1011), decided February 19,
1985, the Supreme Court not only ruled in favor of Garcia
but took the opportunity to overrule the Usery decision.
Taking note of the confused efforts to classify some
activities as "traditional," Mr. Justice Blackmun wrote:
"We find it difficult, if not impossible, to identify an
organizing principle that places each of the cases in the
first group on one side of a line and each of the cases in
the second group on the other side. The Constitutional
distinction between licensing drivers and regulating
traffic, for example, or between operating a highway
authority and operating a mental health facility is
elusive at best." Nor was historical precedent likely to
help identify such a principle since, taken strictly, an
historical approach would prevent the court " . . . from
accommodating changes in the historical functions of
states, changes that have resulted in a number of
once-private functions like education being assumed by the
States and their subdivisions." Justice Blackmun's
reading of history, in fact, suggested to him that
attempting to place functions into "traditional" or
nontraditional categories could easily be a matter of
"historical nearsightedness", today's self-evidently
"traditional" function is often yesterday's suspect
innovation. Driving this point home in his opinion for
Garcia v. San Antonio Metropolitan Transit Authority,
Blackmun noted that National League of Cities listed parks
and recreation as an example of a traditional service and
observed that:

> A scant 80 years earlier . . . in Shoemaker v. United
> States, 147 U.S. 282 (1893), the Court pointed out
> that city commons originally had been provided not for
> recreation but for grazing domestic animals "in
> common," and that in the memory of men now living, a
> proposition to take private property [by eminent

domain] for a public park . . . would have been
regarded as a novel exercise of legislative power. (p.
15)

For the Court majority, however, efforts to develop
clear distinctions of the sort attempted in National
League of Cities were " . . . unlikely to succeed
regardless of how the distinctions are phrased" because no
such distinction " . . . can be faithful to the role of
federalism in a democratic society."

> The essence of our federal system is that within the
> realm of authority left open to them under the
> Constitution, the States must be equally free to
> engage in any activity that their citizens choose for
> the common weal, no matter how unorthodox or
> unnecessary anyone else - including the
> judiciary--deems state involvement to be. Any rule of
> state immunity that looks to the "traditional,"
> "integral," or "necessary" nature of governmental
> functions inevitably invites an unelected federal
> judiciary to make decisions about which state policies
> it favors and which ones it dislikes . . . . We
> therefore reject, as unsound in principle and
> unworkable in practice, a rule of state immunity from
> federal regulation that turns on a judicial appraisal
> of whether a particular governmental function is
> "integral" or "traditional." (pp. 17-18)

None of this should be taken to suggest that the
Constitution imposes no restraints on governmental
action. Constitutional restraints are real enough but, as
the Court concluded, they are procedural rather than
substantive, inhering " . . . principally in the workings
of the National Government itself, rather than in discrete
limitations on the objects of federal authority" (p. 23).
Or, to put it differently, politics determines the
boundaries of acceptable action. The " . . . principal
and basic limit on the federal Commerce power is that
inherent in all congressional action--the built-in
restraints that our system provides through state
participation in federal government action. The political
process ensures that laws that unduly burden the States
will not be promulgated" (p. 27).
What, then, are the appropriate boundaries between
national purpose and states' rights? After Garcia it must
now be clear that the best answer is, Whatever current

politicians can agree they should be. Politicians doubtless will continue to justify their policy preferences by appealing to Constitutional "principle," and such appeals will continue to seem plausible because of the ambiguity of Constitutional language. The most important contribution of the Constitution, however, is not some set of imaginary principles by which to determine the allocation of power, but a framework to guide the continuing debate over who should do what. The Constitution does not answer questions of power allocation so much as it provides a structure through which answers can be found.

Constitutional ambiguity means that no answers to the allocation question are ever "final"; every election carries within it the possibility of a new and different answer. Politicians seek these new formulae under conditions that are necessarily conflictual. Proposals for new governmental programs are certain to be opposed by those who believe that new actions are unwarranted or the responsibility of "some other" level of government. Reforms proposed in the name of efficiency are virtually certain to be opposed by those who either support the allegedly inefficient officials or who believe that participation is a more important value than efficiency. Under the protective umbrella of Constitutional indeterminacy, the fires of federal politics burn continuously, fueled by the unending tension between efficiency and participation, and between national purpose and states' rights.

Federalism As An Analytic Issue

The political question, Who should do what on whose budget?, can also be phrased as an issue for scholarly analysis: What theory guides, or should guide, the allocation of governmental responsibilities in a multi-unit political system? When asked as a normative question, answers yield information about the principles or theories that various analysts believe should guide the division of power among governmental units. When asked descriptively, answers to the question yield information about the behavior of politicians and the ideas used to motivate that behavior. Given the continuing political interest in the issue, it is not surprising that scholars have developed some insightful normative models, nor is it surprising that large numbers of descriptive studies have been done with increasing frequency in the past decade. The following review considers both the relevance of existing normative models and the possibility that the thousands of available empirical studies may be converging on a usable empirical model of intergovernmental political behavior.

Fiscal Federalism

One popular model, derived largely from the work of Professor Richard A. Musgrave but developed further by a number of other economists, provides a rationale for dividing government responsibilities within a larger economic system. Dividing the appropriate functions of government into three classes made it possible for Musgrave to offer a clear rationale for the allocation of responsibilities in a multi-unit system. One function was stabilization, or the control of economic cycles through the use of monetary and fiscal policy. These activities obviously had to be applicable on a national scale to be effective and thus were clearly functions of the national government. Distribution, or the provision of economic resources to the population, was also an appropriate function for national authorities. Market failure to distribute resources adequately was most likely to be felt by society's poor, but subnational governments were unlikely to be effective in managing this function. Hence, this too was a national responsibility. Subnational governments, however, had an important contribution to make to the third function, which was allocation: the division of resources between public goods, available to all, and private goods, available only to those who could pay for them. Particularly in a large nation, with many different groupings of people and varied tastes for public services, no single agency was likely to be capable of responding to these differences. Local and state agencies, with more limited geographic coverage and thus better awareness of local tastes for public services, clearly had to be important participants in the allocation function, within an economic framework provided by national responsibility for stabilization and distribution.[8]

Varied participation in the provision of public goods by state and local governments, however, often leads to serious imbalances between the distribution of benefits and costs, creating problems of both efficiency and equity. The efficiency problem arises because the public benefits produced by one government are often distributed to people who live outside the producing jurisdiction--these kinds of benefits are said to "spill over" into other jurisdictions. From the point of view of the recipient jurisdiction, the benefits that "spill in" are pure gain: individuals obtain a public benefit for which they paid nothing. From the point of view of the producing jurisdiction, however, the spill-overs represent costs for which no benefit is received. The producing jurisdiction, accordingly, has an incentive to cut back its production of spilled-over benefits until its benefits more nearly match its costs. Since the receiving jurisdiction has no similar incentive to produce the benefits (it was not producing them to begin with), the availability of the benefits might fall below socially desirable standards, producing an inefficient allocation of public resources.

Inefficient allocations are also produced by spill-overs that are not so pleasant. For example, a city may dump untreated sewerage into a nearby river that may provide water for several downstream communities. If the city does not experience the "cost" of polluted water, it has little incentive to provide treatment. Downstream communities may bear most of this cost but, since they do not cause the problem, they have less incentive to solve it. In either case, the allocation of resources is inefficient.

The equity problem arises from differences in resources among jurisdictions. Quite apart from spill-overs or spill-ins, some governments may be unable to offer services similar to those available in other jurisdictions because they do not have enough wealth, either in property values or personal income, to support such services. Fiscal disparities of this kind often result in a lower level of public goods than is desirable, particularly for low-income populations, in services such as education or health.

Recognizing the problems caused by benefit-burden imbalances, the framework of fiscal federalism offers a clear solution: grants from higher-level governments to promote efficiency and equity. In cases where spill-overs lead to inefficient resource allocation, fiscal federalism recommends that grants be made to producing jurisdictions equal to the portion of any given benefit that actually spills over into other jurisdictions. Thus, if 30% of the patrons of a city library are residents of other jurisdictions, a grant amounting to 30% of the library budget would be justified. Or, if 10% of a state's health care services are provided to residents of other states, than a national grant of 10% of the state's health budget would be in order. Similarly, fiscal federalism promotes the use of grants to improve the resource base of poor jurisdictions, using the larger tax base available to higher-level governments to compensate for resource shortages among lower-level units. An important normative goal of fiscal federalism, obviously, is that beneficiaries of public benefits should pay the costs of those benefits. Since the "fit" between benefit incidence and cost incidence is unlikely to be perfect in multi-unit systems, however, assistance from higher-level governments provides a vehicle for using a larger tax base to encourage efficiency and promote equity in public service availability.

Fiscal federalism is an undeniably attractive analytic framework, sophisticated in its location of appropriate national and subnational governmental functions, parsimonious in its use of benefit and cost incidence as major tools of analysis, and relatively clear in its recommendations for dealing with benefit-burden imbalances. Its main difficulty is the considerable distance between what the framework asserts--as fact or recommendation--and what occurs in the real political world.

To some extent this difficulty arises from conceptual ambiguity. As a practical matter, clear distinctions between allocation, distribution and stabilization are often impossible to draw. Most major governmental activities, in fact, probably could be placed in more than one of these categories. Some, such as public welfare programs or social security, obviously distribute resources, but they also allocate resources to these public services, which are so large in monetary value that they clearly have an impact on economic stabilization. The apparently neat trichotomy that provides a basis for dividing public power thus turns out to be not so neat at all, but rather muddled when applied to specific cases.

It is also clear that the major analytic tools used in fiscal federalism assume a level of measurement that is, for the most part, beyond our reach. Consider an assertion that might be derived from fiscal federalism: policing is a necessary public good; therefore cities should receive state or federal grants (or both) to support that portion of their police budgets that is devoted to servicing nonresidents. How would one measure the "nonresident" portion of police budgets? One measure might be the nonresident fraction of total arrests, or total citations. But doesn't an arrest or citation of a nonresident also provide a benefit to residents—indeed, would such actions not be a greater service to residents than to others? Or perhaps one could identify the number of nonresidents present in the city on a daily or weekly basis as a proportion of resident population and use that proportion to calculate an appropriate grant. The assumption here would be that both residents and nonresidents enjoy equal benefits. But do residents and nonresidents benefit equally? If nonresidents are mostly workers in city firms, their stay in the city is limited to eight or nine hours, compared to residents, most of whom are present 24 hours per day. Or, if the city is New York, many of the nonresidents are tourists, who flock to the city for varying periods of time, including weeks of daylong residence, particularly in Manhattan. How do we take account of such complications?

The answer, of course, is that we do not, because quite often we cannot. Major public goods such as policing, education, the provision of clean water and clean air, or public transportation cannot be precisely allocated—even in principle—among resident and nonresident beneficiaries because providing the service to one class is providing the service to the other. Fuzzy estimates of the size of each class are possible, but to move beyond such estimates would require data that are not now available and that, in all probability, could not be made available without inquiries that most Americans would find quite distasteful. "Beneficiaries should pay" is a fine principle, but it is more applicable to special services to separable populations than to the public goods that are the staple of modern government. "Compensation for spill-overs" is similarly a fine principle, so long as we remember that the measurement of spill-overs is fuzzy at best, and nowhere close to the level of precision implied by fiscal federalism.

Despite its undeniable attractions, then, fiscal federalism remains more a hope than a practice in American governance. Fiscal disparities between governments remain large and, in the case of many central cities and their surrounding suburbs in the North, are becoming larger, yet neither the national government nor the states have adopted general policies to equalize fiscal capacity among relevant jurisdictions. Many states have adopted

equalization plans for their public schools, mostly under
court orders to do so, but even in these states, public
services are otherwise quite unevenly funded. Both the
national government and the states have expanded their
assistance programs quite dramatically in recent years,
but compensation for spill-overs or spill-ins appears to
have had little to do with the expansion. Program
innovation to deal with serious problems, including
environmental decay, energy, social services, and economic
stimulation have dominated national government actions,
while tax relief has tended to dominate state actions
until the past half decade. Fiscal federalism is an
interesting and important analytic model, but it does not
yet capture much of the behavior of American politicians.

Public Choice

An alternative model of American federalism attempts
to combine insights from both economics and political
analyses into a "public choice" perspective.[9] Like the
fiscal federalism model, the public choice framework
assumes the superiority of markets as mechanisms for
producing and distributing benefits, justifying government
intervention only in cases of market failure.
Externalities (or spill-overs) for which the market would
be unlikely to compensate, the use of common property
resources (e.g., rivers) which a market could not
regulate, or the need for public goods that markets would
be unlikely to produce, all justify government action in
this model, as in the fiscal federalism framework.

The public choice model, however, does not assume that
existing governmental structures are necessarily
acceptable; indeed, existing structures are challenged on
both empirical and conceptual grounds. Empirically,
evidence from studies of government program operations is
used to document the frequent failure of public
bureaucracies to perform effectively or to respond to
citizen interests. Large governmental agencies are
especially likely to be seen as rigid in their adherence
to established procedures, regardless of the effect of
those procedures on the services or products such agencies
were established to provide. The goods and services
provided by government thus are likely to be quite
standardized, even in situations where nonstandard
products would be more effective in meeting agency goals,
and lethargic in delivery, even in situations where speed

of response affects utilization. Moreover, because the officials who make policy in public bureaucracies are often isolated from the recipients of public services by several layers of organization, adjustments in agency procedures are difficult to make.

Officials who have the power to bring about adjustments often do not know what is going on, while those who know what is going on seldom have the power to bring about change. As a result, public agencies often stumble ahead blindly, pursuing outdated policies without regard to either their effectiveness or their efficiency.

The conceptual weakness associated with these weaknesses in performance, of course, is excessive reliance on hierarchy as the major alternative to the market. Since goods and services produced by government do not have a "price" similar to the the price attached to market products, producers of government products have no easy way to judge public demand for what they produce. And, because careers in public agencies often depend on doing or producing more each year, public officials have incentives to expand their activities, regardless of consumer demand for those activities. The greater the reliance on hierarchical bureaucracy as a service delivery mechanism, the fewer the units involved in those services, the weaker the feedback on demand for the services, and the greater the domination of producer rather than consumer interests in the production of goods that may be neither desired nor beneficial. Reliance on large and centralized bureaucracies to produce the public goods made necessary by market failure, in short, can generate a cure worse than the original disease (Ostrom 1973).

If both markets and bureaucracies suffer inherent weaknesses, what can be done? The answer, from a public choice point of view, is twofold. First, emphasize citizen control over the type and quantity of public benefits, and second, recognize that structures for the delivery of those benefits can be as varied as the benefits themselves.

When governments are viewed as producers of benefits demanded by citizens, every good produced by government reflects the common interests of some group of citizens large enough to create a benefit to satisfy its interests. In this sense, any governmental program becomes an expression of some community of interest around that program. In a diverse society, public benefit programs are likely to be similarly diverse, often serving highly specialized communities of interest with programs

specifically tailored to those narrow interests. Multiple
and thus small service jurisdictions are themselves
benefits, however, since programs can be precisely
tailored to fit the preferences of small groups of
citizens. Since all programs are responses to articulated
demands, moreover, control over programs can be exercised
directly by the citizens who demand the narrow service.
Instead of large and distant bureaucracies exerting
control over benefits, citizens in their role of consumers
exert political control by electing to support or not
support the benefits they receive.

To resolve inevitable disputes among a large number of
small program jurisdictions a higher level of authority
would be essential in this kind of system. For similar
benefits provided by a large number of primary
jurisdictions, a higher level of government could also
serve as a central production unit, taking advantage of
economies of scale to offer some benefits at a lower unit
cost than might otherwise be available. Or the higher
unit might develop new services and offer them to the
primary units under quasi-market conditions. In this kind
of system, accordingly, there would be a large, number of
different services provided, some on a very narrow basis,
some on a large-scale and centralized basis, depending on
the kind of benefit and the demand for that benefit among
various communities of interest. Since some communities
of individual interest would be broad, there would be a
sufficient supply of public goods. But since many
communities would be narrow, bureaucratic control would be
unnecessary. Political control over service benefits,
exercised through jurisdictions of various sizes and
interests, would assure a variety of public programs,
responsive to diverse interests, and accountable through
politics to the citizens served (Ostrom 1973).

The public choice framework is appealing because it
appears to move us away from the extremist formulations of
those who believe that the market is the only legitimate
collective institution or those at the opposite extreme
who believe that monopolistic hierarchy is the best
possible model for public service delivery. It also seems
to come close to the American experience in its emphasis
on service demand as a source of governmental structure.
Despite these undeniable virtues, the framework remains
unpersuasive.

Although the model seems to apply reasonably well to
the development of American special district governments,
which provide a single service to narrowly defined

constituencies that pay for that service, its relevance
for the more complex governments of our larger cities and
states seems questionable. Citizens in these more
complicated environments may or may not have enough
information about existing services to calculate their
interests in supporting or withholding support from those
services--assuming that institutional means to express
support or opposition were available. Even with a great
deal of information, citizens would have great difficulty
deriving specific prescriptions from the public choice
framework. Injunctions to "heed citizen-consumers" or
"consider organizational alternatives to large
bureaucracies" are sensible enough, but wholly lacking the
detail that would be necessary to apply such advice in
particular circumstances. Nor does the framework offer
any clear guidelines for dividing responsibilities between
primary and higher-level jurisdictions, or between
services that could be directly controlled by consumer
choice and those that might require a more bureaucratic
form of organization. In the end, therefore, the public
choice framework amounts to an argument for more market
and fewer bureaucratic solutions to public problems,
without the details necessary to render the argument
persuasive rather than just plausible.

Hierarchy As A Federal Model

An alternative model that appears regularly in both
political and analytic discourse is hierarchy: a system of
authority, graded by rank, in which higher ranks exert
control over lower ranks, following directives issued by
the highest authority. Although it may seem strange that
this model could be popular in a system with so many
governments, very few of which would willingly accept a
"subordinate" role, the image of hierarchy has strong
political and intellectual roots in the United States.
To begin with, it is entirely plausible to view the
structure of our governing system as a hierarchy. It is
well-established in law that local governments are
creatures of the states and thus totally subordinate to
them. Furthermore, the same Constitution that guarantees
the continued existence of the states also asserts, in the
famous Supremacy Clause, that both the Constitution and
the laws of the United States " . . . shall be the supreme
Law of the Land; and the Judges in every State shall be
bound thereby, any Thing in the Constitution or Laws of

any State to the Contrary notwithstanding" (Article VI).
Clearly, if national law has precedence over state law,
and state laws control local governments, than the
structure of the system seems quite hierarchical indeed.
If the system actually worked this way, then public
policies would be promulgated by the national government,
enforced by all the states, and implemented by the local
governments. The states, rather than being autonomous
units in a federal system, would be little more than
administrative instrumentalities of a centralized,
national system.

Few politicians or analysts would accept the reality
or argue the desirability of such a centralized system for
the United States, but the intellectual appeal of
hierarchy remains strong. American scholars have been
strongly influenced by a tradition of scholarship, dating
back to the early years of this century, focusing on
"bureaucracy" as a form of social organization (Weber
1947). This form of organization, made up of officials
who are trained for their jobs, recruited on the basis of
competence, and evaluated on the basis of performance
within a carefully graded system of authority, has had a
powerful appeal to American reformers as well,
particularly those activated by recurrent scandals or
evidence of waste. These images also have fit nicely with
American governmental ideologies, which value democratic
participation but, as Herbert Kaufman has demonstrated,
value executive leadership and nonpartisan competence as
well (Kaufman 1956). Indeed, strong governmental leaders
who have been able to resolve difficult problems or
produce major accomplishments--Robert Moses in New York or
Richard Daley in Chicago are examples--are often regarded
as folk heroes, the people who can "cut through the red
tape" to "get things done." They are the "fixers," to
borrow a phrase from Eugene Bardach (1979), whose
activities are necessary to overcome the fragmented and
decentralized inertia built into our system of many
governments.

Hierarchy thus appeals to many intellectuals, and not
a few politicians, as an alternative to existing
structures, usually proposed in reaction to evidence of
inefficiency or corruption in those structures. The
diagnosis is usually the same: duplication of services is
rampant, causing inefficient waste of tax dollars; there
is a lack of coordination among the different agencies
involved in the service; citizens are confused by the
complexity of who is doing what and are thus unable to

hold officials accountable for their wasteful actions.
The hierarchical prescription for these problems also is
usually the same: centralize! Eliminate most of the
duplicating agencies or programs; establish a central
authority over the remaining units, with power to
coordinate and evaluate their activities; establish
procedures through which this centralized authority can be
held accountable, then hold it accountable. Both the
diagnosis of fragmentation and the prescription of
hierarchical integration have a long history in American
politics. Precisely these ideas were applied to city
governments at the turn of the century, to state
governments in the 1920s, to presidential-congressional
relations in the 1930s, to metropolitan areas in the 1950s
and 1960s, and more recently to the organization of the
federal government as a whole. Although not always
successful in reducing fragmentation, the ideas remain
powerful as an alternative model of government
organization.[10]

Hierarchy continues to be utilized as a model of
reform at the state and local levels, largely because it
provides a device for pursuing the efficiency and
rationality values that are so ingrained in the American
political temperament. Applying the hierarchy model to
relationships between the national government and the
states, however, is more problematic. From a
Constitutional point of view, it would be difficult to
argue that states derive their authority from the national
government. The states not only preceded the national
government, but accepted doctrine holds that both the
states and the national government derive their authority
from the same source, namely, the people.[11] If state
authority originates in the people, it cannot come from
the national government. The notion of a hierarchical
relationship between Washington and the several state
governments thus appears impossible to reconcile with
existing Constitutional principles. Even the Supremacy
Clause, after all, applies only to national legislation
that conflicts with state law. If there is no national
law, or if there is national law but it is consistent with
state laws, the Supremacy Clause has no impact.[12]

Apart from Constitutional principle, there is an
insurmountable political defect in the idea of national
hierarchy: the absence of a national party system.
American political parties are organized by state, and
party ideologies tend to be organized by region, to the
extent that they are organized at all. Although

Republican and Democrat labels are used nationally,
eastern Republicans are very different from mid-western
Republicans, southern Democrats are poles apart from
northern Democrats, and western politicians are different
from everybody else. Within states, strong political
party organizations are rare. Instead, individual
politicians choose their affiliation, mount their own
campaigns with money they raise mostly by themselves, and
push issues that may or may not have anything to do with
national or state party platforms. Once elected to state
or national office, therefore, these politicians have very
little reason to accept party direction, except when it
benefits them, and very little incentive to work hard at
developing "national" policy agendas. Under these
circumstances it is impossible to imagine how national
supremacy could work, since it would require unified
support by a continuing majority of locally oriented
legislators for actions that could only result in some
loss of local discretion. Political party
decentralization, in short, undermines the political base
necessary for national hierarchy.

Finally, there is a practical matter to consider.
National hierarchy implies a unified perspective that can
be articulated and imposed on state and local
governments. Congress, dominated by locally oriented
politicians, cannot be expected to develop such unity.
Can the executive branch be expected to do any better?
The answer, almost certainly, is no. A strong President
can occasionally marshall sufficient influence to develop
a unified policy view among executive agencies, but the
agencies and their programs have lifespans that exceed any
President's tenure by a wide margin. Those programs are
so different from agency to agency, and supported by such
different political coalitions, that a unified executive
branch view on any given policy is likely to be extremely
rare. In this sense, the national government is no
different from other American governments. Its executive
agencies are as fragmented by purpose and personnel as are
state and local governments, and overcoming fragmentation
is no less difficult in Washington than it is in Chicago,
or Seattle. Hierarchy, however much it may appeal to our
desires for rationality and effective government action,
does not describe, and cannot prescribe, the politics of
federalism in the United States.

The Organizational Coalition Model

Fiscal federalism, public choice and hierarchy are essentially normative models: their strengths lie primarily in prescribing what should be rather than in describing what is. They are valuable precisely because they express a central insight in a form that allows us to understand a general relationship that may be obscured or contradicted by the particular details of daily events. Because they are empirically weak, these models leave open the question how to summarize the actual patterns of intergovernmental behavior. This has proven to be an extraordinarily difficult question to deal with, precisely because the real world of federal politics is infinitely more complicated than any simple model can capture. Nevertheless, much of the extraordinarily rich empirical literature published in the past few years contains an implicit model that deserves to be made explicit: we may think of it as the organizational process model.

Central to this framework is an idea derived from economics, that government programs are best conceived as benefits, distributed to identifiable population groups, whose costs are borne by population groups that are not necessarily the same but who are in principle identifiable. These benefits are developed, distributed, and supported by organizations that, to borrow an insight from organization theory (Cyert and March 1963), are best understood as coalitions of power, based on interest. Given this view of public programs and their origins, political logic suggests that the main question to be answered in accounting for a given public program is not, What purpose is this program designed to achieve?, but rather, Who benefits from the program? Within this framework, accordingly, rationalistic inquiries into program purpose are less significant than political inquiries into program beneficiaries. [13]

Viewed as coalitions of power, the organizations we know as local, state and national governments reflect characteristically different beneficiary interests through different patterns of public policy. The United Automobile Workers in Michigan and the tobacco farmers in North Carolina, for example, are both powerful coalition participants in their states, but the policy results reflect very different patterns of benefits. Coalition-based variety in public programs does not imply an absence of pattern, however. Leibert has shown that the scope of local government activity varies

systematically with age of government and region, while
Paul Peterson recently has conceptualized the implicit
structure of local, state, and national policies as
predominantly developmental, allocational, and
redistributive (Leibert 1976; Peterson 1981). There is
considerable variety in interests present within
jurisdictions, but there is pattern within variety as
well.

It is important to understand that, within the
American structure, each governmental unit constitutes an
interest that is part of the political environment of
other governments. In addition to simple organizational
maintenance, therefore, all American governments engage in
political representation of organizational and
constituency interests. From a local point of view, the
state and federal governments provide much of the revenue
and all of the regulations that constrain local actions,
while other local governments pursue interests or provide
resources that often require sustained attention.

From a state point of view, legal and financial
responsibility for local government actions combine with
localized legislative representation to determine much of
state policy, while the administration of programs
partially funded by the national government makes national
agencies daily participants in state action.

From a national point of view, localized
representation in Congress and the locally specialized
interests of national administrative agencies--i.e., HUD
to serve northeastern cities, Interior to service the
joint federal-state interests in western states, Defense
to interact largely with southern and coastal
regions--give much of national policy its traditionally
localized configuration. Shared responsibilities, in
short, guarantee that many governments will be represented
in political coalitions. Politically, therefore,
intergovernmental relationships are themselves part of the
"structure."

The fact that one government is always part of the
relevant political environment of other governmental
jurisdictions implies that intergovermental systems are
inherently unstable. Since expenditures by one unit are
often revenues for another, changes in taxing or spending
policies have extensive ripple effects beyond the
boundaries of the unit offering such changes. Annual or
biennial budget cycles, strongly encouraged by
citizen-based taxpayer coalitions, guarantee that
occasions for changes in budget policies will occur at

least annually. Unanticipated events, such as unusually heavy snowstorms or floods, provide less predictable but repeated opportunities to adjust financial priorities. In a sense, therefore, coalitions that support existing financial priorities are constantly "on guard" against raids by new coalitions thrown up by unanticipated events or by the routinized questioning of budget cycles.

Should new or different coalitions prevail in one jurisdiction, some effects will be felt and will cause action in others; a shift in state expenditures may induce an increase in local taxes, or new national programs may induce substantial reductions in older, state-funded programs. Despite the appearance of considerable structural stability in core program responsibilities, the intergovernmental system is inherently dynamic, constantly responding to changes in coalition structure.

Conceptualizing federal politics as patterned interactions among interest-based coalitions, where the products of such interactions are benefits for members (including governments) of victorious coalitions, has several advantages. One is that the framework requires no heroic assumptions about individual knowledge or ability to calculate rationally the costs and benefits of public action. What actors know and how they use or fail to use information in the process of building and maintaining coalitions are questions for investigation, not assumption. Use of the framework thus encourages a search for understanding without prejudging the rationality or effectiveness of coalition behavior.

A second advantage is that this formulation can easily accommodate the rich empirical literature now available. Indeed, it is precisely this perspective that seems implicit in much of that literature, including the many recent studies of local implementation of, or reaction to, federal policies (Pressman and Wildavsky 1974; Nathan, Manvel and Calkins 1975; Dommel 1982; Nathan and Doolittle 1983; Palmer and Sawhill, eds. 1984; Stein 1984b). Use of the framework, accordingly, may permit us to develop interesting general statements simply by making explicit what seems implicit in many of these studies.

A third very important advantage is that the framework is explicitly dynamic, encouraging a deeper exploration of sources and consequences of important actions no less than the actions themselves. The organizational coalition model, in short, offers the promise of moving us some distance toward a better understanding of how American federalism works.

Conclusion: Where's The Beef?

Federalism in the United States is embedded in a cultural system that places a high value on participation and expresses a similarly high level of distrust of government, particularly government that is too large to be controlled by ordinary citizens. These cultural norms are obviously reflected in American governing institutions. Large in number, generally small in size, and legally intertwined with so many other governments that independent action is all but impossible, American governing bodies seem designed to hinder rather than promote public action. Although inefficiency and waste are tolerated as an acceptable price to pay for high levels of participation, periodic demands for greater efficiency often lead to changes in government structure, procedures, or both. Social changes through time also produce demands for new government activities to deal with newly recognized problems. Such demands raise questions about appropriate responsibilities among different levels of government, and are typically debated as issues of state versus national responsibility. Participation, efficiency, national purpose and state rights thus emerge as enduring issues in the American federal polity.

None of these issues are ever finally resolved, because they cannot be finally resolved. Instead, cycles of political prominence recur, with participation or state authority given more weight in one period, only to be succeeded by a period in which efficiency or national purpose values dominate. Neither Constitutional dogma nor political practice can be expected to alter this situation. Constitutional language provides support for all positions, but lacks sufficient clarity to produce any "final" resolution. The political practices of more than 82,000 governments constantly change and constantly bump into one another, providing endless opportunities to continue the arguments. Short of a second American revolution, it is safe to say that the issues of federalism will be with us for some time to come.

For students of federalism, the continuing debate offers a continuing opportunity to improve our understanding and our ability to contribute to sensible reforms. The normative models reviewed here all have contributed to reformist efforts, albeit with mixed results that stem from the absence of strong empirical support for the insights they express. An empirical model, largely implicit in the work done by many scholars during the past two decades, carries the promise of taking us beyond the "wilderness of single instances" Rufus Davis complained about so elegantly many years ago (Davis 1967). Indeed, enough work is available now to suggest a number of new general conclusions that have emerged from the work of scholars who have viewed federalism as a dynamic interaction among differing coalitions of organizations. This may seem a bold claim, and all of us have learned to be skeptical of such boldness, so let me conclude by offering a few examples of new insights about our federal institutions that have emerged from recent scholarship.

I begin with a study that is not so recent, dating back to 1960, but which has just begun to be appreciated sufficiently, namely, Phillip Monypenny's analysis of grants-in-aid (Monypenny 1960). Monypenny set out to explain the existence and growth of federal grants, as well as their characteristically ambiguous designations of purpose. Viewing grants as a product of coalition behavior, he noted the difficulty of mobilizing coalitions around the narrow interests that thrive in the American political climate if programs are defined in terms of those narrow interests. By joining with similar groups from other local jurisdictions, however, groups too weak to secure their ends in local jurisdictions may mobilize sufficient support to gain financial assistance from another government. Since it is financial support that is proposed to other governments, the details of program purpose that inhibit political success elsewhere need not be addressed. Grant purposes can be stated in general terms, allowing the granting unit to be supportive but at the same time allowing recipient units to pursue localized interests that typically vary considerably. Thus, state aid to local school districts typically provides for some minimum state program while allowing considerable latitude for local program differences. Or, federal aid for highways provides for a semblance of a national program while allowing states to decide whether they prefer a more or less extensive system of highways. From a political point of view, accordingly,

. . . federal aid programs are an outcome of a loose coalition which resorts to a mixed federal-state program because it is not strong enough in individual states to secure its program, and because it is not united enough to be able to achieve a wholly federal

program against the opposition which a specific
program would engender. (Monypenny 1960: 15)

Placing coalition behavior at the center of analysis
enables Monypenny to show the inherently political nature
of governmental programs in general as well as the
particular case of federal grants. He not only calls
attention to the significance of political support; he
also shows dynamic interactions between coalition behavior
and program design that are wholly consistent with federal
programs. Such interactions include federal aid to
aviation, through which tiny local minorities have been
able to secure large national subsidies for 2,224 general
aviation airports "of primarily local interest"
(Congressional Budget Office 1983: 116). Monypenny's
explanation of why grant programs typically have vague
objectives anticipates many recent studies that document
ambiguous legislative language[14], as well as other
studies that document the diverse local or state uses of
federal program dollars.[15] Monypenny's insights, in
short, may be regarded as a precursor of much recent
scholarship.

If both politics and program design permit wide local
discretion in the use of federal aid dollars, how do we
explain the actual uses of such dollars? In a brilliant
analysis, Larkey used insights from organization theory as
well as sophisticated computer modeling techniques to
argue that federal General Revenue Sharing funds were
largely absorbed into pre-existing budgetary routines in
five large cities. Local priorities, as determined by
organizational actors in local budget processes,
determined the actual uses of federal dollars from this
ambiguously defined program (Larkey 1979).

Using data derived from the "field network evaluation
studies" organized by Richard Nathan (1982), however,
James Fossett has argued that the degree of discretion
allowed in federal grant design and the level of local
political organization also play a role in determining
local uses of federal dollars. Fossett's conclusions are
not inconsistent with Larkey's but they call attention to
citizen, as well as organizational, coalitions and, by
examining several grant programs rather than a single
program, illuminate different levels of federal constraint
on local spending practices (Fossett 1983). Fossett's
conclusion that the level of discretion permitted by
federal program design is an important factor in local

spending decisions was based on analyses in 13 large
cities.

In another important analysis, Stein systematically
examined the effect of six different design
characteristics, used in some 569 federal grant programs,
on the spending practices of several hundred cities.
Stein (1984a: 183) concludes that " . . . legal provisions
of different grant programs have a significant impact on
the fiscal response of aid recipients . . . ", thus adding
considerable empirical support for Fossett's conclusion.

Many other studies of federal program impact might be
cited, particularly the recent paper by Liebschutz on
local uses of Community Development Block Grant funds
(Liebschutz 1984), or other studies from the field network
evaluation series (Schmandt, Wendel and Tomey 1983;
McManus 1983; or Dommel 1982), to demonstrate our growing
appreciation of federal-local behavioral interactions.
What seems to me really important about this stream of
work, however, is the progress it reveals. Larkey
proposes a model derived from organization theory and
tests the model productively. Fossett proposes a more
comprehensive model, emphasizing additional variables, and
tests it. Stein examines one of the variables shown to be
important in Fossett's work (as well as others) and
confirms its significance quite persuasively. I would
argue that we are now far better equipped to model the
federal-local connection than ever before and coming much
closer to discovering the conditions under which each of
several variables becomes important. This is theoretical
progress, but it is also potentially important from a
practical point of view, since discovery of important
empirical relationships can be used to improve the design
of federal programs.

Monypenny's coalition explanation of federal aid
policy and the recent stream of work on national-local
relations together suggest an insight that recently has
been formalized by Richard Nathan (Nathan 1983). In a
simple but powerful exposition, Nathan refers to
bargaining as the dominant mode of interaction among
federal actors and goes on to suggest the need for a
two-dimensional understanding of bargaining over federal
programs:

> The best way to think about this process is that there
> is a <u>horizontal</u> policy bargaining process that
> consists of decision-making about policy goals and
> instruments for the country as a whole, and a <u>vertical</u>

> dimension, involving the way in which a particular
> grant is defined and executed by individual recipient
> jurisdictions . . . . Federal grants, especially
> larger ones, need to be viewed as involving both a
> horizontal and vertical political bargaining process.
> The vertical bargaining process--the ways grants are
> treated by the recipient state and local
> government--has a great deal to do with the way grants
> work. (Nathan 1983: 48, 57)

Nathan offered this formulation after years of
observing countless vertical as well as horizontal
bargains through his field network evaluation studies.
While abstract enough to capture important general
relationships, therefore, it is also supported by enough
empirical detail to give it substantial credibility as a
way of understanding the federal policy process--including
details regarding the types of coalitions that become
involved in different aid programs. The formulation also
provides an entry into a better appreciation of federal
policy dynamics.

Several years ago I proposed a political model of
federal program development that emphasized the initial
ambiguity of intent among politicians, the inherent
changeability of program goals across time, and the
shifting bases of coalition support for programs
associated with changes in goals (Anton 1980). In an
interesting recent paper, Stein has extended these ideas
by adapting a legislative "universalism" interpretation of
national policy development, supplemented by an analysis
of benefit distributions from community development
programs to approximate the vertical policy dimension.
More importantly, by extending his analysis over a 35-year
period, Stein is able to present a more refined dynamic
model that is both plausible and amenable to further
refinement. According to Stein, most federal aid programs
begin as narrowly focused conditional programs, with broad
eligibility but small funding. However,

> With time, narrow purpose project grants with high
> application costs evolve into broad based,
> non-conditional entitlements and block grants.
> Moreover, participation and legislative support for
> these programs similarly grows from small sized
> minimum winning coalitions to oversized and eventually
> universal coalitions. Fiscal as well as participatory
> growth is the most visible consequence of this

process. A less obvious, but potentially more
important consequence of this evolution is decreasing
federal control over the implementation of federal aid
programs,and hence control over the direction of
federal policy . . . . This condition leads to a
reversal in the evolution of federal aid programs,
returning grant legislation back to its earlier
conditional character . . . . To protect their
electoral positions, representatives seek to
reestablish their control over federal domestic
spending programs by instituting program requirements
for previously nonconditional aid program. (Stein 1985)

Stein's cyclical view of federal aid development is
appealing, in part because it makes good use of both
horizontal and vertical dimensions of federal
policy-making, in part because its dynamic quality permits
analysis of decline as well as increase in funding, and in
part because it identifies important variables that can be
tested through longitudinal analysis of other programs.
It is a good example of recent scholarship that builds
upon past insights to generate a new synthesis that can
itself stimulate further testing and conceptual
refinement.

Although drawn entirely from the literature on federal
aid programs, these examples tell us a good deal about the
federal system as a whole, and even more about the new
thrust of scholarship in the field of intergovernmental
relations. Although political and normative interests
remain strong, there is also a widespread interest in
developing empirical models that can provide better
statements of what is generally true, rather than
particularly interesting. There is a more concerted
effort to build upon past scholarship rather than discard
it. And there is certainly a new appreciation of the
importance of time as an analytic variable in
understanding the dynamics of federal policy-making. None
of these developments can be regarded as a revolutionary
breakthrough, perhaps, but together they offer encouraging
signs of even better things to come.

NOTES

1. For an elaboration of the many available
definitions of federalism, see Rufus Davis, The Federal

Principle. (Berkeley, CA: University of California
Press, 1978).

2. For examples of autonomous behavior in presumably
centralized systems, see William Taubman, Governing Soviet
Cities: Bureaucratic Politics and Urban Development in
the U.S.S.R. (New York: Praeger, 1973), and Michael
Oksenberg, Policy Formulation in Communist China, Ph.D.
dissertation, Columbia University, 1969.

3. For examples, see Terry N. Clark ed.,
Comparative Community Politics. (Beverly Hills, CA: Sage
Publications, Inc., 1974).

4. These developments are reviewed in Thomas J.
Anton, "The Pursuit of Efficiency," ibid.

5. Innovation among the states has been examined by
Jack L. Walker, "The Diffusion of Innovations Among The
American States," American Political Science Review, 63
(September 1969): 880-889, and Virginia Gray, "Innovations
in the States. A Diffusion Study," American Political
Science Review 67, (December 1973): 1174-1185. For a
review of recent innovations in economic development
policy, see Thomas J. Anton and Rebecca Reynolds, "Old
Federalism and New Policies for State Economic
Development," Publius: The Journal of Federalism.
(forthcoming).

6. For a review of the American approach to local
government, see Anwar Syed, The Political Theory of
American Local Government (New York: Random House, 1966).

7. The Tenth Amendment reads: "The powers not
delegated to the United States by the Constitution, nor
prohibited by it to the States, are reserved to the States
respectively, or to the people."

8. See Richard A. Musgrave (1959) and Wallace E.
Oates, Fiscal Federalism. (New York: Harcourt Brace
Jovanovich, 1972).

9. I rely here primarily on Vincent Ostrom's useful
paper, "Can Federalism Make a Difference?" (Ostrom 1973).

10. For a review and an application of these ideas,
see Advisory Commission on Intergovernmental Relations,
The Federal Role in the Federal System: The Dynamics of
Growth; An Agenda for American Federalism: Restoring
Confidence and Competence. (Washington, D.C.: ACIR,
Publication A-86, June 1981).

11. The Preamble, while technically not a part of the
Constitution, proclaims the accepted understanding that
"the people" are the source of the Constitution's
authority. See Corwin (1978: 1-3).

12. For a discussion of the "Supremacy Clause," see Corwin (1978: 273-280).

13. For applications of this view, see Thomas J. Anton, <u>Moving Money</u>, (Cambridge, MA: Oelgeschlager, Gunn & Hain, 1980, Chapter 5); and Barry S. Rundquist, <u>Political Benefits: Empirical Studies of American Public Programs</u>, (Lexington, MA: Lexington Books, 1980).

14. See Larkey (1979).

15. See Martha Derthick, <u>Uncontrollable Spending for Social Services Grants</u>, (Washington, D.C.: The Brookings Institution, 1975); and Paul R. Dommel and Associates (1982).

34

REFERENCES

Anton, Thomas J. 1980. Federal Assistance Programs: The
    Politics of System Transformation. In Douglas E.
    Ashford, ed., National Resources and Urban Policy.
    New York: Methuen Inc., pp. 15-44.

_____. 1985. Decay and Reconstruction in the Study of
    American Intergovernmental Relations. Publius: The
    Journal of Federalism, 15 (Winter): 65-97.

Bardach, Eugene. 1979. The Implementation Game: What
    Happens After a Bill Becomes a Law. Cambridge, MA:
    MIT Press.

Bureau of the Census. 1985. 1985 Census of Governments,
    Topical Studies, Vol. 6, No. 3: State Payments to
    Local Governments. Washington, D.C.: Government
    Printing Office.

Congressional Budget Office. 1983. Public Works
    Infrastructure: Policy Considerations for the
    1980's. Washington, D.C.: Government Printing
    Office, p. 116.

Corwin, Edward S. 1978. The Constitution and What It
    Means Today. Princeton: Princeton University Press.

Cyert, Richard M. and James G. March. 1963. A Behavioral
    Theory of the Firm. Englewood Cliffs: Prentice Hall.

Davis, Rufus. 1967. The Federal Principle
    "Reconsidered." In Aaron Wildavsky, ed., American
    Federalism in Perspective. Boston: Little Brown and
    Co.

Dommel, Paul R. and Associates. 1982. Decentralizing
    Urban Policy: Case Studies in Community Development.
    Washington, D.C.: The Brookings Institution.

Downs, George and Patrick D. Larkey. 1985. The Search
    for Government Efficiency. New York: Random House.

Executive Office of the President, Office of Management
    and Budget. 1983. budget of the United States
    Government. Washington, D.C.: Government Printing
    Office.

Fossett, James W. 1983. _Federal Aid to Big Cities: The_ _Politics of Dependence_. Washington, D.C.: The Brookings Institution.

Kaufman, Herbert. 1956. Emerging Conficts in the Doctrines of Public Administration. _American_ _Political Science Review_, 50 (December): 1057-1073.

Larkey, Patrick D. 1979. _Evaluating Public Programs: The_ _Impact of General Revenue Sharing on Municipal_ _Government_. Princeton. Princeton University Press.

Leibert, Roland J. 1976. The Partial Eclipse of Community Government: The Trend Toward Functional Specialization. _Social Science Quarterly_, 56: 210-224.

Liebschutz, S.F. 1984. Community Development Dynamics: National Goals and Local Priorities. _Environment and_ _Planning C: Government and Policy_, 2:295-305.

McManus, Susan. 1983. _Federal Aid to Houston_. Washington, D.C.: The Brookings Institution.

Monypenny, Phillip. 1960. Federal Grants-in-Aid to State Governments: A Political Analysis. _National Tax_ _Journal_, 13 (no. 1): 1-16.

Musgrave, Richard A. 1959. _The Theory of Public_ _Finance_. New York: McGraw Hill.

Nathan, Richard P. 1982. The Methodology for Field Network Evaluation Studies. In Walter Williams, ed., _Studying Implementation_. Chatham, N.J.: Chatham House Publishers, pp. 73-79.

_____. 1983. State and Local Governments Under Federal Grants: Toward a Predictive Theory. _Political Science Quarterly_, 98 (Spring): 47-57.

Nathan, Richard P. and Fred C. Doolittle and Associates. 1983. _The Consequences of Cuts_. Princeton: Princeton University Press.

Nathan, Richard P., Allen D. Manvel, and Susannah E. Calkins, et al. 1975. _Monitoring Revenue Sharing_. Washington, D.C.: The Brookings Institution.

Ostrom, Vincent. 1973. Can Federalism Make a
    Difference? Publius: The Journal of Federalism, 3
    (Fall): 197-237.

Palmer, John L. and Isabel V. Sawhill, eds. 1984. The
    Reagan Record. Cambridge, MA: Ballinger Publishing
    Co., Urban Institute Study.

Peterson, Paul E. 1981. City Limits. Chicago:
    University of Chicago Press.

Pressman, Jeffrey L. and Aaron Wildavsky. 1974.
    Implementation: How Great Expectations in Washington
    Are Dashed in Oakland: Or, Why It's Amazing That
    Federal Programs Work at All. Berkeley: University
    of California Press.

Schmandt, Henry J., George D. Wendel, and E. Allan Tomey.
    1983. Federal Aid to St. Louis. Washington, D.C.:
    The Brookings Institution.

Stein, Robert M. 1984a. The Structural Character of
    Federal Aid. Research in Urban Economics, 4: 167 85.

_____. 1984b. Policy Implementation in the Federal
    Aid System. In G. Edwards, ed., Public Policy
    Implementation. New York: JAI Press.

_____. 1985. Growth and Change in the U.S. Federal
    Aid System. Proceedings of Southern Political Science
    Association Meeting, Savannah, Ga., Nov. 3-5, 1984.

Weber, Max. 1947. The Theory of Social and Economic
    Organization. New York: Oxford University Press.

Wechsler, Herbert. 1954. The Political Safeguards of
    Federalism: The Role of the States in the Composition
    and Selection of the National Government. Columbia
    Law Review, 54:543-560.

2

How Federalism Matters
in Natural Resources Policy

Dorotha M. Bradley
and Helen M. Ingram

It is almost obligatory for anyone writing on
federalism today to note the multiple ways of looking at
intergovernmental relations which abound in the
literature. Scholars and politicians continually find it
necessary to invent new names, create new models, or make
up new metaphors for federalism. The list is enormous.
To name just a few there are: dual federalism,
cooperative federalism, creative federalism, new
federalism, picket-fence federalism, fiscal federalism,
permissive federalism, and, the most notable, layer-cake
and marble-cake federalism. William H. Stewart (1982:
5-24) has helpfully compiled an inventory of 326 metaphors
and models of federalism ranging from "the serious to the
silly" (Elazar 1982: 2). As Sally Fairfax (1982: 979)
notes, "no recasting of federalism theory [has been] worth
a fig without a snappy slogan."
Some of these ways of looking at federalism are
descriptive of what people think they see; others are
evaluative and often pejorative, reflecting what they
would like to see. Our purpose in this paper is to look
at the real world of federal-state relations unfettered by
the constraint of a particular framework. We propose to
review federal-state relations in the broad area of
natural resources, concentrating particularly on forest,
range, and water policy. Three questions have focused our
study: What is the role of federalism? Have some
interests been served over others? How has the federal
system structured the sorts of politics that have gone on
in these location-based natural resources?

PUBLIC LANDS POLICY

The history of public lands policy can generally be
divided into four eras: acquisition, disposition,
reservation, and management. Much of the narrative
history in the succeeding four sections, unless otherwise
noted. has been extracted from Dana and Fairfax (1980).

Acquisition

After the Revolutionary War, the thirteen states
claimed ownership of all British Crown lands which were
not privately owned. Massachusetts, Connecticut, New
York, Virginia, North and South Carolina, and Virginia all
claimed extensive lands based on colonial boundaries drawn
far to the west. Maryland led the remaining six states in
an effort to force the cession of these western lands to
the central government. Their purpose was to equalize
land resources among the states, to provide assets for the
central government to use in meeting the national debt,
and to foster feelings of political and economic
solidarity resulting from common ownership of vast,
valuable territory. Between 1781 and 1802 the proposed
cessions were made comprising a total of 233 million acres.
The following year, 1803, 523 million acres were
acquired from France as part of the Louisiana Purchase.
In 1819, Florida was purchased from Spain adding 43
million acres. The "Oregon Compromise" with Great Britain
avoided war and added 181 million acres in the Pacific
Northwest. As a result of the treaty ending the war with
Mexico in 1848, 335 million acres in the Southwest were
acquired. Texas sold 79 million acres to the federal
government in 1859. The southern borders of Arizona and
New Mexico were acquired by the Gadsden Purchase of 19
million acres in 1853. Finally, Alaska's 365 million
acres were purchased from Russia in 1867. These
acquisitions totaled approximately 1804 million acres of
land and 33 million acres of water. Together they
comprised the public domain lands which Congress has over
the years largely disposed of in various attempts to raise
money or to promote the orderly settlement of the
continent. At the peak of acquisition, three-fourths of
the land lying between the Atlantic and the Pacific and
between Canada and Mexico (about 1441 million acres) was
included in the public domain. Only about 411 million
acres, 29 percent, of the original public domain remained

in federal ownership by 1980. In addition to the
remaining public domain lands, public lands now include
additional lands acquired or reserved by the federal
government for national monuments, parks, forests, and
other specified uses.

Disposition

Although there are enormous overlaps, the disposition
era may be described as lasting from 1776 until 1891. At
that latter date Congress authorized the President to
proclaim forest reserves, even though practically speaking
the period of disposition ended with the adoption of the
Taylor Grazing Act in 1934 and technically it ended with
the passage of the Federal Lands Policy Management Act
(FLPMA) in 1976. The period of reservation when lands
were reserved or withheld from disposition lasted from
1891 until 1905. Beginning in 1905, programs to manage
actively rather than to retain the public domain became
prominent.

What to do with the public domain lands and their
resources has been a persistent question throughout our
history. The earliest disposals reflected the young
nation's lack of money. Land boundaries were promised to
encourage military enlistments during the Revolutionary
War and were offered later to reward soldiers for
service. The General Ordinance of 1785 provided that
after survey and division into saleable tracts, lands were
to be sold at auction to the highest bidders.

In part because surveying and land sales offerings
proceeded slowly, squatting on public lands became
commonplace. Eastern Congressional representatives
strongly objected to this practice because it was not
orderly and did not bring the maximum price for the
lands. But by 1828 the composition of Congress had begun
to shift as more and more representatives from newly
admitted states took their seats. In the newer states
squatters were regarded as pioneer settlers whose
enterprise should permit them to buy the land they had
settled without competition. Preemption acts, which in
effect legalized squatting, were passed in 1830 and 1841
and extended in 1853, 1854, and 1862. These acts
constituted victories for the West (the area between the
original thirteen states and the Mississippi River) for
they emphasized actual settlement over revenue
production. The East not only objected to the failure to

retire the national debt, they feared that Western settlement would drain the East of labor resulting in increased wages. Nevertheless, as territories became states, disposal policies became increasingly generous.

The General Ordinance of 1785, which had provided for the surveying and sales of the public domain, also reserved Section 16 in every township for the states to support education. As the West gained political clout these grants increased. Thus, twelve states received one section per township, fourteen received two, and three states received four. If granted sections were not available due to previous occupation or reservation, the state could choose alternate lands. These have become known as "in lieu" selections--and several states have still not selected all the lands due them. Nevada, upon admission in 1864, demanded money instead of land arguing that the land they were to receive was worthless desert. Recently Nevadans have claimed that the state was inadequately compensated by Congress and have demanded their land selection rights. In other states, wilderness study areas and designated wilderness areas also run afoul of the "in lieu" lands, reducing the pool from which the states can choose (Fairfax 1982: 972).

The Morrill Acts of 1862 and 1890 further aided education by providing the states with public land for establishing colleges of agriculture and mechanic arts. In addition grants were made to support wagon roads, river improvement, canals, swamp drainage, and other internal improvements. Railroad grants overshadowed all the others amounting to more than 132 million acres of which 37 million acres went to the states to benefit the railroads. These grants were intended to encourage improved transportation between the Midwest, Far West and the East. The South feared this linkage of the agricultural West and industrial East out of concern for economic competition and because better transportation would encourage Western settlement. Since the West generally opposed the extension of slavery, the South worried that increased settlement would lead to increased numbers of Western states and Western representatives, resulting in Southerners being outvoted in Congress.

Thus it was in 1862, in the absence of most of its Southern members, that Congress passed the first Homestead Act offering 160 acres to citizens who occupied and cultivated the land for five years. Contrary to the myth that the West was primarily opened and settled by these homesteaders, the truth is that most of the best land was occupied before 1862 and successful homesteading mostly occurred in the upper Midwest. The incredible efforts of homesteaders in the Great Basin generally resulted in physical and financial ruin due to drought, blizzards, dust storms, and the fact that 160 acres of semi-arid land was insufficient to support a family. New laws were passed liberalizing the number of acres and reducing the time periods required but these were unsuccessful, and the attempts to farm the Great Plains resulted in the severe dust bowl conditions of the 1930s. Similar efforts to encourage timber growing and irrigation on public land were also failures. More than 70 percent of the original public domain was transferred to other ownership. Of this about 69 percent went to individuals and institutions, 22 percent to the states and 9 percent to the railroads.

The bounty of the public domain was a treasure unique in world history that has profoundly influenced American development. Soil, timber, forage, wildlife, and minerals were widely available and it was easy and respectable to evade laws designed to control their disposal and exploitation. Yet by the turn of the century this laissez-faire approach to the frontier was under severe attack as the crusade for conservation and efficient use of resources was begun by concerned Easterners.

Reservation

The period of disposal was replaced by the period of reservation and withdrawals, and was initiated largely due to fears about forest depletions and resulting watershed destruction. Reservations and withdrawals can both be made largely at the discretion of the President and the Secretary of the Interior. However, reservations designate areas to be retained in government ownership for specific purposes. Withdrawals remove certain areas from disposal without necessarily reserving them for any specific purpose. Reserved lands sometimes allow additional uses if they are not deemed incompatible; for example, mining is acceptable in forest reserves but not in national parks.

Early reservations were concerned with preservation rather than management and the differences between parks and forests were not widely understood. In 1864 Congress ceded Yosemite Valley and Mariposa Big Tree Grove to the State of California for public recreation. There was widespread dissatisfaction with California's

administration and the land was receded to the federal
government in 1906. Two million acres in Yellowstone were
reserved for park purposes by Congress in 1872 but no
attempt was made to provide for their administration or
protection from fire or trespass. Ultimately the U.S.
Cavalry provided supervision until the National Park
Service was established in 1916 after vigorous and
sustained Eastern lobbying. By that time thirteen areas
had already been designated for park use.

The earliest forest reserves were begun by New York in
the Adirondacks in 1872 and were part of the national
trend to preserve scenic areas and watersheds by
withholding them from use. Early conservationists shared
with preservationists the idea that retention of lands and
resources by the federal government was the crucial first
step. And in 1891 the Forest Reserve Act was passed
authorizing the President "to set apart and reserve"
timbered areas on the public lands.

Interestingly, the commonly accepted notion that the
West declared war on the reserves when the President began
to create them has recently been called into question.
The contemporary press in the West and elsewhere voiced no
dire forebodings. In fact, most of the reserves created
between 1891 and 1897 resulted from petitions by citizens
in the reserve areas requesting such actions. Still,
these reserves were not unanimously well received. Some
critics objected to the fact that no provision was made
for administration and protection. Others, including
potential settlers, miners, stock raisers and lumbermen
objected to withdrawing these lands from all use. Few
were satisfied completely and a National Academy of
Sciences Commission was appointed to make legislative
recommendations. Before it did so, however, President
Cleveland neared the end of his term and in the closing
days created thirteen new reserves, more than doubling the
existing reserved areas. This action was taken on the
basis of inadequate studies made primarily by Eastern
academics and without consultation with either governors
or elected representatives from the affected areas.

Congress was furious--unlike previous reservations
these new reserves included cities, towns, agricultural
lands and important developments. In an appropriations
bill rider no mention was made of revoking the reserves,
but President Cleveland was authorized to modify the
boundaries presumably to eliminate the unwise inclusions.
Cleveland pocket vetoed the bill, leaving McKinley to call
a special session on appropriations. At this session the

Organic Act for the Forest Service was passed as a rider
to the 1897 appropriations bill. Main opposition to the
bill came from Western irrigation interests who saw any
use of the forests as detrimental to protecting the
watersheds. They especially objected to grazing and
timber harvesting on forest reserves. On the other hand,
Western commodity users joined forest management advocates
and many preservationists to support the bill.

Management

The beginning of the management era in natural
resources policy is commonly associated with the
Presidency of Theodore Roosevelt and with his Head of the
Division of Forestry, Gifford Pinchot. These men led what
was to become nearly a moral crusade to prevent the
destruction, waste, or monopoly of the public resources.
To them conservation meant the wise and efficient use of
natural resources to provide "the greatest good for the
greatest number for the longest time." Like other
Progressives they embraced the principles of scientific
management, technical efficiency, and nonpartisan good
government.

There were three basic parts to Roosevelt's
conservation vision. First, he emphasized retention of
the public domain and during his administration he
attempted to secure federal ownership of all but the
clearly agricultural lands. Second, he attempted to
create a self-supporting funding system under which
revenues generated from timber, minerals, and grazing on
the public lands could be used for the administration and
further development of federal lands. Finally, resource
issues were viewed as matters requiring technical and
professional expertise rather than political
consideration. Therefore, he attempted to institute
scientific management of all natural resources.

FOREST AND RANGE POLICY

Soon after Roosevelt's election in 1904, the forest
reserves were transferred from Interior to Agriculture and
receipts from forest reserves were placed in a fund for
use in protecting, extending, and improving the reserves.
Pinchot quickly reorganized the agency stressing
decentralized decision-making under national direction.

Though enormously successful in recruiting professionally trained foresters and fostering a strong esprit de corps, the Forest Service, as it came to be called, was not able to steer itself clear of all conflict. The Agricultural Appropriations Act of 1907, for example, reflected the hostility of some Westerners and some Western Congressmen when it abolished the special fund created from forest reserve receipts and required the Forest Service to provide detailed accounts of all revenues and expenditures. In addition, it forbade creation of further reserves in Washington, Oregon, Idaho, Montana, Wyoming, and Colorado without Congressional approval.

Since these states had the most desirable timberlands, Roosevelt responded by proclaiming 16 million acres of forest reserves in these areas just before he signed the 1907 appropriations bill into law. Once again executive action had flouted Congressional intent and once again Congress was infuriated. Recognizing the need to build public support, Roosevelt called the governors of all the states and territories to a conference on the conservation of the nation's natural resources. They were joined by many members of Congress, professional organizations and the press. This was the first time governors had gathered to discuss national issues and the conference was quite successful. Follow-up conferences and commissions also supported Presidential initiatives and urged continued cooperation along these lines between states and between the states and federal government.

Hostility from the West was related to the fact that despite emphasis on conservation as wise use, the administration of Teddy Roosevelt had withdrawn and reserved millions of acres of public land. Since the development of the West was so closely tied to the use of these resources anger surfaced when these resources were withheld. The idea of states' rights to develop natural resources located in the West was then and is now a powerful political force. Efforts were continually made to get federal lands ceded to the states with the underlying purpose being to remove them from public to private control. The zealousness of Pinchot's young foresters did not win friends in the West. Neither did the fact that many foresters were hostile to the use of the forests for grazing, resenting that range problems took more time and attention than did the silviculture for which they were professionally trained. The "locking up" of water, minerals, and power sites which had been available to the East in its development was strongly resented. Further objections were based on the idea that removing lands from settlement and development removes them from tax rolls and thereby imposes an unfair burden on the area. Finally, for Westerners national forests were controversial and in case of doubt, they preferred federal spending directed toward developing water projects and other resources crucial to the West.

Interestingly, at the same time that cession of public lands to the states was being advocated and enthusiasm for the Forest Service was at a low ebb in the West, support in the East for national parks and national forests was growing. Beginning about 1880 the idea of governmental purchase to protect large areas of land in the East steadily increased. Eastern support came from three sources. First, Eastern loggers, having logged their lands, wanted to sell these cutover lands to the federal government as they believed they were otherwise worthless. Second, Eastern preservationists, conservationists, and naturalists favored acquiring these lands as a preservation measure. Third, these cutover lands posed tremendous fire hazards and a great deal of the support in the East was tied to the reputation of the Forest Service as a successful fire control agent.

The Weeks Act of 1911 ultimately provided for the purchase of lands for national forests without specifying geographic limits. Thus the Forest Service extended their work beyond the Western public lands and became truly national. The consent of state legislatures where purchases were planned was required in order not to infringe on state wishes. Most states were enthusiastic and the consent requirement did not interfere significantly with acquisition. A second provision of the Weeks Act appropriated funds for the Secretary of Agriculture to cooperate with any state or group of states in protecting private or state forests from fire in order to protect the watersheds of navigable streams. Although the funds were limited, this action encouraged many states to adopt effective fire control laws and to establish fire control organizations.

After 1912 when Congress appropriated money for roads for management and fire protection, Congressional attention began to shift elsewhere. And with the coming of World War I, resource policy drastically shifted from conservation to exploitation.

Even when actions were underway to protect forest lands, no such measures were being undertaken on behalf of public grazing lands. Initially stock raisers obtained land ostensibly for other uses or more commonly simply used the range as trespassers. Concern for title often did not extend beyond needed water holes. After the invention of barbed wire, huge areas were fenced off by large cattle barons despite 1885 legislation forbidding such enclosures and authorizing their destruction. These laws were rarely enforced and, in general, little was done to protect the public domain lands from overgrazing.

Livestock grazing on the forest reserves was also not without problems. Foresters, as has been noted, were often hostile to this use of the land despite the fact that in the early years the most numerous users of forest lands were stockmen. Minimal range fees were charged beginning in 1906, yet grazing revenues exceeded timber receipts from 1906 to 1910, equalled them from 1911 to 1917, and far surpassed them from 1917 until 1921. After 1910 range protection was given attention by the Forest Service but often even meager management efforts met with hostility from the livestock industry.

However, livestock operators did not constitute a unified single-interest group. Cattle growers warred against sheepmen. And both opposed homesteaders and settlements that would limit their use of the range or block cattle drives from winter to summer range. Often matters were settled with violence and bloodshed.

Because of the totally unregulated situation on the unreserved public domain, grazing conditions there continued to deteriorate. By contrast, on the forest reserves Forest Service efforts to impose minimal fees and limit overgrazing eventually engendered some support. In two crucial cases the U.S. Supreme Court in 1911 reversed a number of lower court decisions and upheld the Secretary's authority to regulate use of the forest reserves. Stockmen who were originally hostile gradually came to see the advantages of having the Forest Service carefully draw grazing allocations to protect water supplies, tree growth, and the range itself. Grazing permits were issued with officially recognized livestock boards successfully reducing inevitable friction. Efforts to initiate a similar leasing plan for the public domain repeatedly failed. Still, on 400,000 acres in California, range conditions became so bad that cattle and sheep operators joined together to persuade Congress to add these lands to the Modoc National Forest. When that bill passed, similar requests flooded in from all over the West.

Other than the Stockraising Homestead Act of 1916, however, little was done to limit grazing use on the public domain. The 1916 Act provided for 640-acre ranch homesteads, recognizing the impossibility of success on 160- and 320-acre parcels in the arid West. Six hundred forty acres also proved too small and the Act added a further problem when mineral title was severed from the title to surface resources and the former was retained by the government. By the 1960s and 1970s serious conflicts arose when the government began leasing the coal which underlies the ranch homesteads.

World War I brought over-exploitation of both the range and forest lands. On the public domain there were no controls on overgrazing. On Forest Service lands the Forest Service was pressured into issuing "temporary" permits to increase range use. Demand for meat was high and increased production was encouraged. The results were disastrous for the depleted range and for the artificially over-expanded industry. Economic hardship which followed made control even more difficult in the succeeding years. By the mid-1920s severe drought coupled with the desire of the federal government to raise grazing fees to help pay off the World War I debt brought on major conflicts. Ultimately the whole concept of range management was challenged. The fracas was conducted on a highly emotional level with tremendous press and editorial attention. To conservationists, the Society of American Foresters, the American Forestry Association, and many Easterners, the stock operators' demands were unreasonable--even evil. In such an atmosphere no constructive legislation could be agreed upon. Furthermore, in the bitter dispute the Forest Service lost the support it had been developing among the livestock industry.

The situation was critical when in 1929 Herbert Hoover became President. His Secretaries of Interior and Agriculture agreed that a leasing plan for the public range was needed but they could not agree on which department should administer it. Faced with no consensus, Congress again failed to act. Hoover then decided that the land should be transferred to the states because they could not do worse and might do better. Congress held hearings on the proposal but never seriously considered its passage since opposition was nearly universal. Eastern states and conservationists who had a stake in keeping the lands as a national resource feared private control and further deterioration and voiced expected criticisms. But even Western states were not enthusiastic. The lands were so "beat out" that they were considered a liability and two potential income sources were at stake: Mineral rights were to be retained by the federal government and the states stood to lose highway funds distributed on the basis of the amount of federal land in each state.

The Great Depression and the severe drought and Dust Bowl conditions which followed finally forced Congressional action. The result was the Taylor Grazing Act of 1934. This legislation ended the period of free access to the public domain and represents the first widespread effort to manage, conserve, or improve the public domain lands. Following its passage, President Franklin Roosevelt withdrew these lands from all further homestead entry. Stock operators were now required to secure grazing permits, pay fees and use the public lands as prescribed by the Department of Interior. Unfortunately, the operators had used these lands as their own for sixty years and they were not about to give up their accustomed advantages. When provisions for allocating the range were implemented, the most prosperous of the traditional users completely dominated the permit process. Nomadic sheep grazers and cattle operators, hard hit by the drought and economic collapse, were virtually locked out.

Furthermore, in order to win approval of the Act, Interior Secretary Ickes struck bargains which continued overgrazing for four more decades. Among his promises were: that there would be no extensive bureaucracy to regulate the use of the lands; that fees for grazing would be tied to administration costs, not fair market value; and that Interior could administer these lands for about $150,000 annually compared to the Forest Service estimate of $1.5 to $2 million. Thus he ensured both low grazing fees and a weak collection and regulatory agency while implicitly promising to protect and revitalize the public lands. Furthermore, the conservation groups provided no counterweight. They were either preoccupied with forest-to-park land transfers or refused support to any effort not run by the Forest Service. In this way the public domain lands became grazing lands, and the Grazing Service came to be run by the stock operators who controlled the Grazing Advisory Boards.

Range conditions deteriorated even further in World War II than they had in World War I. The war and the markets it created were as beneficial to the livestock industry as they were devastating to the land. The industry emerged stronger than ever and was virtually

unwilling to tolerate any interference with the use of
"their" range. The Grazing Service proved totally
inadequate to provide range protection. Wildlife was also
hard hit as ranchers did everything they could to rid
themselves of wildlife. Forest lands fared somewhat
better as the Forest Service tried diligently to prevent a
recurrence of the World War I overgrazing disaster.
Nevertheless, the emergence of powerful livestock and
forest industries during the war meant that forest and
range policy came to be dominated by them.

The postwar years began to reflect a change in the
nation's values. Dana and Fairfax (1980: 180) argue that
for the first half of the twentieth century the
conservation movement had primarily been government
defined and government led. Concerned interest groups had
arrayed themselves to support accepted government
leadership and programs. In the 1950s, however, new
groups began to appear which were not so easily
accommodated. Ultimately a third great wave of
conservation developed in which the initiative slipped
from the government and was taken up by the demands of new
interest groups.

On the public domain lands yet another grazing fee
controversy arose in the mid-1940s. An attempt to triple
the fees charged by the Grazing Service (a rate half that
levied by the Forest Service) was met with a harsh
response by Senator Pat McCarren of Nevada, head of the
Senate Public Lands Committee. The Grazing Service was
caught between McCarren's committee, which demanded lower
fees, and the House Appropriations Committee, which
insisted on higher fees. As a result, the Service
suffered an 85 percent budget reduction and virtually
ceased to exist. Out of the wreckage, by executive
reorganization, the remnants of the Grazing Service were
merged with the General Land Office (GLO) to form the
Bureau of Land Management (BLM) in 1946.

The BLM began with distinct disadvantages. It had "no
coherent mission, no authority, and no statutorily defined
existence. It was rather like the lands it managed, a
residual category, assigned to administer the loose ends
of over 3500 statutes randomly enacted over the previously
150 years" (Dana and Fairfax 1980: 187). Further, it had
an acute financial crisis and almost no personnel. The
grazing boards ultimately contributed money to pay BLM
salaries. Finally, tying the BLM to the GLO was at best
confusing. It meant that the BLM inherited the GLO's
responsibilities for all mineral leasing as well as for

processing and recording all sales, entries, withdrawals, and leases on the public domain. The reorganization was primarily the work of supporters of the large livestock operators and was not intended to be the beginning of an era of land stewardship. Despite the growing importance of preservation groups and recreationists in other areas, the BLM continued to be ignored by the public and dominated by commodity interests for the next twenty years.

Responding to new pressures, the Forest Service, on the other hand, pushed through Congress its own Multiple Use and Sustained Yield Act in 1960. At the time only the Sierra Club objected, noting that the Act gave the Forest Service nearly absolute discretion in setting priorities and provided no clear criteria for evaluating competing multiple uses.

The 1960s generally reflected the growing strength of the wilderness and recreation interests and saw the creation of the National Wilderness Preservation System (1964), the National Wildlife Refuge System (1966), the Wild and Scenic Rivers System (1968), the National Trail System (1968), the North Cascades National Park (1968), and the expansion of the Redwood National Park (1968). In the Forest Service a big controversy developed over their clear-cutting practices—a commercial harvesting method that is quite ugly—and fueled opponents' arguments that the Forest Service had "sold out" to industry.

The public domain lands continued to be unattended to and underfunded. For example, they were completely ignored in the 1964 Wilderness Act. However, some progress was eventually made by the BLM due to the Public Land Law Review Commission undertaken by Representative Wayne Aspinall of Colorado. As a result of the Commission's report, for the first time in its history the BLM was authorized to inventory and gather information about the lands and resources under its jurisdiction. The decade ended with the passage of the National Environmental Policy Act of 1969 (NEPA) which mandated consideration of the environmental impacts of major federal activities through preparation of environmental impact statements (EISs).

Environmental quality rather than concern about specific resource uses became an issue in the 1970s. These years saw the passage of the Clean Air Acts of 1970 and 1977, the Federal Water Pollution Control Act of 1972, and the 1977 Clean Water Act all of which greatly enhanced the federal role in environmental issues. However, they did so in a manner which reflected the Nixon

administration's particular brand of federalism. They
relied on the states, with federal financial aid, to carry
out most of the required regulatory functions. They hoped
to move control closer to the state and local levels, yet
provisions for federal overview of state programs and
creation of the Environmental Protection Agency prevented
total delegation of authority to the states.

For the public domain lands the 1970s were
particularly significant. The BLM finally was given its
own organic act when the Federal Land Policy and
Management Act (FLPMA) was passed in 1976. This Act was

> . . . truly landmark legislation. It provided for the
> first time a clear and coherent statement from
> Congress on the administration of the nation's public
> lands. . . . It set policy and standards for the
> Bureau to plan, manage, and protect the public lands
> and their resources. (U.S. Congress 1980: 1)

Furthermore, for the first time the policy of federal
public lands was formally declared: that the public lands
should remain in federal ownership and should be managed
under the principles of balanced multiple use and
sustained yield.

Nevada cattlemen holding grazing permits from BLM
perceived a threat to their interests in the multiple use
emphasis as it was interpreted and implemented by the
Carter administration. And the result was the
organization and spread of the Sagebrush Rebellion—the
movement to transfer ownership and control of public lands
from BLM to the states in which they are located. Soon
other Western state legislatures joined Nevada; bills were
also introduced in Congress and hearings were held. In
many respects, Sagebrush is the recent version of the
older conflicts which troubled BLM's predecessors, the
General Land Office and the Taylor Grazing Service.

In this same vein it is noteworthy that the election
of Ronald Reagan, a self-proclaimed Sagebrush Rebel and
rancher, and his appointments of "Rebels" James Watt as
Interior Secretary and Robert Burford as BLM Director did
not end the controversies surrounding the agency (Culhane
1984: 293-94; Clarke and McCool 1985: 115-18). As Culhane
(1984: 314) notes, "[Watt's] unpopular policies and his
highly visible verbal pratfalls ultimately proved so
intolerable as to elicit a Senate 'no confidence'
motion." Watt resigned under pressure in October 1983 and
was replaced by William P. Clark. He, in turn, was

succeeded by Donald P. Hodel. Burford has retained his
position but his policies are challenged on numerous
fronts. Grazing policies believed to be turning the
public rangelands into desert and highly controversial
wilderness and mineral leasing policies are among those
most criticized.

Once again grazing fee controversies have reached near
range war proportions. On December 31, 1985, the 1978
Public Rangelands Improvement Act is due to expire. This
Act governs how much sheep and cattle operators must pay
to graze their animals on BLM and Forest Service lands.
Once again the controversy hinges on whether to continue
the current practice of tying grazing fees to the cost of
raising and selling livestock (which keeps the fees low)
or whether to increase the price paid to reflect the cost
of grazing on similar private land. A BLM and Forest
Service draft study reports that current fees on public
lands are $1.35 per animal per month. Comparable private
fees are $6.65.

Operators and conservationists can find no areas of
agreement and the rhetoric is emotional and highly
reminiscent of the earlier grazing fee fights. A leader
of the National Cattlemen's Association insists that "the
wildlife community doesn't realize that the best friend
they've got is the rancher. We're trying to establish a
cooperative working relationship with wildlife people,
conservationists and environmentalists to get them to
recognize those values [of the cowboy] and quit the
bickering" (Stanfield 1985: 1623). On the other hand, a
Wilderness Society representative argues, "That they [the
operators] won't even support something as weak-kneed as
[the subcommittee's draft] symbolizes that they want to
continue the status quo of overgrazing, bad management and
the abuse of public lands in their own selfish interests
rather than acting responsibly in the public interest"
(Stanfield 1985: 1623).

Federal range managers are also divided on the issue.
The Forest Service apparently favors higher fees; the BLM,
lower ones. Although there have been numerous attempts at
compromise, the two sides seem a long way from resolving
the current edition of this 100-year old controversy. As
Stanfield notes:

The problem is that the issue of grazing fees and
public land management is so loaded with the passion
of cowboy mystique, the western power politics that
has predominated in Congress on this issue for 100

> years, and the long-simmering frustration of the
> perpetually rebuffed conservationists that the cowboys
> and the conservationists appear unlikely to
> accommodate each others' point of view (1985: 1623).

Interestingly, although "only two percent of the nation's
beef producers graze their cattle on public lands, the
issue is a battle cry for the entire industry and the
West" (Stanfield 1985: 1625). And this is true

> even though only 8 percent of western beef producers
> graze their cattle on public lands, [somehow] few if
> any of the 92 percent that don't benefit from the
> federal subsidy complain about their comparative
> disadvantage. And others who live in the West take
> the cause of the public land grazers to heart
> (Stanfield 1985: 1625).

WATER POLICY

The history of water policy has always been closely
linked with that of the land. In tracing this history,
our discussion will be divided into four eras: (1)
navigation and flood control; (2) construction and
development; (3) interagency conflict; and (4)
devolution. Simultaneously with the early territorial
acquisitions, exploration of the new lands and rivers were
undertaken. The Army Corps of Engineers was created in
1802 and from the beginning it assumed a central role in
the exploration, protection, and utilization of the
nation's waterways.

Navigation and Flood Control

In 1824 Congress authorized the Corps to investigate
and improve navigation on the Mississippi and Ohio
Rivers. This led to a series of bills covering rivers and
harbors that over time have resulted in numerous "internal
improvements" including river channelization, dredge and
fill activities, and beach erosion control.
By 1850, Congress had added flood prevention to the
growing list of authorized Corps responsibilities. The
Mississippi River Commission was established in 1879 to
investigate and improve both navigation and flood control
in the Mississippi Basin. The Corps was chosen director

necessarily involving them in river basin planning and
intergovernmental relations (Clarke and McCool 1985:
15-18).

Construction and Development

As settlement extended into the more arid lands of the
West, water became an ever more crucial consideration.
Recognizing the near impossibility of expecting individual
landholders to carry out effective irrigation programs by
themselves, the Congress in 1894 passed the Carey Act. It
attempted to lure the states into participation by
promising them land. This plan had little success and by
the end of the century it was clear that federal help was
needed. Nearly all feasible irrigation projects that
could be developed by individuals, private corporations,
or the states were already underway (Dana and Fairfax
1980: 76). Pressure from the West, where economic
development depended on water, and support from Teddy
Roosevelt's White House led to the passage of the
Reclamation Act of 1902, the beginning of federal
irrigation activities. Initially the Reclamation Service
was organized within the U.S. Geological Survey to
administer the Act. But in 1907 the Service was made an
independent bureau and in 1923 it was renamed the Bureau
of Reclamation. Its mission was to transform the arid
West of cowtowns and barren desert waste into prosperous
modern communities supported by lush farmland (Clarke and
McCool 1985: 27).
To accomplish this, irrigation works were to be
created in the seventeen Western states funded by the
sales of public lands which were earmarked for the
reclamation fund. It was expected that once these
projects were underway, the estimated costs of
construction would be used to calculate charges per acre
which the water users would then pay back over a ten-year
period. Numerous problems developed in the ensuing years,
some technical, some financial. Sales of public lands did
not produce sufficient revenues to cover project costs and
water users were unable to meet the ten-year repayment
schedules. The deadlines were extended to twenty years
and in 1921 supplementary monies were found by diverting
part of the oil, potash, and potassium royalties from
public lands into the reclamation fund. Still, money
remained a big problem, forcing the Director of the
Service to admit in a 1926 appropriations hearing that,

due to the number of uncompleted projects and the present
state of the fund, it would be inadvisable to take up any
new work for some years (Clarke and McCool 1985: 26-31).

Meanwhile the Corps' mission had again been extended
by Congress. Early river and harbor acts had dealt mainly
with removing obstructions from waterways. Then,
typically, other functions had been added ad hoc with
particular situations and projects leading to general
statutes and guidelines for future projects (Allee and
Ingram 1972: 2-30).

The 1909 Rivers and Harbors Act had authorized the
Corps to add hydroelectric power development to its
project studies (Clarke and McCool 1985: 19). A broad
planning function began in 1927 with the "308" reports.
Some 200 reports on the potential of various rivers for
multiple purpose development were prepared over the next
ten years emphasizing navigation, flood control,
irrigation, and hydroelectric power. Thus, in addition to
its historic mission of navigation and flood control, and
later shore protection and power, the Corps has become
involved in a wide variety of other water development.
For example, irrigation was added in 1944, hurricane
protection in 1955, water supply in 1958, fish and
wildlife management in 1958, storage for water quality in
1961 and recreation in 1944 (expanded in 1965) (Allee and
Ingram 1972: 2-30).

Liberal readings of its authorities suggest the Corps
should have no difficulty in responding to almost any
water-related activity suggested by local interests.
Nevertheless, there is evidence that Corps involvement in
these other activities has sometimes continued to be
justified as necessary for flood control. In one case a
wildlife preserve was recommended for an urban floodway
but pains were taken to point out that this was the only
feasible method for handling the potentially large amount
of floodwater in the area. In another case the
recreational uses of a site were expanded until they were
well over half the total expected benefits--still Congress
was assured that this was primarily a flood control
project (Allee and Ingram 1972: 2-31).

The New Deal years saw a resurgence of the Bureau of
Reclamation. When jobs were scarce, the best engineering
graduates from Western universities proudly joined the
Bureau. In addition, the agency was refinanced and the
repayment period was extended to forty years.
Hydroelectric power generation had become an important
part of water resources development and the Bureau's

Boulder Dam was an impressive feat. Revenues from power sales also helped the agency re-establish itself (Clarke and McCool 1985: 32-35).

Interagency Conflict

By the 1950s, however, there was growing competition between the Bureau of Reclamation and the Corps of Engineers. Though the Bureau tried to expand its mission to include Alaska, it was reminded that its activities were limited to the seventeen Western states. Congressional concern about duplication of effort was resolved in favor of the Corps. Increasingly, reclamation projects were justified on the basis of recreational benefits (Clarke and McCool 1985: 35-36).

By the 1960s the Bureau's interagency struggles became quite bitter. As good dam sites became scarce, wilderness areas, national parks and monuments were scouted by the agency. This involved the Bureau in fights with conservationists and the National Park Service in addition to their continuing competition with the Corps. In a major defeat, for example, the Colorado River Basin Bill of 1968 turned back a Bureau proposal to build two dams in the Grand Canyon (Clarke and McCool 1985: 97-98).

Meanwhile the Corps had become a virtual monopoly, doing more water resources development planning and construction than the Bureau even in the Bureau's "own" area--particularly the Pacific Northwest (Clarke and McCool 1985: 98-99). By the 1970s when the environmental movement had grown strong, the Corps was able to lay claim to a long-standing interest in pollution control. It now began involving itself in the new urban studies and expanded permits programs (Clarke and McCool 1985: 17). The Bureau of Reclamation, on the other hand, was condemned by environmentalists and had great difficulty meeting the extensive requirements inherent in the environmental impact statements mandated by the 1969 National Environmental Policy Act (NEPA). In addition, their earth-filled Teton Dam collapsed causing extensive loss of life and property and further eroding confidence in the agency (Clarke and McCool 1985: 99).

Devolution

The election of Jimmy Carter in 1976 did not improve
matters. In a challenge to "water politics as usual,"
Carter tried to cut federal funds for nineteen ongoing
water projects. Of this "hit list," eleven projects were
under construction by the Corps (Clarke and McCool 1985:
19), and eight were being built by the Bureau of
Reclamation (Clarke and McCool 1985: 99). Southern and
Western members of Congress reacted angrily and were
joined by Western governors. The storm of protest
apparently took the Carter administration by surprise
since seventy-four members of Congress had just sent a
letter supporting the President's efforts at water
reform. Four problems seemed paramount: (1) careerists
in the Corps and Bureau of Reclamation did not share the
administration's interest in limiting structural water
development projects; (2) governors and members of
Congress were not warned in advance about which specific
projects were to be included; (3) the seventy-four
Congressional letter writers claimed they had intended
their support for limiting new projects, not those that
were already underway; and, (4) 1976 and 1977 were years
of drought when interest in water development was
especially salient in the West (Clarke and McCool 1985:
20).

Since four of the five largest Western water projects
were on the hit list, Westerners were particularly upset.
Interest groups such as the Western States Water Council
and the National Water Resources Association joined with
Congressional allies, the Bureau of Reclamation and the
Corps, to fight for funding of all the projects. The six
Western senators on the Senate Appropriations Committee
and the fifteen Western representatives on the House
Appropriations Committee led the struggle. Ultimately, in
a compromise bill, the Congress decided to withhold
funding on the Auburn Dam pending completion of safety
studies and to delete funds for Fruitland Mesa, Narrows
Unit, Oahe, and Savory Pot Hook--all Bureau projects.
Funds were reduced for the Central Arizona Project (CAP)
(Clarke and McCool 1985: 100).

Northern legislators who voiced strong objections to
paying for big Western water projects were influential in
the decision. Local opposition was the cause of Congress
deleting funds for at least two of the projects: the Oahe
Diversion Project in South Dakota where farmers and
ranchers, the ostensible beneficiaries, objected, and the

Narrows Unit in Colorado. Further, the CAP, generally
supported in Arizona, is opposed by an organized local
group called Citizens Concerned About the Project (Clarke
and McCool 1985: 100-101).

Even those who fought the hit list recognize that
times have changed for Western water projects. Governor
Lamm of Colorado, for example, notes lowered expectations
and sees the days of Western water projects coming to an
end. He strongly believes that "there is a limit to the
carrying capacity of the West" (Clarke and McCool 1985:
100-101). Governor Lamm is not alone. In addition, the
Coalition for Water Project Review was formed by more than
twenty environmental groups in opposition to Corps
projects. Both environmental and economic objections were
raised. And as the conflict broadened, the National
Taxpayers Union, the League of Women Voters and Common
Cause also got involved (Clark and McCool 1985: 21-22).

In addition to his efforts to reform water policy by
cutting funds, President Carter called for increased cost
sharing between the states and federal government. Carter
suggested that the states pay five to ten percent of
project costs. Secretary of Interior Andrus claimed that
states with good projects would be ". . . willing to put
their money where their mouth is" (Clarke and McCool 1985:
23-24). Congress refused to go along.

The Reagan administration promised a new beginning in
Western water development. Interior Secretary Watt told
Western governors that Carter's "War on the West" was
over. Sensitive to the strong support Reagan received
from Western agriculture, ranchers and associated
businesses, the administration appeared more sympathetic
to the dependence of Western states on federal water
projects. Accordingly, a 21 percent increase in the FY
1983 Bureau of Reclamation budget was followed by another
significant increase for FY 1984. In addition, the agency
was now renamed the Bureau of Reclamation after having
been reorganized and named the Water and Power Service in
1979 (Clarke and McCool 1985: 105).

Interestingly, the FY 1983 budget also contained a
request for a 26 percent decrease in Corps funding.
Congress, however, continued the funding levels of the
previous two years. President Reagan also has tried to
require the states to pay a substantial portion of project
costs (Clarke and McCool 1985: 29). Faced with enormous
federal budget deficits, the Congress seems likely to
agree.

Currently pending before the Congress are omnibus water project bills which provide for major up-front funding of water projects. The provisions were worked out in an agreement between the Senate leadership and the administration. Under this agreement, feasibility studies would require a 50 percent cost sharing by local sponsors; hydroelectric, municipal, and industrial projects would require 100 percent up-front funding; and irrigation projects (Corps only) would require 35 percent up-front. Alhough there are some significant differences between the House and Senate versions, both contain many of the same cost sharing provisions. Neither bill addresses the Bureau of Reclamation projects but similar requirements are expected to follow (National Water Line 1985).

Meanwhile, the House in a 203-202 vote agreed to strip 31 water projects from a supplemental 1985 spending bill. Appropriations Committee Chairman Jamie L. Whitten (D-Miss.) strongly argued for funding all 62 Corps projects, noting that there have been no new starts on federal water projects in ten years. He added these are "not pork barrel . . . . When did it get to be bad to look after your own country?" (Shapiro 1985: A4).

Other problems also beset federal-state relations in water. Federal courts are chipping away at the power of states to keep water within their own borders for their own citizens. The traditional notion that states somehow "own" the water within their borders has been modified recently by the U.S. Supreme Court in the Sporhase decision (Weatherford, Ingram, and Brown 1984-85: 6). Along the same vein, El Paso, Texas, is trying to import large quantities of groundwater from an unwilling New Mexico. The San Diego County Water Authority is trying to purchase the opportunity to receive some 300,000 acre-feet of water from a private reservoir on the Yampa River in Colorado. These waters are at least partially allocated by interstate compacts and there has been an assumption underlying "the law of the river" that the water allocated to each state is to be consumed in that state. Proposed "water market" transactions will severely test that assumption (Weatherford et al. 1984-85: 6). Furthermore, some believe that if the states are unable to resolve their differences, Congress can and will act (Clyde 1984-85: 9-10).

Large Indian water claims also have yet to be resolved. In 1908 the U.S. Supreme Court held that when the United States created Indian reservations it also indirectly reserved enough water to accomplish the

purposes of the reservation (Winters v. U.S., 1908, 207
U.S. 564). Throughout the West, the amount of water thus
reserved for Indians greatly exceeds the amounts currently
being used on reservations (Clyde 1984-85: 11).
Non-Indian users are likely to be displaced as the tribes
put their promised water to use. This will undoubtedly
impose some hardship and increase friction. It is
probable that the federal government will be called upon
to offer assistance or compensation (Weatherford et al.
1984-85: 6).

As the Mexican population and related water demand
grows, it is conceivable that pressure could build to
reopen negotiations concerning the division and quality of
the Colorado River water flowing into Mexico. To the
degree that our national security is seen as being
dependent on Mexican goodwill and oil, the interests of
the Colorado River Basin states may be compromised in the
name of overriding national needs. Additional concerns
include aggravated salinity problems and possible water
contamination by commonplace and exotic chemicals
(Weatherford et al. 1984-85: 6, 17).

CONCLUSIONS

There has been considerable political controversy in
the field of natural resources which could be classified
under the rubric of the pejorative federalism models. For
example, federal dominance of decision-making over
resources located within the boundaries of various Western
states has attracted a great deal of attention. Not
surprisingly, the states' rights model, dual federalism,
has recently become important in discussions of the Carter
"hit list" and the Sagebrush Rebellion. This has happened
despite the fact that scholars have generally agreed that
"dual federalism 'passed' during the period of the
Depression and World War II" (Fairfax 1982: 952).

Over time various other models have also come in and
out of fashion. At times particular interests have made
up new models or definitions of federalism as a means of
providing themselves with some intellectual
justification. Classically, new definitions and models
have been used to obscure the real issues or as a cloak to
hide the real interests behind. For these reasons, we
have decided that the place to begin is not with these
models because they may blind one to what is really going
on. Rather, we have preferred to relate a narrative from

which can be drawn certain lessons of federal-state relations.

We have been struck by at least five lessons as we have reviewed the history of federal land and water policy.

Lesson One

First, much of the conflict that has been masked as a federal-state conflict is really interstate conflict. As early as the acquisition era, there were conflicts between the seven states with large colonial claims to Western territories and the six states without such lands. Later as the federal government aided the West in its push for settlement and use of Western resources, Easterners began "to agitate for conservation, husbandry, and efficient use of the lands" (Dana and Fairfax 1980: 31). Meanwhile, with federal grants to the railroads, the South worried about losing out to a combination of the industrial East and the agricultural West.

In water, Southern agriculture has long competed with Western irrigators for federal water projects. More recently there is controversy between the Frostbelt and the Sunbelt as the latter grows and develops—sometimes at the expense of the former.

Lesson Two

A second lesson follows fairly closely from the first: federal projects and federal lands are federal in name only. Sally Fairfax has argued that it is misleading to view federal authority as all powerful. She recognizes the U.S. Supreme Court decision in Kleppe v. New Mexico which sustained "a federal statute that preempted long-standing state wildlife programs, and held that federal authority over federal lands was 'without limit'" (Fairfax 1982: 970). But she argues that there are numerous factors which tend to limit potential federal authority. The BLM, for example, has been expected to fulfill enormous land management responsibilities with far less money and far fewer personnel than comparable federal resource agencies (Fairfax 1982: 974; Clarke and McCool 1985). "Operating in an intensely politicized, frequently polarized political arena, BLM personnel do not always consider bold assertion of federal prerogatives to be their top priority" (Fairfax 1982: 978).

Furthermore, for the BLM especially, federal lands are
a misnomer. Unlike the Park Service and the Forest
Service which are at times troubled by "inholdings"
(privately-held lands within their areas of jurisdiction),
the BLM only occasionally administers "blocked in" lands.
More often BLM lands are a checkerboard of fragmented
parcels mixed in with federal parks and monuments,
forests, wildlife refuges, and Indian and military
reservations, as well as with state or privately-owned
lands. "The result is not 'federal lands' but a crazy
quilt of landowners, management goals, resources and
constraints. The states and localities therefore emerge
as particularly important participants in BLM's management
efforts" (Fairfax 1982: 975).

Earlier, in a classic study of the administration of
the public domain lands, Phillip O. Foss also emphasized
the importance of local interests in federal grazing
policy. He detailed a decision-making process which is
dominated by prosperous, influential stockmen acting
through District Grazing Advisory Boards effectively to
"capture" the BLM (Foss 1960: 199-201).

Whether or not the BLM remains "captured" to the same
degree, it is still true as Foss (1960: 197) argued that
for many stockmen the federal range is an integral,
necessary part of their operation. And grazers continue
to make the claim that federal grazing permits are
commonly capitalized into the value of privately held
ranches when they are bought and sold. This dependence
along with the individualistic nature of Western livestock
operators has inevitably fueled opposition to any sign of
federal government "interference."

In the area of federal water policy, there is also
ample evidence of the influence of local and state
interests. Federal water projects are most often locally
initiated. And if they are to have much hope of success,
they must be able to demonstrate unified local support.
In addition, basin-wide agreement among states involved
"is as important in getting a reclamation package through
Congress as local agreement is in getting a single project
into the package" (Ingram 1978: 70).

Furthermore, once projects have been completed, the
proceeds from hydroelectric power generation have gone to
basin-wide development accounts or to fund further
development. Economists have long been critical of this
"raid on the federal treasury" as benefits are seen to be
heaped on the project area at the expense of the general
national interest (Ingram 1978: 62).

Still, the notion of too much federal control dies hard. We think that what looks like federal control may be more accurately described as reflecting the perspective of scientific management. For the most part the federal resource agencies still aspire to live up to the ideals of the "golden era of Roosevelt and Pinchot." Thus, a cadre of resource professionals have emerged at the national level who believe in rational, comprehensive, scientific planning and management. And this has seemed to mean that they favor centralized decision-making. We think it likely that this is not so much a concern for centralization or decentralization as it is an issue of choosing among theories of decision-making. Thus the question has become one of scientific management versus local control. The scientific principles that resource professionals know and uniformly apply are better implemented through hierarchical structures, but this does not necessarily mean centralization or decentralization even though it is commonly so identified. Reconciling professional knowledge about what ought to be done with local concerns is not easy.

The Corps of Engineers, for example, has been credited with making a more conscientious attempt to accommodate itself to the calls for increased public participation in Corps decision-making than other resource agencies. Yet when "fishbowl planning" and other extensive efforts to involve the public did not result in a consensus on the best project alternative or in rating highly the alternatives believed best by the Corps, the agency lost enthusiasm for innovative planning programs (Mazmanian and Nienaber 1979: 167).

R.W. Behan points to this same concern in the Forest Service when he writes of the myth of the omnipotent forester. According to him young foresters are imbued with the myth that what they must do is "have enough guts to stand up and tell the public how [its] lands should be managed. As professional foresters, we know what's best for the land" (Behan 1966: 398).

The very creation of the BLM within Interior provides a further example. Former Secretary of Interior Ickes promised the livestock industry and its Congressional supporters an agency that would ameliorate overgrazing and range destruction but one that would be weak compared to the Forest Service. A handful of range managers with a small budget would not be able to impose much scientific decision-making on an unwilling livestock community.

Lesson Three

   A third lesson derived from our review is that
multiple interests operate through the federal system to
form bargaining arenas sensitive to their concerns. Often
what looks like federal-state conflict on the surface may
turn out to be a jostling among various interests for the
forum which best advantages each of them.
   In water policy, the federal Boulder Canyon Project
Act, for example, clearly advantaged California interests
over those of Arizona so much so that Arizona refused to
sign the Colorado River Compact (Goslin 1978: 35).
   Currently, the new Clean Water bill presents a funding
formula for sewage treatment plants that advantages
smaller states over larger ones and certain areas of the
country over others. "'I don't know what the Founding
Fathers would have to say about the logarithms of sewage
needs cubed, but I don't think they would be surprised to
see Rhode Island, Connecticut and Maine ganging up on New
York' said Sen. David F. Durenberger (R-Minn.), who
complained that Great Lakes states stand to lose $156
million under the new formula" (Peterson 1985: A23).
   In public lands policy as early as the disposition
era, Eastern states objected to federal policies for
Western public lands not out of concern for the West but
out of worry that increased Western settlement would
negatively affect Eastern labor and wages. Later,
commodity interests repeatedly pushed for federal
involvement and funding. Western commodity interests,
preservationists and foresters joined forces to support
the Forest Service Organic Act in 1897. Cattle and sheep
operators overcame their innate hostility long enough to
get together and persuade Congress to add 400,000 acres of
depleted California range to the Modoc National Forest.
   By the 1930s, an experimental range scheme which
permitted state and federal assistance to stock operators
in one area was so well-received that soon other areas
were requesting Congressional authorization to create
their own grazing districts (Dana and Fairfax 1980: 160).
The result was the Taylor Grazing Act in which the more
prosperous and influential users locked out less
advantaged operators. The executive reorganization of
1946 which created the BLM also was primarily the work of
the large livestock operators and their allies.
   Interestingly, this has not meant that
environmentalists are opposed to federal involvement. As
we have noted, preservationists and conservationists

actively supported the early Forest Service, and
conservation groups allowed the federal takeover of the
grazing districts in part because the conservation groups
were so involved in the battle between the Forest Service
and the Park Service over wilderness designations and land
transfers between the Services. Further,
environmentalists supported the passage of the BLM's
organic act, FLPMA, in 1976 which mandated multiple use of
the public lands. In fact, Culhane argues that

> The environmental movement . . . constituted a
> powerful tool that the service and the bureau used to
> reinforce the resource-protection half of the
> multiple-use policy. Environmentalists' criticisms. .
> . and warnings . . . were visible public pressures
> that agency offices could use to justify increasingly
> stringent restrictions on consumptive users'
> activities. The militant preservationist demands of
> many environmentalists added punch to such pressures
> because the demands confronted traditional users with
> a choice between complying with the agencies'
> restrictions on defending themselves against efforts
> to place more and more federal land off-limits to the
> "despoilers." (1981: 228)

On the other hand, we have found no consistent pattern of
support or opposition from either environmentalists or
commodity users and development interests. In water
policy environmentalists have strongly opposed the
activities of both the Bureau of Reclamation and the Corps
of Engineers. And they have willingly worked with the
President for devolution--pushing water project
responsibilities back to the states. Eastern states, who
happily claimed federal ownership of Western lands when
they were bringing in money, have seen them as a local
responsibility when they became a drain on the federal
treasury.

Established grazers who benefited from the Taylor
Grazing Act wanted a new, separate agency instead of the
stronger Forest Service, but they too have wanted federal
intervention to improve range conditions during the bad
times. In the Hoover era, neither the federal government
nor the states wanted involvement. And now, when the
grazing permittees are fighting fee increases and
pressures for other uses of the public lands, they prefer
other, more favorable decision-making arenas.

In sum, multiple interests have played out their
concerns using the federal system to take advantage of
whichever forum will provide them the best hearing, but
the situation is highly fluid and flexible. "Interactions
are complex, and mutual interests are typically partial
and not arrayed around levels of government" (Fairfax
1982: 973-974).

Lesson Four

Our fourth lesson considers the problem of hidden
costs. And we note that not only are there costs to the
federal treasury when the federal government takes the
burden of decisions but there are costs to the recipients
as well. Many critics, especially economists, have long
been outspoken on the failure to perceive the real costs
to the nation of federal water development. They have
expressed concern about "raid-the-treasury" games where
benefits are heaped on the interests of the project area
while the more general, diffuse interests of the federal
taxpayer suffer. Evaluation criteria have been criticized
for exaggerating project benefits, and financial
arrangements have been scored for extended pay-out periods
and low interest rates. Even when stringent benefit-cost
criteria and realistic interest rates have been employed,
it has been argued that the national interest has been
sacrificed. Opportunity costs are paid when one federal
program is chosen over another. Then, too, the large
federal bureaucracies with cadres of skilled professionals
represent a significant federal resource which might be
better employed to serve different national goals (Ingram
1978: 62). Very similar complaints have been made about
the federal land management agencies (Clawson 1983;
Brubaker 1984).

The perception that there are no real costs to the
recipients of federal largesse is also questionable. In
the Colorado River Basin, for example, two landmark pieces
of legislation--the Colorado River Storage Project Act of
1956 and the Colorado River Basin Act of 1968 are
illustrative. The former provided for four major upper
basin storage projects: Glen Canyon, Navajo, Flaming
Gorge, and a conditional Curecanti. The latter provided
for the Central Arizona Project (CAP) in the lower basin,
but also included projects affecting Utah, Colorado, New
Mexico, and Nevada (Ingram 1978: 62-63).

Generally, Western interests perceive these projects
as the vehicle through which they get their fair slice of
a much larger national subsidy pie that is distributed
across the country. And as such there is a reluctance to
review these projects critically. Nevertheless, the
recipients have paid costs found in foregoing choice, in
acting with insufficient information, and in forfeiting
the development of their own planning and decision-making
capability (Ingram 1978: 62-63).

The big choice for basin residents to make is among
alternative futures. Will there be continued population
growth and industrial expansion, or will they choose to
maintain wide-open spaces with low population densities
and limited industries? Will resources be exploited for
the benefit of the nation as a whole or will development
be foregone in favor of maintaining a relatively unspoiled
environment? Will the existing distribution of wealth be
maintained or will resource development be used to
redistribute riches to less privileged groups including
Indians and marginal farmers? Specific water development
projects make sense when they provide means of achieving
the desired future. However, in the politics of federal
water development the focus is on specific local projects
and whether the state or locality will be chosen to
receive the federal project, not on where the basin could
or should be going. And federal agencies have
traditionally played the key role in identifying dam sites
and selecting local projects (Ingram 1978: 65).

Federal authorization and appropriations have meant
compliance with federal evaluation procedures. In turn,
this has resulted in over-emphasis of national economic
efficiency often at the expense of broader social and
environmental considerations. The Animas-La Plata
project, part of the Colorado River Basin Act package,
provides a not uncommon example. Local support for the
project came from farmers and two Ute Indian tribes who
believed project irrigation water would improve the
quality of their lives. However, without taking into
account indirect social benefits, the benefit-cost ratio
was unfavorable and the project was rejected. Congressman
Wayne Aspinall of Colorado, who particularly wanted the
Animas-La Plata and four other projects in order to put
Colorado's entitlement in the upper basin to use, had the
political clout to block the CAP unless the Colorado
projects were authorized. In their hurried reworking of
the project to achieve a better benefit-cost ratio, the
Bureau of Reclamation dropped the plans to irrigate

marginal lands, including most of the Indian lands.
Instead, they offered increased industrial allocations to
Peabody Coal for development on the Ute reservation.
Farmington, New Mexico, was also approached to purchase
water for additional municipal development. Thus choices
about development were narrowed; for the Indians,
agriculture was not to take place. There was very little
time or opportunity for debate (Ingram 1978: 66-68).

Recipients commonly must act without sufficient
information about the project, its implications, or
alternative choices for two reasons: pressures for unity
and pressures for early action. We have already noted the
importance of local and basin-wide unity if a project is
to be approved. Our concern here is that the pressure
imposed by the need for unity effectively dampens debate.
Before the decision was made to authorize the CAP, for
example, two agricultural economists asserted in the
Arizona Review on the basis of research that Arizona had
enough groundwater to last 170 years and that
redistribution of water from agricultural to municipal and
industrial use was preferable to the CAP (Young and Martin
1969). The pair were roughly castigated by the Arizona
Daily Star and disowned by Congressman Morris Udall of
Arizona, the core activist behind the CAP who believed
they had done Arizona a disservice (Ingram 1978: 69-70).

Pressures for early action also limit information.
States have a strong motivation to sew up entitlements,
that is, to make sure that federal money does not result
in a state s water being forever lost to allocations
outside the state's boundaries. There are compelling
political reasons for states to settle upon any project
that might pass muster under federal evaluation procedures
and get it included in an omnibus basin bill. The effect
is to rush projects into authorization without sufficient
time or information. The hasty revision of the Animas-La
Plata is a case in point (Ingram 1978: 71).

Recipients have also paid costs by forfeiting the
development of their own planning capabilities.
Dependence on federal water development and focus on the
complexities of federal water politics have discouraged
states from developing their own decision-making and
long-range planning capabilities. Even as late as 1973,
only two of the basin states could claim to have completed
state water plans. Most admitted that they had not yet
developed the capability for an independent position
vis-a-vis the federal government (Ingram 1978: 72).

In public lands policy, the Sagebrush Rebellion reflects many of these same kinds of concerns. Costs are paid when the federal government acts as a remote absentee landlord. States encounter numerous difficulties trying to manage their "school lands." These dispersed holdings are often completely surrounded by federal lands. Sometimes even getting access is problematic. Frequently the states are "unable to manage their lands according to their own priorities when they conflict with BLM plans for federal lands" (Fairfax 1982: 972). Western governors have also voiced objections when federal landholdings in their states have appeared to be likely targets for siting MX-missiles, nuclear facilities, toxic dumps, and other controversial public projects (Fairfax 1982: 973).

Often hidden costs also result from the difficulty of getting a local or regional problem on the national agenda. When Congressional decisions are made in the logrolling mode, members of Congress frequently vote on things they do not care about. And these tradeoff decisions are connected with other choices which also do not get considered on their merits. For example, neither of the two Colorado River bills we have detailed were very logical or consistent. They encompassed no overall plan of development. Different projects and provisions were not complementary. Both paid insufficient attention to the physical limits of the basin and both failed to take into account general environmental impacts (Ingram 1978: 73).

Thus, it is not only the federal treasury that pays when federal decision-making dominates, but also the recipients. The latter, pleased to be included, think they are deferring costs to others and they often do not look to see whether they are getting what they really want. The political rules require that they get certain sorts of things which usually means that they must accept whatever is on the agencies' agendas.

At the same time, however, the federal government can serve as a place where weaker interests can find a forum. Some interests that are poorly represented locally have far more weight at the national level. Environmentalists, for instance, were able to build enough national support to prevent additional dams in the Grand Canyon. And federal decision-making allows sufficient scope for developing bureaucracies strong enough to counter influential private interests. The federal government can amass influence sufficient to challenge large-scale

private developers better than the small-scale state
bureaucracies can.

Lesson Five

Looking at all of these things, some people have
argued that federalism does not matter. William H. Riker,
for example, has argued that judgments made about
federalism ". . . are a way of saying that it is not very
significant as an institution" (1975: 159). Our final
lesson, therefore, is that federalism must be considered
within the context of substantive public policy. We have
found no general propositions and no ideal types, but
neither have we found that federalism can be disregarded.
It is not that federalism is a sham or that it does not
matter, but that the way it works is highly dependent on
the policy area and the stage of evolution of the policy.
What we have learned by focusing on federalism in
natural resources policy is that the federal structure
provides a stage upon which the struggle among interests
can be played out. It is within the role of federalism to
determine the locations where decisions are made, who gets
to participate and on what terms and by which rules. We
have concluded that more federalism research needs to be
done, particularly in substantive areas as we have done,
or in policy types. Much can be learned about federalism
by comparing how it operates in different policy areas.

REFERENCES

Allee, D., and H. Ingram. 1972. Authorization and
Appropriation Processes for Water Resource
Development. Final Report. Prepared for the National
Water Commission by Cornell University.

Behan, R.W. 1966. The Myth of the Omnipotent Forester.
Journal of Forestry (June).

Brubaker, S. 1984. Rethinking the Federal Lands.
Washington, D.C.: Resources for the Future.

Clarke, J.N., and D. McCool. 1985. Staking Out the
Terrain: Power Differentials Among Natural Resource
Management Agencies. Albany: State University of New
York Press.

Clawson, M. 1983. The Federal Lands Revisited.
Washington, D.C.: Resources for the Future.

Clyde, E.W. 1984-85. The Colorado River--An Overview.
Arizona Waterline (Fall/Winter), pp. 1-2, 9-11.

Culhane, P.J. 1981. Public Lands Politics. Baltimore:
The Johns Hopkins University Press.

Culhane, P.J. 1984. Sagebrush Rebels in Office: Jim
Watt's Land and Water Politics. In N.J. Vig and M.E.
Kraft, ed., Environmental Policy in the 1980s:
Reagan's New Agenda. Washington, D.C.: Congressional
Quarterly, Inc.

Dana, S.T., and S.K. Fairfax. 1980. Forest and Range
Policy. New York: McGraw-Hill.

Elazar, D.J. 1982. Intergovernmental Functions and the
Metaphors of Federalism. Publius (Spring), pp. 5-24.

Fairfax, S. 1982. Old Recipes for New Federalism.
Environmental Law, 12: 945-980.

Foss, P.O. 1960. Politics and Grass: The Administration
of Grazing the Public Domain. Seattle: University of
Washington Press.

Goslin, I. 1978. Colorado River Development. In D.F. Peterson and A.B. Crawford, eds., Values and Choices in the Development of the Colorado River Basin. Tucson: University of Arizona Press.

Ingram, H. 1978. Politics of Water Allocation. In D.F. Peterson and A.B. Crawford, eds., Values and Choices in the Development of the Colorado River Basin. Tucson: University of Arizona Press.

Mazmanian, D.A. and J. Nienaber. 1979. Can Organizations Change? Washington, D.C.: The Brookings Institution.

National Water Line. 1985. Washington, D.C.: National Water Resources Association, Vol. 9, No. 14 (July).

Peterson, C. 1985. Water Act Sent to Floor of Senate. Washington Post, May 5, p. A23.

Riker, W.H. 1975. Federalism. In F.I. Greenstein and N.W. Polsby, eds., Handbook of Political Science, Vol. 5. Reading, MA: Addison-Wesley Publishing Co.

Shapiro, M. 1985. House Narrowly Deletes 31 Water Projects. Washington Post, June 7, p. A4.

Stanfield, R.L. 1985. Cowboys and Conservationists in Range War Over Grazing Fees on Public Lands. National Journal, July 13, pp. 1623-25.

Stewart, W.H. 1982. Metaphors, Models, and the Development of Federal Theory. Publius (Spring), pp. 1-3.

U.S Congress. house of Representatives. Subcommittee on Mines and Mining. November 22, 1980. Sagebrush Rebellion. Impacts on Energy and Minerals. Oversight hearing. Salt Lake City, Utah. Committee Serial No. 96-39. Washington, D.C.: Government Printing Office.

Weatherford, G., H. Ingram, and F.L. Brown. 1984-85. The Future of the Colorado River. Arizona Waterline (Fall/Winter).

Young, Robert A. and William E. Martin. 1967. "The
    Economics of Arizona's Water Problem." <u>Arizona Review</u>
    (March). College of Business and Public
    Administration, University of Arizona.

3

Ocean Resources and Intergovernmental Relations: The Record to 1980

Maynard Silva
and Lauriston King

It has only been since the late 1950s that issues
concerning the development, use, and management of marine
and coastal resources have been perceived as deserving
sustained national policy attention. This recent
awareness has made the oceans and their resources the
newest family of natural resources to compel the attention
of the political system. As a result, the character of
relations between state, local, and national governments
is still in the process of sorting out and adjusting.

The nature of intergovernmental relations in marine
resources management prior to 1980 reflected the broad
pattern of the post-New Deal years, namely a shift in
governmental authority away from the states and toward
Washington. This general trend, though of more recent
vintage, has also characterized management efforts in
fisheries, marine mammals, pollution, and coastal
management. Many of the policies behind the management
efforts were the product of the burgeoning amount of
environmental legislation passed during the 1970s, much of
which was directed at ocean resources. Indeed, the 1970s
were an unusually productive period of innovation in
legislation designed to develop, preserve, and protect
marine resources. Even a partial list is impressive:
Coastal Zone Management Act (1972); Marine Mammal
Protection Act (1972); Marine Protection, Research, and
Sanctuaries Act (1972); Federal Water Pollution Control
Act Amendments (1972); Endangered Species Act (1973);
Deepwater Ports Act (1974); Magnuson Fishery Conservation
and Management Act (1976); Outer Continental Shelf Land
Act Amendments (1978).

This burst of legislative creativity was one product
of an active Congress influenced by national concerns for

energy and the environment, active and passive resistance
by the Executive Branch, separate groups promoting the
interests of their members, and a growing number of
conflicts between different levels and agencies of
government. The result was increased government activity
at all levels of marine affairs, a use-by-use rather than
comprehensive approach to ocean resources, an expanded
federal role, and the creation of innovative management
arrangements such as the regional fisheries management
councils (Cicin-Sain 1982a).

Not surprisingly, the character of relations between
and among state, federal, and local governments was
determined far more by a mix of political feasibility,
perceptions of the authority needed to get the job done,
and the desires of shifting coalitions of interest groups,
than by any comprehensive philosophical concern for the
distribution of power, authority and competence in the
federal system. For the most part these laws were drafted
to meet the special needs of each resource and shared only
the marine environment as their common element. The
result through 1980 was an ad hoc set of arrangements
where intergovernmental relations took their distinctive
contours for each resource or use from legislation, court
decisions, and the experience of implementation. This
chapter will review briefly the nature of these
relationships by describing the key policies for
fisheries, marine mammals, offshore hydrocarbons and
minerals, marine pollution, and coastal resource
management.

MARINE FISHERIES

The powers vested in Congress by the commerce clause
of the Constitution provide for the management of
fisheries by the federal level of government. For most of
this country's history, however, the management of fishery
resources was left to state governments. In some cases
fisheries management authority was delegated to local
government. The most notable example of local fishery
management has been the town management of shellfish beds
in New England.

Beginning in the mid-nineteenth century states,
generally without federal interference, began to manage
fisheries (Nielsen 1976). While most states confined
themselves to management of fisheries within the
three-mile territorial sea, there were some that extended

their efforts beyond this line. To do so, these states had to prove a legitimate interest such as enforcement or conservation and, further, an established legal basis (for example, landing laws or citizenship) for asserting jurisdiction over fishermen (Greenberg and Shapiro 1982; Montgomery 1976).

It was not until the 1940s that federal involvement with fisheries management began in any significant way (Greenberg and Shapiro 1982; Gordon 1982; Nielsen 1976). Prior to World War II, most fisheries management was conducted by the states, usually with little coordination between states. The federal government virtually abstained from involvement in marine fisheries. Because of the migratory, transboundary nature of most fisheries resources, however, no one state could possibly hope to manage a fish stock successfully. The growing realization that fisheries were regional resources whose management required interstate planning and implementation precipitated a series of regional state marine fisheries commissions. Because they were federal interstate compacts, each commission had to be consented to and approved by acts of Congress (Wiggins 1985). The Atlantic States Marine Fisheries Commission was established in 1942; in 1947 the three west coast states joined in the Pacific Marine Fisheries Commission (later joined by Alaska and Idaho); and the five states of the Gulf Coast formed the Gulf States Marine Fisheries Commission in 1949 (Gordon 1982).

While the marine states fisheries commissions were constituted with the objective of fostering interstate cooperation in fisheries management, the structure and authority of the commissions did not allow actual interstate management. They lacked the power to require individual states to adopt particular management techniques, so they functioned primarily as a means for interstate consultation and cooperation on common stocks, problems, and, ideally, solutions.

One result was a perceptible shift from the kinds of intergovernmental relations of the pre-war to those where interstate fisheries organizations had emerged but the management decisions were fundamentally those of the individual states. Nonetheless, initial modifications of the intergovernmental system for fisheries management had occurred. Though not intended as such, they represented a more complex structure for fisheries management in the U.S. federal system. For the next fifteen years, the management structure for fisheries in the United States

remained fairly stable. States were the primary
managers. They cooperated through the
federally-established fisheries commissions. The
fisheries infrastructure at the federal level devoted its
attention to international fisheries problems and research.

This pattern changed in 1964 with Congressional
passage of the Bartlett Act (P.L. No. 88-308) and its
supplement, the Contiguous Fisheries Zone Act of 1966
(P.L. No. 88-658). The former declared that foreign
fishermen were to be excluded from the U.S. territorial
sea; the latter created a "contiguous zone" which extended
beyond the three-mile territorial sea to twelve miles and
excluded most foreign fishing. Both acts, then, were
intended to eliminate foreign fishermen from nearshore
waters. Day-to-day management remained with the states
even though Congress had declared in the passage of the
Bartlett Act that the states were not to receive
regulatory jurisdiction in the 3-to-12 mile contiguous
zone. The federal government continued to limit its
activities in the territorial sea and contiguous zone to
the gathering of data and enforcement (Greenberg and
Shapiro 1982). Even though the federal government chose
not to exercise regulatory authority in the contiguous
zone, the Bartlett Act and the Continguous Fisheries Zone
Act provided precedents for expansion of the federal
government into fisheries management.

In 1969 the influential report of the Commission on
Marine Science, Engineering and Resources, commonly
referred to as the Stratton Commission, was published. It
described the U.S. fishing industry as suffering from a
variety of woes which the Commission attributed, in part,
to a lack of intergovernmental cooperation.

> A major impediment [to sound management] is the welter
> of conflicting, overlapping, and restrictive laws and
> regulations applying to fishing operations in the
> United States. With jurisdiction over fishery
> management and development largely in the hands of the
> States and with lines of authority between State and
> Federal Governments ill-defined, the responsibility
> for action is hopelessly splintered. Moreover, the
> tendency toward parochialism in the individual States
> has led to a mass of protective legislation that
> militates against research, development and innovation
> . . . . Interstate cooperation has been relatively
> unsuccessful. These interstate commissions exist . .
> . . But none has the regulatory powers nor adequate

staff . . . . Under existing statutes, the Federal
Government has no explicit role in the management of
fisheries within U.S. territorial waters. In view of
the discouraging lack of coordination among State
programs, the Commission concludes that Federal
leadership and guidance--and when necessary,
regulatory power--must be asserted. (U.S. Congress,
House, 1969: 95-96).

The Stratton Commission's recommendations for a completely
restructured system of fisheries management, including an
expanded and more substantive role for the federal
government, would not be immediately accepted. In
retrospect, however, the philosophical underpinning of the
Commission's recommendations, i.e., the need for a more
integrated system of intergovernmental fisheries
management, had taken hold. Change would follow.

The National Marine Fisheries Service (NMFS) responded
to the Stratton Commission report in 1971 by establishing
its State/Federal Fisheries Management Program. The
existing state marine fishery commissions were used to
plan and coordinate activities of the program (Gordon
1982; Kreps et al. 1978). By encouraging state fishery
administrators to cooperate with their counterparts from
other states and with the federal government, this program
resulted in several management plans for fisheries within
the territorial sea (Fritschie 1980; Gordon 1982).

For the next several years, a great deal of discussion
took place concerning the future of U.S. fisheries
management. One of the major themes in this national
debate was the enhancement of the federal role. Then in
1976, Congress passed the Fishery Conservation and
Management Act (for which the title was later amended to
the Magnuson Fisheries Conservation and Management Act,
Magnuson Act or MFCMA). The Magnuson Act (16 U.S.C., 1801
et seq.) represented a major regime change for the
intergovernmental management of fisheries. No longer
would the states be preeminent, especially in waters
beyond three miles, nor would the coordination of
management efforts be left to fortuitous or haphazard
cooperation. For the National Marine Fisheries Service as
the principal fisheries agency at the federal (Department
of Commerce) level, passage of the MFCMA represented a
major reformulation of its position in the structure of
intergovernmental relations vis-a-vis fisheries. From
being a research and data-gathering agency that assisted
state management of fisheries, it became the leading

entity for the management of marine fisheries in the
United States.

The most succinct way to summarize this new regime is
to review several key aspects of the legislation. First,
Section 101 of the legislation created a 197-mile wide
fishery conservation zone (FCZ)--from the outer edge of
each state's territorial sea out to 200 nautical miles.
Section 302 of the MFCMA declares that the management of
fisheries resources within the FCZ will be conducted by
eight regional fishery management councils. Membership of
the councils is comprised of designated representatives
from federal and state fisheries management agencies,
public representatives of the states in each region, and
nonvoting members of other relevant federal agencies
(e.g., the State Department, the Coast Guard). The duly
constituted councils are to formulate fishery management
plans (FMPs) (Section 303), which are to be reviewed by
NMFS and, ultimately, approved by the Secretary of
Commerce (Section 304). Finally, under Section 306, the
states retain jurisdiction over fisheries in the 3-mile
territorial sea.

These features of the MFCMA are important to the
discussion of fisheries management and U.S. federalism
because they directly respond to the goal of the Magnuson
Act which "is a unified approach to management of
fisheries throughout their range. The MFCMA attempts to
accomplish this through a coordinated state, regional, and
federal effort" (Bubier and Rieser 1984).

It would seem that the MFCMA had created what in an
earlier day might have been designated as a system of
cooperative federalism, that is, a system which recognizes
"layers of government" but which blurs the functional
distinction between those layers. Though prescribing
cooperation between the blurred layers, cooperative
federalism assumes federal supremacy in order to foster,
coordinate, and force state programs to comply with
nationally defined goals (Fairfax 1982: 956-57). The
states, the public, and the federal government would work
together under federal leadership to develop fishery
management plans that would conserve the nation's valuable
commercial and recreational fish stocks. One commentator
saw the councils of the MFCMA as unique in the U.S.
federal system in that the "regional councils, composed of
federal, state and public representatives, are not modeled
after any other authority; rather they were shaped by the
demands of compromise and necessity" (Rogalski 1980).
Implicit in this view is that the MFCMA established a

cooperative system of fisheries management by virtue of
state representation on the councils. This would indicate
to some that the councils were neither state nor federal
but rather (as their name implies) regional bodies.
However, this view has been challenged by,

[l]egal opinions issued by NOAA [National Oceanic and
Atmospheric Administration], the Civil Service
Commission, the Department of Justice, the Office of
Management and Budget, the General Services
Administration, and the General Accounting Office
yield the following agency consensus definition of the
legal status of the Councils at the present time:

(a) the Regional Fishery Management Council [sic]
are Federal instrumentalities created by statute to
fulfill a Federal junction--the preparation of
management for fishery resources in the Federal
Fishery Conservation Zone. (U.S. Congress, House,
1982).

In addition, Section 306(b) of the MFCMA clearly
undermines the cooperative character of the legislation in
its provision for federal preemption of state management
authority if state management adversely affects the
functioning of the federal fishery management plan (Burke
1982). In the opinion of Greenberg and Shapiro, the MFCMA
is so strong that, "if a Council or the Secretary [of
Commerce] determines that there should be no management of
a fishery, any state regulation, even of 'registered'
vessels, would be inconsistent with that determination and
could not stand." (1982: 669).
Thus, by 1980, the intergovernmental regime for
fisheries management was one adjusting to major
modifications and provisions that remained somewhat
unclear. On one hand, the MFCMA had created a system for
integrated management of the resource and a council
structure that would facilitate cooperative interaction
among and between the levels of government. On the other
hand, legal interpretations of council status and Section
306 can be viewed as establishing a federally dominated
system with state interests in a potentially subordinate
position. Only further experience with its implementation
could indicate the exact form of intergovernmental
relations that would develop from the MFCMA.

MARINE MAMMALS

Unlike the case of marine fisheries where an increased
federal management role evolved over forty years, the
domestic management of mammals shifted abruptly from one
almost entirely dominated by state governments to one in
which the federal government became preeminent. This
occurred with the passage of the Marine Mammal Protection
Act of 1972 (MMPA) and the Endangered Species Act of 1973
(ESA).

For most of this century, marine mammals, including
whales, dolphins, seals, sea otters, walruses, polar
bears, and other similar species, were the management
concern of state governments. Except for species-specific
international treaties to which the U.S. government was a
party, (e.g., International Whaling Commission, Fur Seal
Act of 1944), the federal government had not been actively
involved with the management of marine mammals (Cicin-Sain
1982b). For example, the California sea otter had been
managed and protected, including the establishment of a
refuge, by the California Department of Fish and Game
since 1913.

Passage of MMPA changed this. Its purpose was to
maintain viable and healthy populations of marine
mammals. To achieve this the MMPA established a permanent
moratorium on the "taking" of marine mammals. As Smith
has observed,

> "taking" is so broadly defined that virtually any
> interaction that disturbs the natural behavior
> patterns of a marine mammal is in violation of the
> statute or of regulations promulgated pursuant to
> statutory authority. Virtually any interaction with
> marine mammals requires prior authorization. (Smith
> 1982: 181).

In a somewhat unusual move, Congress divided the
responsibility for implementation and administration of
the MMPA between the Department of Commerce (NOAA
designated as responsible agency) and the Department of
Interior [U.S. Fish and Wildlife Service (USFWS)]. NOAA
is responsible for cetaceans and pinnipeds (excluding
walruses) and the USFWS is to manage all other covered
marine mammals [Sections 3(12)(A) and (B)]. To assist and
advise these agencies, the MMPA also authorized the
creation of the Marine Mammal Commission and a Committee
of Scientific Advisors on Marine Mammals.

In terms of state participation, the MMPA states in
Section 109(a)(1), "except as otherwise provided in this
section, no state may adopt any law or regulation relating
to the taking of marine mammals within its jurisdiction."
The general exception found later in this Section is in
those instances when the state regulation is found
consistent, by either the secretaries of Commerce or
Interior (depending on species), with the provisions of
the MMPA. Remember that the broad definition of "taking"
would therefore preclude any independent action by states
or their agencies.

Further provisions of Section 109 were seen as holding
out the possibility of a return to state management of
certain marine mammals under certain conditions (Armstrong
1979; Smith 1982). Eight years after passage, this
possibility had not become a reality. Alaska, for
example, tried to have authority for marine mammals
returned from the passage of the Act.

This sole dependence on federal management caused
concern in some circles. These critics felt that
exclusion of state participation had led to ineffective
management. This is demonstrated in the following
comments drawn from 1981 hearings by the Subcommittee on
Fisheries and Wildlife Conservation and the Environment on
the MMPA.

Lonnie L. Williamson of the Wildlife Management
Institute noted that

> In our view, the problem stems primarily from the
> Federal preemption of State authority for control of
> marine mammal species, and from the vague and
> imprecise regulations established for implementation
> of the program. The result has been, in too many
> instances, ineffectual administration, inadequate or
> incomplete enforcement and a disservice to the cause
> of resource conservation. (U.S. Congress, House, 1981:
> 9)

Representing Alaska, Ronald Skoog noted

> Jurisdictional responsibility for all these animals
> was shifted to the Federal government--polar bear,
> walrus, and sea otter to the U.S. Department of
> Interior, and sea lion, seal, and whales to the U.S.
> Department of Commerce. Certain provisions of the
> MMPA supposedly provide for the resumption of marine
> mammal management by a state. Alaska applied for

return of management of the 10 species listed above in
January 1973. Alaska's continual attempts to resume a
marine mammal conservation program and the 8-year
failure of the responsible Federal agencies to return
management or develop their own programs is a history
of bureaucratic absurdity. (U.S. Congress, House,
1981: 17)

A final example that the MMPA had possibly
precipitated disharmony between levels of government is
provided by C. Dale Snow of Oregon's Department of Fish
and Wildlife,

The necessity to involve the expertise and resources
of coastal states in properly managing marine mammals
of the continental shelf can only be realized by
revising the Act. Federal preemption of important
state functions, in the absence of federal action to
accomplish those tasks, does nothing for the health or
stability of marine mammal populations. (U.S.
Congress, House, 1981: 30)

The Endangered Species Act (1973) is more limited in
its application. For a marine mammal to be managed (i.e.,
protected) under the provisions of the ESA, the Secretary
of the Interior must have designated that species as
either "endangered" or "threatened" (with endangered
signifying the greater susceptibility to extinction).
Once protected, however, that protection is complete. So
much so, that all federal agencies must carry out their
functions, whether they be actual activities or
regulation, licensing or permitting, in a manner
consistent with the well-being of endangered or threatened
species.
    Smith (1982) has commented on the effect of the ESA on
state-federal cooperation.

Although the federal government is instructed to carry
out programs authorized by the ESA in cooperation with
affected states "to the maximum extent practicable,"
the statute also contains a preemption provision
limiting the applicability of state laws. With regard
to interstate commerce in, or exportation or
importation of, threatened or endangered species, no
state law may permit what is prohibited or prevent
what is allowed by the ESA. . . . In a section
comparable to provisions in the MMPA, the ESA allows

state management of threatened and endangered species upon approval of the state's authorization statutes and proposed management scheme. (p. 186)

With marine fisheries, there was some ambiguity as to the intergovernmental regime established by the MFCMA. With marine mammals it seems clear: the states, by the beginning of the 1980s, clearly had been relegated to a subsidiary role. The structural arrangement for managing fisheries extant in 1980 was one in which the federal government occupies a dominant position.

OUTER CONTINENTAL SHELF HYDROCARBONS AND MINERALS

To a large degree, the record to 1980 of intergovernmental relations vis-a-vis outer continental shelf (OCS) resources is that of oil and gas. By 1980, mineral resources had not yet begun to be exploited in economically significant ammounts, and any preliminary discussions of management regimes were inspired by those already in place for OCS oil and gas.

In looking at the legal framework that has formed the patterns of intergovernmental relations in the context of OCS hydrocarbons, it is important to recognize two components. The first is the body of legislation that influences, either directly or indirectly, the manner in which management decisions about the leasing, exploration, development, and production of OCS hydrocarbons takes place. The second component is comprised of those court rulings that have sustained or modified the locus, practice and/or the execution of OCS leasing decisions, the regulation of development activities, and determined the relative importance of the various levels of government to a much greater degree than other areas of marine resource management.

In the early years of OCS oil and gas development, the OCS management process was rather unencumbered by legislative or judicial mandates. Oil and gas began to be extracted from sources underlying the ocean in 1896, but was not managed until 1926 when California began to regulate OCS hydrocarbons by issuing leases (Cicin-Sain 1986). Beginning in 1937, the federal government began to contest the authority of the states to regulate and garner income from OCS oil and gas resources (Richardson 1985).

In 1945, President Truman proclaimed management authority over the seabed and resources of the U.S. OCS.

This action partially cleared the way for the federal
government to begin leasing the OCS for oil and gas. What
remained in the federal government's path were those
coastal states that continued to believe that they were
entitled to leasing and management rights to offshore oil
and gas.

This issue was resolved in a two-stage process, the
first being judicial and the second legislative. The
first stage consisted of a legal challenge brought against
the State of California by the federal government. The
suit sought to prohibit California from letting leases for
offshore oil and gas exploration. In this case, U.S. v.
California (1947), the Supreme Court found with the
plaintiffs--the states had no right to authorize or profit
from the development of offshore hydrocarbons. That
power, it was decided, resided with the federal
government. The second stage is represented by the
response of Congress to the Supreme Court decision in U.S.
v. California. That response was the enactment of two
pieces of legislation which combined the situations that
existed before and after the suit. That is, with the
Submerged Lands Act (SLA) of 1953, Congress declared that
the states would be the principal agents in the leasing of
ocean bottom for oil and gas development out to three
miles (i.e., the limit of the territorial sea). With the
companion Outer Continental Shelf Lands Act (1953),
Congress reserved for the federal government the right to
offer leases beyond the three-mile territorial sea. Thus
both levels of government could claim primacy in the
management and regulation of OCS hydrocarbons, though in
restricted and separate areas. State governments would
have control out to three miles; beyond that boundary the
federal government would be the responsible entity.

For approximately twenty years little changed in the
relative roles and jurisdictions of the two levels of
government. Then in the late 1960s, concern for the
environment became a major issue on the public's agenda.
As this concern grew, there came with it a spate of
environmental legislation much of which had a major
impact, either directly or indirectly, on the "business"
of leasing OCS oil and gas development sites. This
legislative activity would also affect the
intergovernmental arrangements for OCS management.

The level of legislative activity vis-a-vis the
environment in general and ocean resources in particular
was unprecedented and has not been duplicated since.
Between 1969 and 1973 at least seven major pieces of

legislation, which would have a bearing on the manner in which OCS leasing would be conducted, were adopted or significantly amended. These were the National Environmental Policy Act of 1969 (NEPA), amendments to the Clean Air Act (CAA), amendments to the Federal Water Pollution Control Act (FWPCA), the Marine Protection, Research, and Sanctuaries Act of 1972 (the Sanctuaries Act), the Marine Mammal Protection Act of 1972, the Coastal Zone Management Act of 1972 (CZMA), and the Endangered Species Act of 1973 (ESA).

For this discussion, perhaps the most important was the Coastal Zone Management Act of 1972. In terms of OCS leasing, the CZMA has probably been the most controversial of this legislative bundle. This controversy results from the provisions of Section 307. These provisions declare that for any state with a federally approved coastal zone management plan, that state has the right to review any federal activity, including federal licensing or permitting, which directly affects its coastal zone. The review is to determine whether or not the federal action is consistent with that state's coastal zone management plan. If inconsistent, i.e., if it is contrary to the goals and objectives of the state's plan, then the activity in question must be modified or halted. Prior to and continuing into the 1980s, many states had used the CZMA consistency provisions to block or force alteration of federal OCS activities.

In addition to the environmental legislation of the early 1970s, other factors were at work that would alter state-federal (and sometimes local) interactions in this area. Most notable were upheavals in the world petroleum system. In 1973 the OPEC oil boycott shocked the United States.

Several pieces of legislation had a direct bearing on efforts to cope with this blow to the energy economy, one involving efforts to expand imports of foreign petroleum, the other to accelerate oil and gas production along the coastal margin of the United States. During the late 1960s and early 1970s, there was growing concern for the increasing demand and rising cost of importing crude oil into the United States. One option to the expensive and environmentally undesirable proposals to dredge deeper channels to accommodate the new class of supertankers was to build deepwater ports outside the territorial sea. Although a number of proposals to construct deep water ports in the United States existed, none had been built prior to 1974 because there was no coherent policy to authorize and regulate their construction, operation, and use.

The ports were promoted as a less expensive way to bring in large volumes of oil at less cost than conventional methods, as less dangerous to the environment, and as a means for stimulating local coastal economies. After an intense debate on environmental issues, federal agency jurisdiction, and the role of the coastal states in awarding these permits, the Congress passed the Deepwater Ports Act on December 17, 1974. The Act charged the Secretary of Transportation with issuing licenses for the ownership, construction, and operation of deepwater ports after determining that the project was consistent with national security and other national interests including energy sufficiency and protection of the environment. For intergovernmental relations the key point was that any adjacent state, or a state connected by pipeline to such a port, or within 15 miles of such a port, which was threatened with pollution, could veto the construction application.

In a decision with far greater ramifications for intergovernmental relations and marine resource development, President Nixon proposed to accelerate greatly the pace at which hydrocarbons were developed on federal OCS lands. The response, in turn, from the states and those concerned for the environment was an attempt to slow the rate of this acceleration. The ensuing Congressional debate led to significant amendments to several pieces of legislation affecting OCS hydrocarbons and their management in an intergovernmental context. Of particular interest were amendments to the CZMA, the Clean Water Act (CWA), and the OCSLA. The CZMA amendments established a mechanism and a source of funding, the Coastal Energy Impact Program, to help the states plan for and mitigate the onshore impacts of a variety of coastal energy developments including OCS oil and gas development (Bish 1978).

The Clean Water Act Amendments of 1977 (CWAA) established two important substantive changes for OCS development: 1) extended federal jurisdiction over oil spills from 12 miles out to 200 miles; and 2) included oil spills from OCS drilling platforms under the aegis of the CWA.

After several years of discussions, hearings, and consideration of alternative bills by the the U.S. Congress, the OCSLA was amended in 1978. Among the extensive changes or additions to the federal OCS leasing

program mandated by the OCSLA Amendments was the
requirement that the Secretary of the Interior prepare and
submit to Congress, on a periodic basis, five-year plans
indicating the timing and location of future lease sales.
This was to assist the states in anticipating and
responding to those federal actions. The amendments also
provided for more involvement by the public and by the
states, establishment of additional environmental
safeguards, the use of the best available (in terms of
safety) technologies, and a process whereby the Secretary
of the Interior can terminate a lease for environmental
purposes (Murphy 1980).

In terms of greater state participation (beyond that
provided for by the CZMA consistency provisions mentioned
above), the addition of Section 19 by the OCSLAA is also
relevant. It established that the Secretary of the
Interior must consult and solicit comments from the
governors of states likely to be affected by oil and gas
activities on the federal OCS. Further, this section
allows for the comments of local governments to be
transmitted to the Department of the Interior through the
governor's office.

In terms of judicial activity, there was one important
case during this period. In Maine v. U.S., the Supreme
Court rejected the position of Maine that it should be the
state and not the federal government that would have the
authority and responsibility for offering leases for OCS
exploration and development beyond the territorial sea.
In essence, the Court upheld its position in the 1947 U.S.
v. California case.

Thus for OCS hydrocarbons the pattern of
intergovernmental relations between 1940 and 1980 was
characterized by a displacement of earlier state authority
in leasing offshore waters, a compromise restoring a
portion of that authority to the states for their
territorial waters, and increasingly, the authority to
stall or curtail certain federal activities in the area
outside the territorial sea. For example, by 1980,
governors of affected states had to be informed by the
Secretary of the Interior of any federal OCS activities.
Further, the secretary was required to take note of any
comments made by the governors. Added influence was given
to the states in the form of the CZMA consistency
requirements. At the inception of the 1980s, it was clear
that OCS management was a partnership, although a somewhat
reluctant one on the part of the federal government.

MARINE POLLUTION

Public concern for environmental deterioration during
the 1960s embraced both land and sea. Increased disposal
of sewage sludge, dredged materials, industrial wastes,
and toxic chemicals in the ocean prompted scientists and
environmentalists to warn about the unknown threats to the
health of the oceans if such indiscriminate dumping
continued. For example, in the period between 1949 and
1953, the amount of waste dumped in the ocean was about
1.7 million tons a year; it rose to 7.4 million tons a
year for the years between 1964 to 1968 (Council on
Environmental Quality 1970: 8). There was no reason to
believe the trend would be reversed.

President Nixon, sensitive to the growing strength of
environmental sentiment in the nation, requested in the
spring of 1969 that the Council on Environmental Quality
(CEQ) conduct a study of ocean dumping. His charge to the
Council was to examine the effects of ocean dumping on the
environment, the amounts of toxic wastes dumped in
specific locations, and alternatives to ocean disposal.

The brief report called for a comprehensive approach
to ocean disposal that would regulate dumping and ban
disposal of harmful materials (Council on Environmental
Quality 1970). Although various agencies, including the
Army Corps of Engineers, the Atomic Energy Commission, the
Water Control Administration, and a variety of state
agencies had authority over specific aspects of ocean
dumping, none had the comprehensive authority needed to
address the growing magnitude of the problem. The Council
singled out for particular concern the disposal of
polluted dredged materials, sewage sludge, and industrial
wastes. Among the key recommendations were that dumping
of undigested sewage be halted; that dumping of digested
and other stabilized sludge be phased out; that any need
to continue certain kinds of dumping be considered interim
measures until options were identified; that dumping of
industrial wastes be stopped as soon as possible; and that
dumping of toxic wastes be stopped immediately.

The administration moved quickly to send legislation
to the Congress based on the CEQ report. Here it became
entangled in the usual pulling and hauling over committee
jurisdictions and legislative mandates, but finally
emerged as the Marine Protection, Research, and
Sanctuaries Act, or Ocean Dumping Act. President Nixon
signed the bill on October 23, 1972. The law spelled out
the rules for ocean dumping, mandated a research program

on the impact of man's activities on the marine
environment, and established conditions for creating
marine sanctuaries. The approach was to regulate the
dumping of any material that would "adversely affect human
health, welfare, or amenities, or the marine environment,
ecological system, or economic potentialities." It flatly
prohibited the ocean transportation and dumping of any
radiological, chemical, or biological warfare agents, or
high-level radioactive wastes in the territorial sea and
contiguous zone.

The key provisions relating to dumping are those
dealing with permits, ocean waste disposal in general, and
the dumping of dredged materials. Responsibility for
carrying out the dumping policy was given to the
Environmental Protection Agency (EPA) and the Army Corps
of Engineers (COE). Evaluation of permit requests had to
be measured against the need for dumping, its impact on
human health and welfare as well as its persistence,
volume, and nature, and alternatives to dumping. Congress
resolved its jurisdictional fight over the respective
roles the Environmental Protection Agency and the Army
Corps of Engineers would play by granting authority to the
Corps to prepare permits for dredge spoil disposal but to
notify the EPA of its intent before granting the permit.
In cases of conflict the EPA had the last word.

On another jurisdictional question Congress made the
Ocean Dumping Act applicable "beyond the baseline of the
territorial sea." The internal and territorial waters
were exempted because Congress had just passed amendments
to the Clean Water Act which applied to those areas.
Neither bill resolved the overlap in jurisdiction over
disposal operations in the territorial sea other than that
of municipal sewage wastes from pipes which were addressed
only in the water pollution act (National Advisory
Committee on Oceans and Atmosphere 1981: 13).

Despite containing conflicts over the requirements of
the dumping act, particularly establishing a December 31,
1981 deadline for the disposal of municipal sewage sludge,
the act appeared to reverse the steady increase in wastes
dumped in the oceans. For example, in 1973 some 12
million tons of wastes were dumped, over 90 percent of
which were sewage sludge and manufacturing wastes. Just
two years later dumping had been halted in the Pacific and
reduced in the Gulf of Mexico. Although industrial
dumping had decreased a bit in the Atlantic, the total
figure of 8.7 million tons was still higher than the 1968

figure because of the increase in sewage sludge dumping
(Environmental Protection Agency 1977).

At the same time the Congress was hammering out the
ocean dumping act, it was engaged in a major overhaul of
the Federal Water Pollution Control Act, the basic law for
cleaning up the nation's water. The approach of the act
and its subsequent amendments was to provide state and
interstate water pollution control agencies with
construction and other grants, enforcement procedures,
research programs, and a grant program to cities for
building sewage treatment plants. Several provisions of
the act sought to control deterioration of water quality
in the territorial sea, the contiguous zone, and the open
ocean. Specifically, it regulates discharge of nondredged
materials from onshore outfall pipes, from all point
sources out to three miles, and from sources other than
vessels out to twelve miles. The Environmental Protection
Agency is also charged with making the rules for dumping
dredge spoils, and the Secretary of the Army, working
through the Corps of Engineers, to award permits for the
disposal of dredged or fill material.

Policies to control--and ultimately eliminate--the
disposal of noxious wastes in coastal waters provided no
real departure from the earlier pattern of increased
federal responsibility for protecting environmental
quality. The Environmental Protection Agency and the
Corps of Engineers were made responsible for reviewing and
issuing permits, monitoring compliance, and, with the
National Oceanic and Atmospheric Administration, for
design of research on the effects of ocean dumping.
Although the Submerged Lands Act (1953) granted
substantial authority to the states for managing the
coastal ocean, Congress did not extend this authority to
the control of ocean dumping. Indeed, the Congress
specifically preempted state authority for dumping.
Although the EPA Administrator is urged in the legislation
to consider suggestions from coastal states, it is not
required. The extent of this preemption is reflected in
Section 106(d) of the Ocean Dumping Act which states that
once the law comes into force, "no state shall adopt or
enforce any rule or regulation relating to any activity
regulated by this title." Under the Clean Water Act the
states were charged with conducting their own discharge
permit programs, but only if approved by the EPA. Like
most of the other marine management measures passed in the
early and mid-1970s, both the Ocean Dumping and Clean
Water Acts were amended to clarify and sharpen the

original legislation. These adjustments did not, however, alter the hegemony of the federal government in the management of marine pollution.

COASTAL ZONE MANAGEMENT

For the most part the ocean management prescriptions of the 1970s were directed toward specific resources--fish, oil, gas, water, thermal energy or seabed minerals. The major exception, however, was the Coastal Zone Management Act of 1972, which sought to take a comprehensive approach to reconciling pressures for both conservation and development along the nation's shorelines. Increased coastal population, pressures for commercial and recreational development on beaches, wetlands, and barrier islands, shrinking wetland habitats, and the burgeoning amount of garbage dumped into coastal waters, all conspired to direct attention to the need for comprehensive rather than piecemeal solutions.

The act itself is the product of a number of distinctive legislative interests that evolved through the late 1960s. Specifically, its legislative ancestry drew heavily on four distinctive phases of concern for coastal issues: concern for shrinking recreational opportunities along the coasts; the deteriorating condition of wetlands and estuaries; the economic opportunities for ocean development; and a growing interest in land use policy (Ziles 1974; Popper 1981; Kitsos 1985). The law which emerged sought to incorporate many of the ideas suggested in legislative proposals to deal with these issues. It asserts "a national interest in the effective management, beneficial use, protection, and development of the coastal zone" [sec. 302(a)]. To realize these diverse and frequently conflicting goals the act set up grant-in-aid programs to provide financial incentives for coastal states to "exercise their full authority over the lands and waters in the coastal zone" [sec. 302(g)].

Political feasibility dictated that the program be a voluntary process between the states and the federal government, where the states made specific resource allocations and designed comprehensive plans with federal support and subject to federal approval. To accomplish this partnership the coastal management act established a procedural framework within which states have a good deal of discretion in designing programs which fit their

particular political, geographical, and environmental
circumstances.

In order to take part, the states had to develop
management programs that would: (1) identify important
resources, areas, and uses within a state's coastal zone
requiring management or protection; (2) establish a policy
framework to guide decisions about appropriate resource
use and protection; (3) identify the landward and seaward
boundaries of the coastal zone; (4) provide for the
consideration of the national interest in the planning for
and siting of facilities that meet more than local needs;
and (5) include sufficient legal authorities and
organizational arrangements to implement the program and
insure compliance.

The initial incentive for state participation was
federal money to support up to 80 percent of the costs of
developing a plan. Once a state plan had been approved by
federal officials in the National Oceanic and Atmospheric
Administration it became eligible for awards to administer
the approved program. Funds were also available to
establish estuarine sanctuaries and promote beach access.
Additional incentives were added in 1976 through the
Coastal Energy Impact Program which provided additional
grants and loans to coastal states taking part in the
management program and confronting the shoreside effects
of offshore energy development. An added administrative
incentive for the states was the prospect of checking
federal agency actions not compatible with the coastal
management program. Federal activity directly affecting
the coastal zone must be, to the maximum extent
practicable, consistent with approved state management
programs. In effect, the provision acknowledged the
primary management authority of the states.

By 1978, 24 states had established new coastal
management agencies, subunits of agencies, or management
commissions. Identifiable progress had been made in the
protection of coastal resources such as wetlands, beaches
and dunes, reefs, and barrier islands; in the management
of coastal development, particularly for areas vulnerable
to erosion, flood plains, dredge disposal sites, and
energy facilities; and for increased protection of the
recreational and cultural resources of the coasts (Office
of Coastal Zone Management 1979). By 1981, 26 states and
territories had approved programs, accounting for over 78
percent of the nation's shoreline.

It is no overstatement to claim that any chance for
the Coastal Zone Management Act to succeed hinged on the

pattern of bargaining and negotiation between federal, state, and local governments. The program is voluntary. There are no federal sanctions on states such as Texas that refuse to participate. Conversely, those states which do take part are charged with designing plans that address issues of national interest like beach access and wetlands protection, reconciling state and national interests in coastal siting of energy facilities, and meeting a variety of procedural requirements ranging from new legislation and regulations to submitting to federal evaluations. To repeat, it is the states, not the federal government that determine policy for these substantive issues. This state authority is given added force by the consistency provisions of the law (Greenberg 1981; Harvey 1984; Husing 1984). These provide that federal agencies may not grant permits for activities affecting a state's coastal zone unless the permit applicant certifies, and the state agrees, that the activity is consistent with the state's coastal program.

Given the eclectic nature of the CZMA's origins, it is hardly surprising that the Coastal Zone Management Act incorporated a number of mechanisms from other environmental and resource management legislation. For example, the provision that state programs be approved by a federal agency in order to receive funds is similar to the pollution control statutes, although the coastal act gives states more discretion in shaping their programs than the pollution laws. It is also similar to other federal resource development laws like the Federal Land Policy and Management Act that granted states influence over federal resource development efforts which affect them. Finally, like the review-and-comment procedures, the coastal act's consistency requirements apply to all federal agencies (Conservation Foundation 1984).

Despite these rather modest opportunities to tilt the pattern of federal dominance in marine resource management toward the states, the fact remains that prior to 1980 the act did little to alter existing relations between federal, state, and local governments. There are two reasons for this: the first is that many state programs did not have approved plans. For example, by the end of 1978 only 13 states had approved programs; by 1980, an additional 13 states and territories had received approval. The second, and more fundamental reason, is that the expansive charge to the states to accommodate national, state, and local interests, as well as to preserve and protect the natural marine environment is sharply constrained by a provision [sec. 307(e)] which declares that no federal or state rights or laws are to be diminished, superceded, modified or repealed by the act or by state coastal management programs. It also specifies that the requirements of the Federal Water Pollution Control Act and the Clean Air Act shall be the water and air pollution control provisions of state coastal management programs.

Constitutional, political, and administrative barriers have made it impossible for either federal or state governments to play a predominant role in the comprehensive management of coastal resources. Prior to the passage of the Coastal Zone Management Act, the courts were about the only way to resolve new fights between federal and state governments over the distribution of authority for marine resource issues. The act displaced this frequently ambiguous and unpredictable situation with one defined by a clear statement that the states, using their full authority, were the best units of government to establish a national program of coastal zone management, and that these programs would provide a mechanism for negotiating and formalizing a distribution of power and authority (Armstrong and Ryner 1978: 32). In a more general sense, "it is not just empty rhetoric to assert that any successful coastal water management and planning effort will require a partnership of both federal and state interests, since under current law neither source has full or sufficient power to unilaterally establish a comprehensive management program" (Armstrong and Ryner 1978: 33).

CONCLUSIONS

Reflecting on the history of intergovernmental relations in the five ocean and coastal resources areas we have briefly surveyed, four summary observations are suggested. In addition, this brief background survey would seem to lend support to conclusions reached by Anton, and Bradley and Ingram in chapters 1 and 2. We will begin by discussing our summary statements. These will then be placed in the context of the Anton and Bradley and Ingram chapters.

First, the period between 1940 and 1980 was a rather busy period for the reformulation of the intergovernmental relations arrangements for ocean and coastal resources. In every area that we have examined, the patterns of

structures, responsibilities, and authorities were much
changed in 1980 from what they had been four decades
earlier. This is not to suggest that there was continued
evolution of these patterns during this period. Nor is it
to suggest that each area's arrangements were
metamorphosing at the same rate or at the time within the
period. Rather, this survey suggests that by a series of
adjustments, each of the five resource areas arrived at
1980 with a much different arrangement for
intergovernmental relations than it had started with in
1940. Further, the adjustments were not coeval. For
some, there were adjustments throughout the period (e.g.,
fisheries, hydrocarbons). For the others, much of the
adjustment came during the 1970s.

Second, in the previous paragraph we refer to the
"arrangements" for intergovernmental relations. We use
the plural explicitly. Each area has its own character
and approach to intergovernmental relations. Fisheries
management had become a more cooperative and integrated
arrangement, although a threat of federal dominance could
be identified. Marine mammals management had clearly come
under the exclusive purview of the federal government. In
terms of ocean dumping and related activities, the federal
government had mandated standards which the states had to
adhere to. At the same time, however, it was providing
funds to assist the states in meeting those requirements.
Thus it could be said that a collaborative relationship
had been developed between the levels of government. For
coastal zone management, the states had maintained their
primacy although their positions had been strengthened by
federal actions and dollars.

Third, adjustments occurred primarily through
legislative actions of the U.S. Congress. The Magnuson
Fishery Conservation and Management Act, the Coastal Zone
Management Act, the Marine Mammal Protection Act, the
Outer Continental Shelf Lands Act, the Clean Water Act,
and other pieces of legislation discussed above each
modified the intergovernmental arrangements extant at the
time of their passage. Legal decisions have also affected
the way in which the various levels of government have
interacted with one another in the management of ocean and
coastal resources. However, except in the case of OCS
hydrocarbons, these legal renderings have not been as
influential as those of Congress.

The fourth observation we can make refers to the
legislative adjustments discussed in our third
observation. In some instances the effects on the system

of intergovernmental relations were explicitly thought out and were perhaps the inspiration for the legislation creating those changes. That is, the notion of improving intergovernmental relations and activities figured heavily in the discussions to adopt various provisions of the legislation. This impetus, for example, can be seen behind changes in coastal zone management and fisheries. In both cases, changes were implemented with the explicit hope of improving the effectiveness or practicality of state-federal relationships. On the other hand, it is not evident that concerns about the arrangements for or functioning of intergovernmental relations played any signifcant role in the formulation and passage, for example, of the Marine Mammal Protection Act.

These summary points and the abbreviated histories of intergovernmental relations in the five areas presented above provide support for Anton's argument in Chapter 1. That is, intergovernmental relations in the United States should not be viewed in terms of any static model. Rather, they should be evaluated in terms of dynamic organizational coalitions. Thus the arrangements we have be able to discern are the result of the various levels of government and other interests attempting to improve their respective positions. This helps to explain the greater dependency on the judicial system observed in the case of OCS hydrocarbons. Compared with the legislative process, some of the interests involved have found the judicial arena more appropriate for the enhancement of their position.

Several of the "lessons" presented by Bradley and Ingram in Chapter 2 also find support in the intergovernmental patterns that emerged between the 1940s and 1980 for the five areas we have examined. For example, they demonstrated that in their cases much of the conflict of the U.S. federal system which had been attributed to federal-state antagonisms were in fact state-state conflicts. The increased role and authority of federal agencies in fisheries management can in part be attributed to the inability of the states to cooperate in the adoption of compatible fishery management plans. Bradley and Ingram also argue that the "arena" in which intergovernmental disputes are acted out will depend upon the perception of the participants. The actors will seek those arenas or configurations that will best promote their interests. As mentioned above, this has been the case with OCS hydrocarbons. Finally, they, like Anton, have urged that no single model or ideal type can be used

to explain U.S. federalism. Each substantive public
policy area will likey have its own unique pattern of
intergovernmental relations. This clearly, is what we
found with fisheries, marine mammals, hydrocarbons, ocean
dumping, and coastal zone management.

Finally, we must agree with Kitsos (1981) that the
1970s should be viewed as the period of legislation for
ocean resources and the 1980s as the real period of
implementation. Therefore, we expect that major changes
will occur in the intergovernmental relations systems for
ocean and coastal resources in this decade. Further, we
anticipate that the remaining chapters in this volume
indicate that some additional modifications have occurred,
not because of any real attempt by the Reagan
administration concertedly to develop a New Federalism,
but because of laws and forces already at work in January
of 1981. Additionally, the internal dynamics of each
intergovernmental area are anticipated to have had as
great an impact as any attempt to forge a single system of
intergovernmental relations for ocean and coastal
resources and activities.

ACKNOWLEDGMENTS

This work is a result of research sponsored in part by
the Texas A&M University Sea Grant College Program through
a grant provided by the National Oceanic and Atmospheric
Administration, Office of Sea Grant, Department of
Commerce.

REFERENCES

Armstrong, James J. 1979. The California Sea Otter:
Emerging Conflicts in Resource Management. San Diego
Law Review, 16: 249-285.

Armstrong, John M. & Peter C. Ryner. 1978. Coastal
Waters - A Management Analysis. Ann Arbor Science
Publishers, Inc.

Bish, Robert. 1978. Local Government Diversity and
Federal Grant Programs: Lessons from the Coastal
Energy Impact Program. In Timothy Hennessey, ed.,
Formulating Marine Policy: Limitations to Rational
Decision Making. Proceedings of the Second Annual
Conference held at the Center for Ocean Management
Studies, June 19-21, 1978. The University of Rhode
Island, Kingston, Rhode Island.

Bubier, Jill and Alison Rieser. 1984. Preemption or
Suppression of StateRegulation in the Territorial
Sea. Territorial Sea, IV: 1-9.

Burke, W.T. 1982. U.S. Fishery Management and the New
Law of the Sea. The American Journal of International
Law, 76: 24-55.

Cicin-Sain, Biliana. 1982a. Managing the Ocean Commons:
U.S. Marine Programs in the Seventies and Eighties."
Marine Technology Society Journal, Fourth Quarter.

_____. 1982b. Sea Otters and Shellfish Fisheries in
California: The Management Framework. In Cicin-Sain
et al., eds., Social Science Perspectives on Managing
Conflicts Between Marine Mammals and Fisheries, pp.
195-232.

_____. 1986. Offshore Oil Development in California:
Challenges to Governments and to the Public Interest.
Public Affairs Report, in press.

Cicin-Sain, Biliana, Phyllis M. Girfman and John B.
Richards, eds. 1982.Social Science Perspectives on
Managing Conflicts Between Marine Mammals and
Fisheries, Proceedings from a Conference on Management
of Sea Otters and Shellfish Fisheries in California,
Held at Auoyo Grande, California, January 9-11, 1981,

Marine Policy Program, Marine Science Institute, University of California at Santa Barbara and University of California Cooperative Extension.

Conservation Foundation. 1984. State of the Environment - An Assessment at Mid-Decade. Washington, D.C.

Council on Environmental Quality. 1970. Ocean Dumping - A National Policy. Washington, D.C.

Environmental Protection Agency. 1977. Ocean Dumping in the United States: Fifth Annual Report.

Fairfax, Sally. 1982. Old Recipes for New Federalism. Environmental Law, 9: 945-980.

Fritschie, Gustave. 1980. Impact of Federal Legislation on Coastal Commercial Fisheries. Mimeo, paper presented at Coastal Zone '80, pp. 8.

Gordon, William G. 1982. Marine Fisheries Management - Another Look at an Old Issue. In Gary Knight, ed., Marine Fisheries Management Reporter, Jonathan Publishing Company, Baton Rouge, Louisiana, pp. 69:9301-61:9306.

Greenberg, Eldon V.C. 1981. Federal Consistency Under the Coastal Zone Management Act: An Emerging Focus of Environmental Controversy in the 1980's. Environmental Law Reporter, 11.

Greenberg, Eldon V.C., and Michael E. Shapiro. 1982. Federalism in Fishery Conservation Zone: A New Role for the States in an Era of Federal Regulatory Reform. Southern California Law Review, 55: 641-690.

Harvey, Susan. 1984. Federal Consistency and OCS Oil and Gas Development: A Review and Assessment of the Directly Affecting Controversy. Ocean Development and International Law, 13 (4).

Husing, Onno. 1984. A Matter of Consistency: A Congressional Perspective of Oil and Gas Development on the Outer Continental Shelf. Coastal Zone Management Journal, 12, (2/3).

Jacobson, Jon, et al., eds. 1985. Federal Fisheries
Management: A Guidebook to the Magnuson Fishery
Conservation and Management Act, Revised Edition.
Ocean and Coastal Law Center, University of Oregon Law
School, Eugene.

Kitsos, Thomas R. 1981. The Implementation of Ocean
Legislation in the Eighties: A Legislative
Perspective. Paper presented at a seminar entitled
"Future Directions in U.S. Marine Policies in the
1980's," sponsored by the Hurcting Center for the
Study of Democratic Institutions at the University of
California, Santa Barbara, June 4-6, 15 pp.

Kitsos, Thomas R. 1985. Coastal Management Politics - A
View from Capitol Hill. Journal of the American
Planning Association, 51.

Kreps, Juanita M., Jerry J. Jasinowski, James W. Curlin,
Robert J. Blackwell, and Richard Frank. 1978. U.S.
Ocean Policy in the 1970s: States and Issues.
Washington, D.C.: U.S. Department of Commerce,
Government Printing Office, 328 pp.

Montgomery, John E. 1976. Amendment One of the Atlantic
States Marine Fisheries Compact as a Basis for Uniform
State Fisheries Regulation. Research sponsored by
NOAA, Office of Sea Grant No. NG-33-72. Mimeo.

Murphy, John M. and Martin H. Belsky. 1980. OCS
Development: A New Law and a New Beginning. Coastal
Zone Management Journal, 7.

National Advisory Committee on Oceans and Atmosphere
(NACOA). 1981. The Role of the Ocean in a Waste
Management Strategy. Washington, D.C.

Nielsen, Larry A. 1976. The Evolution of Fisheries
Management Philosophy. Marine Fisheries Review 38
(December): 15-23, MFR Paper 1226.

Office of Coastal Zone Management, National Oceanic and
Atmospheric Administration. 1979. The First Five
Years of Coastal Zone Management. Washington, D.C.

Popper, Frank J. 1981. The Politics of Land-Use Reform.
University of Wisconsin Press.

Richardson, Frank K. 1985. Tradition and Innovation in Resolving Two Disputes Over the Continental Shelf. In J.D. Nyhart, ed., Coastal Zone and Continental Shelf Conflict Resolution: Improving Ocean Use and Resource Dispute Management. Cambridge, MA: Sea Grant College Program, Massachusetts Institute of Technology, MITSG 85-28, pp. 5-17.

Rogalski, William R. 1980. The Unique Federalism of the Regional Councils Under the Fishery Conservation and Management Act of 1976. Boston College Environmental Affairs Law Review, 9: 163-203.

Smith, Edwin. 1982. Legal Perspectives on the Sea Otter Conflict. In Cicin-Sain et al., eds., Social Science Perspectives on Managing Conflicts Between Marine Mammals and Fisheries, pp. 179-194.

U.S. Congress. House. 1969. Our Nation and the Sea: A Plan for National Action, Report of the Commission on Marine Science, Engineering and Resources. 91st Congress, 1st Sess. H. Doc. 91-42. Washington, D.C., 305 pp.

U.S. Congress. House. Committee on Merchant Marine and Fisheries. 1981. Marine Mammal Protection Act, Hearing before the Subcommittee on Fisheries and Wildlife Conservation and the Environment, 97th Congress, 1st Sess. on Marine Mammal Protection Act Authorization - H.R. 2948, April 7, 1981. Marine Mammal Protection Act Improvement - H.R. 4084, July 13, 1981, Serial 97-8, Washington, D.C.

U.S. Congress. House. 1982. Oversight Report on the Magnuson Fishery Conservation and Management Act of 1976. A Report together with supplemental and additional views of the Committee on Merchant Marine and Fisheries. 97th Congress, 2nd Sess. Rept. 97-438, Union Calendar No. 266, March 2, 1982, Washington, DC, 45 pp.

Wiggins, Charles W. 1985. Intergovernmental Approaches to Cross-Jurisdictional Problems. Paper presented at Conference on States and the Territorial Sea, San Antonio, Texas, December 9-11.

Ziles, Zigurds L. 1974. A Legislative-Political History
    of the Coastal Zone Management Act of 1972. *Coastal
    Zone Management Journal*, 1 (3).

4

Intergovernmental Relations in Marine Fisheries Management

Alison Rieser

Intergovernmental relations in the regulation of U.S. marine fisheries differ from those found in other marine resource management programs, reflecting the unique nature of the resource and its management requirements. This chapter describes the status of intergovernmental relations in marine fisheries in an overview of the last eight years of state-federal experience under the Magnuson Fishery Conservation and Management Act (MFCMA) (16 U.S.C. 1801 et seq.), and considers whether the state-federal relationship should be redefined in light of this experience. It concludes with a brief evaluation of recent proposals for such redefinition.

The Nature of the Resource and its Implications for Intergovernmental Relations

Many fish species spend a portion of their life cycle in the waters of more than one political jurisdiction. They may travel from internal waters (bays, rivers, and estuaries) and the coastal waters of several states into the Fishery Conservation Zone (FCZ), sometimes even ranging beyond the 200-mile limit into international waters or the waters of another country. Nevertheless, the largest and most valuable domestic fisheries take place in state waters. This was true prior to passage of the MFCMA and remains true today, despite the increase in offshore fishing activities of U.S. fishermen with the reduction in foreign fishing fleets.[1] Even with the broad expansion of federal waters, the proportion of landings from state waters has held constant.

A fishery encompasses a number of activities,
including harvesting, processing, and marketing. Several
different groups may be involved in each of these sectors,
for example, harvesters may be commercial or recreational,
and use gear ranging from handlines to mile-long nets
extending across the fishing grounds. Conflicts among
user groups, particularly between recreational and
commercial harvesters, increase as the value of the
fishery grows or as stock sizes decline due to fishing
pressure or environmental conditions affecting
recruitment.[2] With the availability of increasingly
sophisticated technology, fishing operations have become
extremely costly, especially with the dramatic increases
of the last several years in such fixed expenses as fuel,
insurance, and interest rates. When stocks are abundant
and demand and prices are high, the number of harvesters
can increase rapidly as fishermen refit their vessels to
take advantage of new opportunities. When stocks decline,
the competition on the fishing grounds can become intense
and the pressure on management authorities to enact
measures to control fishing increases. If the troubled
fishery occurs in the waters of more than one management
regime, authorities must agree on the sources of the
problem and the most effective means of addressing it.

State Management Institutions

The capacities of individual state governments to
address the range of issues that surround marine fisheries
vary considerably, and states have shown varying degrees
of interest in managing the fisheries found within their
waters. Most states employ one of two basic forms of
organization: the fishery commission or the administrative
department (National Marine Fisheries Service 1983). The
fishery commissions are usually composed of members who
are appointed by the governor to represent the fishing
community, and whose appointments sometimes require the
consent of the legislature. The commissions often have
the power to appoint the director of the fisheries'
agency, to establish policies and to oversee their
implementation, with authority to review the agency's
budgets and programs (NMFS 1983). The agency in turn
administers the data collection, licensing and enforcement
programs, relying on the Commission for policy direction.
Some state fishery commissions have rulemaking authority

as well (e.g., Rhode Island's Marine Fisheries Council;
see R.I. Gen. Laws 20-3-2).

The departments are more typical administrative
agencies, headed by a cabinet-level appointee approved by
the state legislature. The department head or
commissioner may appoint an industry or citizen advisory
committee to review policies and proposed regulations.
Such external review may also be required by state
statute. The authority of state fishery departments
varies depending on the degree of legislative authority
delegated by the state legislature. In some states, the
department has broad discretionary authority to
investigate problems in the fisheries, develop policies,
and promulgate and enforce fishing regulations, including
licensing and management controls. Other state
legislatures retain regulatory authority and enable the
department only to carry out research, licensing, market
development, and public information functions. A third
variation is the partial delegation where the legislature
retains authority over the most significant fisheries of
the state, for example, lobster in the State of Maine,
while allowing the commissioner or director to issue
regulations for other fisheries.

For several years, commentators have described these
limited delegations of authority as severe constraints on
the management capacity of the states (e.g., Council of
State Governments 1975: 4). These limitations were seen
as impediments to interstate cooperation in the management
of migratory fisheries, and efforts were made to encourage
states to adopt a model fisheries act, giving policy and
regulatory responsibility to an administrative agency.
However, it was also recognized that even those states who
had delegated sufficient authority to regulate fisheries
in their own waters were powerless to ensure that
consistent management standards were applied in the waters
of neighboring states.

In the 1940s, Congress and the states established
three interstate fisheries commissions to promote
interstate cooperation in the management of marine
fisheries: the Atlantic States Marine Fisheries
Commission, the Gulf States Marine Fisheries Commission,
and the Pacific States Marine Fisheries Commission (see,
e.g., 16 U.S.C. 667a, Atlantic States Marine Fisheries
Compact). Under the compacts, each state appoints three
members to its commission: the director of the fisheries
agency, a state legislator, and a citizen with knowledge
of the fisheries. The commissions are only empowered to

study and to recommend uniform management measures to the
member states; they cannot promulgate regulations to carry
out their management plans.[3] Nor does adoption of a
management plan by an interstate commission bind the
member states to adopt implementing regulations. The
commissions rely upon the consensus of member states on a
management program. If one state disagrees with a
proposed program, it will not be adopted, and a state is
not required to implement even those measures receiving
consensus support. It has been suggested that the
voluntary nature of the commissions probably accounts for
the open and active participation of states in their
deliberations (Buck and Sale 1985: 27). But despite
several years of work on a number of interstate management
plans for such important species as striped bass and
menhaden, compliance by the member states has been very
uneven (NMFS 1983). The management programs developed by
the commissions have been very sound, despite their
limited implementation (Apollonio 1979).

The Allocation of Authority Under the MFCMA

Before 1976, management problems in the U.S. marine
fisheries were only addressed by the coastal states. The
federal government had promulgated a small number of
fisheries regulations to carry out U.S. obligations under
international fisheries agreements. The declaration of
the 200 mile exclusive fishery conservation zone in 1976
marked a major shift in U.S. policy. Until that time the
U.S. had insisted that international law preserved every
nation's freedom to fish anywhere outside the territorial
waters of another nation. But political pressure from
regions with major commercial fisheries, principally New
England and the Pacific Northwest, eventually outweighed
the international policy considerations of the U.S.
Executive Branch, and the Magnuson Fishery Conservation
and Management Act was passed (Congressional Research
Service 1976). The Act was designed primarily to assert
national control over foreign fishing on stocks within 200
miles of the coastline. To enlist sufficient support for
this seaward extension of authority, however, the Act's
sponsors agreed to maintain traditional state authority
over fisheries within the territorial sea.
    The objectives of the Act were to establish a national
fisheries program, designed to rebuild stocks hurt by the
two decades of intensive foreign fishing, and to develop

the U.S. fishing industry, especially its capacity to harvest the underutilized species found in U.S. waters (MFCMA Section 1801(b)). Another goal was to place management on a rational and scientific basis that was sensitive to biological as well as socioeconomic factors (MFCMA Sections 1802(18) and 1851). These objectives were embodied in the concept of "optimum yield":

> The term "optimum," with respect to the yield from a fishery, means the amount of fish--
> (A) which will provide the greatest overall benefit to the Nation, with particular reference to food production and recreational opportunities; and
> (B) which is prescribed as such on the basis of the maximum sustainable yield from such fishery, as modified by any relevant economic, social, or ecological factor. (MFCMA Section 1802(18)).

Responsibility for achieving these objectives was assigned to the Secretary of Commerce, who acts through the National Marine Fisheries Service (NMFS) of the National Oceanic and Atmospheric Administration (NOAA), and to eight nonfederal entities created by the Act, the regional fishery management councils. These councils are composed of federal and state management officials as well as representatives of the fishing industry. Implicit in the Act is the recognition of the high degree of variation among fisheries in their management needs, and among existing management authorities in their capacity to respond to these needs.

The regional council system was designed to combine local and federal expertise in determining the social and economic needs of fishing communities, the biological requirements of fish stocks, and the national and international interests in fishery products (Jacobson et al. 1985: 44). During the Senate debate on the Act, Senator Magnuson, the chief Senate sponsor of the bill, remarked:

> As is evident, we have attempted to balance the national perspective with that of the individual States. We firmly believe that this institutional arrangement is the best hope we can have of obtaining fishery management decisions which in fact protect the fish and which, at the same time, have the support of the fishermen who are regulated. (Congressional Research Service 1976: 455).

Given the enormous variety among fisheries in the
various regions and the diverse interests that fisheries
management serves, the regional council system was an
innovative and creative response to what was perceived as
the major problem of national fisheries management: the
absence of an institutional framework for the development
and implementation of policy (Rogalski 1980). Thus, it
was not simply a political or legal necessity that states
were given a large role in national fisheries management;
it was a response to the practical difficulties of
formulating and implementing policies for such diverse
resources. The U.S. Senate Commerce Committee (1975:
685-686) stated in its report on the MFCMA:

> unity of management, or at least close cooperation, is
> vital to prevent jurisdictional difference from
> adversely affecting conservation practices. The
> committee recognizes the need to have close
> cooperation between the Federal and State governments
> because of the separation of jurisdiction inherent in
> this Act. This is one of the primary reasons why both
> State and Federal representatives are included in the
> membership on the Regional Fishery Management Councils.

In contrast with the intergovernmental systems in
place for other marine resources such as Outer Continental
Shelf oil and gas, the states, at least collectively, play
a major role in federal management of marine fisheries.
State members outnumber federal voting members. For
example, the New England Fishery Management Council has
seventeen voting members, eleven of whom are appointed
from lists submitted by the governors of the member states
of persons knowledgeable and experienced in the fisheries
of New England. The other six voting members are the NMFS
Regional Director and the principal fishery administrators
of the five New England states (MFCMA Section 1852).
Despite the preponderance of nonfederal voting members on
the councils, an individual state cannot, however, be
assured that its particular policy objectives will be
adopted. The council is charged with developing regional
management policies and measures, which may incorporate
the existing regulations of the adjacent coastal states,
as long as they are consistent with the National Standards
of the Magnuson Act (MFCMA Section 1851).
In addition to providing through the regional councils
a role for each state in developing policies for federal
waters, the MFCMA preserves the existing authority of each

state to manage the fisheries "within its boundaries"
(MFCMA Section 1856(a)). The seaward boundary of state
waters is generally three miles from the shore, except on
the Gulf of Mexico coast of Florida and Texas where the
limit is three marine leagues, approximately nine
miles.[4] Inside state waters, the states are subject to
federal controls only if the Secretary of Commerce
determines that a state regulation (or a state's failure
to adopt regulations) substantially and adversely affects
the carrying out of a federal fishery management plan
(MFCMA Section 1856(b), 50 C.F.R. Part 619). The Act
requires the secretary to make these findings in the
context of a formal adjudicatory hearing. But the state
law may only be preempted where the fishery occurs
predominantly within the FCZ, even if the fishery occurs
in the waters of several states.

Beyond the territorial sea, the states did not retain
the same measure of extraterritorial authority for which
they had received judicial approval in the decades prior
to the MFCMA (see, e.g., Florida v. Skiriotes, 313 U.S. 69
(1941); Bayside Fish Co. v. Gentry, 297 U.S. 422 (1936);
Alaska v. Bundrant, 546 P.2d 530 (Ak. 1976)). State
authority beyond three miles is limited by the Act in two
important ways: First, both direct state regulation and
indirect state controls, such as landing laws or
possession prohibitions, may now only apply to "vessels
registered under the laws of the State" (MFCMA Section
1851(a)). This provision has been interpreted as
permitting a state to control fishing in waters beyond its
seaward boundary only when three conditions are satisfied:
the regulation does not conflict with federal law,
including a Fishery Management Plan (FMP); the state
demonstrates that a legitimate state interest is served;
and the vessels regulated are registered by the state and
operate from state ports (California v. Weeren, 607 P.2d
1279, 1287 (Cal. 1980); State v. F/V Baranof, 677 P.2d
1245 (Ak. 1984)). Second, state regulation even of
registered vessels will be superseded by an FMP regulation
where an actual conflict exists between the rules.

Recent court decisions have held that the Act did not
intend to preempt state regulation in the FCZ in the
absence of a conflict with federal regulations (Bubier
1985a). Although the Act does not define "registered,"
both the Baranof and Weeren decisions suggest that a broad
interpretation is most consistent with the Act. The
crucial question left unresolved is what constitutes a
conflict between state and federal regulations. Very

little guidance has come from the courts on this question
(see, e.g., State v. Sterling, 448 A.2d 785, 787 (R.I.
1982) and Alaska v. Painter, Ak. Ct. App. Opinion No. 446,
Feb. 22, 1985) or from NOAA.

Thus it is perfectly acceptable within the framework
of the MFCMA for individual states to adopt regulations
for their waters that differ from adjacent states and from
any federal regulations adopted for the adjacent portion
of the FCZ. It is only when there is a conflict and a
predominant federal interest that the federal regulations
may be applied throughout the species' range against the
desire of the states.

Intergovernmental Problems in Fisheries Management

To what extent has management under the Magnuson Act
been hampered by the jurisdictional arrangements created
under the Act? There is no question that jurisdictional
problems have arisen. These problems have occurred
despite predictions by members of Congress that the
Council structure and the scientific approach to
management would prevent disagreement among government
agencies:

> The bill [H.R. 200] provides for the maximum amount of
> professional and scientific involvement in the
> preparation and development of management plans and
> strategies; it is the expectation of our committee
> that there will be very little and infrequent conflict
> between States and the Federal Government over
> management of the various fish stocks because of the
> high professional caliber of the fisheries biologists
> who will be involved, whether the payroll they be on
> be Federal or State. (Congressional Research Service
> 1976: 840, statement of Rep. Leggett).

Intergovernmental conflicts have included
disagreements among state and federal management entities
on policies and measures, jurisdictional ambiguity
resulting in no management responsibility being taken, and
the circumvention of federal regulations by segments of
the fishing industry taking advantage of differences in
state management controls. Jurisdictional problems were
identified as serious limitations on the federal system in
the early years of implementation of the MFCMA in two
surveys by the General Accounting Office (Comptroller

General 1979a, 1979b)[5] and by officials then responsible
for federal management (e.g., Leitzell 1979). Conflicts
continue to emerge as more federal plans are implemented
through management measures which differ from existing
state regulations (e.g., Bubier and Rieser 1984b).

Federal fishery management plans have been challenged
in court by states in only four instances, each time
unsuccessfully. The first lawsuit filed under the Act was
brought by the state of Maine, challenging the Atlantic
herring plan (Maine v. Kreps, 563 F.2d 1043 (1st Cir.
1977)). A preliminary plan had been prepared by the
Secretary of Commerce because the New England Regional
Council, in existence for only a few months, had not had
time to develop foreign fishing quotas and regulations. A
preliminary management plan only applies to foreign
fishing. Having no effect on domestic fishing, the
preliminary plan was not in conflict with existing state
regulations. Maine, however, charged that the secretary
had uncritically accepted the quotas and foreign fishing
allocations of the international agency formerly
responsible for the region, the International Convention
for Northwest Atlantic Fisheries (ICNAF), instead of
making an independent determination of the "optimum yield"
for Atlantic herring, as that term is defined by the Act.
The state argued that the foreign fishing level should be
zero because the stocks were below those levels which
could produce the maximum sustainable yield.[6] Favoring
the most rapid rebuilding of the stock, Maine argued that
the interests of domestic fishermen should be paramount.
The federal court rejected the challenge, finding that the
secretary was free to take foreign policy considerations
into account in defining optimum yield, especially in
1977, the transition year between international management
and exclusive U.S. regulation. While technically a
state-federal dispute because of the parties, the suit
concerned federal policy toward foreign allocations, and
not whether state policies and management measures should
prevail over or give way to federal regulations.

Louisiana's legal challenge to the Gulf of Mexico
Council's shrimp management plan was, again, not so much a
federal-state dispute but an outgrowth of a state-state
conflict. The shrimp plan approved in 1981 established a
cooperative seasonal closure of U.S. FCZ waters adjacent
to Texas waters to run concurrently with the Texas shrimp
closure. Texas had for some time closed its waters for a
portion of the year in an effort to prevent the harvesting
of shrimp below the minimum size established under state

law. Louisiana and Texas have had a longstanding
disagreement over state shrimp regulations largely because
of the different demands of their local industries.
Canneries in Louisiana use small to medium shrimp, while
Texas processors produce raw, frozen, or breaded shrimp
and thus require larger shrimp. Not surprisingly, then,
Louisiana objected throughout the Gulf Council's
three-year deliberations to measures that would restrict
the year-round harvesting practices of their shrimp fleet.

When the Secretary of Commerce approved the shrimp
plan and implemented its closure provision through
emergency regulations, Louisiana filed suit in federal
court, claiming the closure to be a violation of the
MFCMA's National Standards (Louisiana v. Baldrige, 538 F.
Supp. 625 (E.D. La. 1982)). The state claimed that the
secretary had improperly approved the plan because he had
not considered Louisiana's scientific evidence that the
closure would be ineffective. By not considering the
"best scientific data available," the secretary had
violated National Standard number two (MFCMA Section
1851(a)(2)). The court, however, found the Secretary's
approval of the Council's plan to be rational and fully
supported by both the administrative record and the best
scientific information available. Although Louisiana
failed to prevail on the merits of its claim, it was
successful in defending its right to bring suit against
the Secretary of Commerce for injuries allegedly sustained
by its citizens. The Justice Department had argued that
Louisiana lacked standing to challenge regulations
promulgated under the MFCMA. In rejecting this claim, the
court reaffirmed the proprietary interest of states in
fisheries within their boundaries, an interest which was
also recognized by the MFCMA in its provision for state
participation in the development of FMPs (Louisiana v.
Baldrige, p. 629).

The only direct challenges to federal fisheries
regulations on grounds of conflict with existing state
laws have been brought by the State of Florida. The suits
raised important fundamental issues regarding conflicting
state and federal policies, but both were settled without
resolving them.

Florida's first suit, filed in March 1983, challenged
the federal mackerel plan and regulations on two separate
grounds (Florida v. Baldrige I, No. TCA-83-7071, N.D.
Fla., 1985). First, Florida claimed that the federal
plan, by allowing fishing vessels to employ purse seines
in the FCZ, failed to meet the Coastal Zone Management

Act's requirement that federal actions "directly affecting the state's coastal zone" be consistent to the maximum extent practicable with existing state coastal laws and policies (CZMA, 16 U.S.C. 1456(c)(1)). Second, the State claimed that the federal regulations had preempted Florida's laws prohibiting the taking of food fish with purse seines without observing the procedural requirements of section 1856(b) of the MFCMA.

The Gulf of Mexico and South Atlantic Councils had wanted to prohibit the use of purse seines for mackerel fishing in the FCZ. Use of this highly efficient and controversial gear had been banned by all the southeastern states, including Florida. NOAA had opposed a blanket prohibition on grounds that it would violate several of the MFCMA National Standards (Taylor and Rieser 1983: 10). The Council's plan, therefore, allowed purse seining in the FCZ, subject to a special set of restrictions.

In response to Florida's argument that the FMP should be consistent with the marine fisheries section of its coastal management program and ban purse seines, NOAA concluded that "consistent" does not mean "identical," where offshore conditions dictate a different approach to management in the FCZ. Where "the state's fishery is protected to the same extent under the FMP approach as under the state's approach, the two plans are consistent" (NOAA 1982: 7-8). NOAA did not challenge application of the consistency requirement to the FMP; it argued that the plan was in fact "consistent to the maximum extent practicable." Florida argued that its gear restriction was more protective of the fishery and should therefore be applied throughout the fishery's range.

Florida's second suit was filed in October 1983, challenging the snapper-grouper FMP regulations (Florida v. Baldrige II, No. TCA-83-7380, N.D. Fla., 1985). In addition to the consistency claim under the CZMA, Florida argued that the federal regulations unlawfully superseded the effect of its ban on the possession and use of fish traps both within the FCZ and the state's waters. The state asserted that fishermen crossing state waters to use fish traps in the FCZ would make it impossible to enforce the state's prohibition in state waters. The practical effect was a preemption of state authority but without the due process provided by the MFCMA.

NOAA refuted the state waters preemption claim, arguing that Florida could still ban the use of fish traps in state waters, it simply could not enforce the ban through a possession prohibition. To do so would interfere with a fisherman's lawful use of the gear in the FCZ. NOAA argued that this type of infringement on state law is constitutionally sanctioned by the supremacy clause of the U.S. Constitution (Article VI, clause 2) (NOAA 1981). With regard to the supersession in the FCZ, NOAA argued that state regulation of fishing in the FCZ is permissible only in the absence of conflict with a federal regulation. Here, the state and federal rules were in clear conflict.

The first Florida v. Baldrige case was settled by an agreement between the parties stipulating that state law can only be enforced in the FCZ "absent a conflict with the lawful exercise of federal fisheries authority and/or jurisdiction under the Magnuson Act." The parties further agreed that Florida's ban on the use of purse seines conflicted with the federal regulations "to the extent that the state law attempts directly and/or indirectly to prohibit use of purse seines to take King and Spanish mackerel in the FCZ."[7]

The second suit, regarding the fish trap prohibition, was also settled by stipulated agreement. This settlement was appropriate, at least in part, because two recent court decisions found that the Florida statute was not intended to apply beyond state waters (Bethell v. Florida, 741 F.2d 1341 (11th Cir. 1984); Southeastern Fisheries Assoc. v. Dep't of Natural Resources, 453 So. 2d 1351 (Fla. 1984)). Neither settlement, however, addressed the issue of federal supersession of state law within state waters nor the consistency requirement of the Coastal Zone Management Act. Florida apparently decided to drop its consistency claims after the Supreme Court narrowly interpreted the geographic scope of the CZMA in Secretary of Interior v. California (464 S.Ct. 312 (1984)). Florida's decision may have been unwarranted. The Supreme Court had ruled that OCS lease sales are not subject to the consistency requirement because, inter alia, they occur outside the state's coastal zone. But NOAA's consistency regulations continue to require federal fishery management plans to be consistent with approved state coastal zone management programs (Federal Register, Vol. 50, p. 35210, Aug. 8, 1985). Moreover, the supersession issue is likely to arise again, and the failure to obtain a definitive answer in the Florida cases eliminated an opportunity to prevent further intergovernmental disputes.

The substantive provisions of the MFCMA and the regulations interpreting them provide only modest guidance

on resolving future conflicts in state and federal
management policy. National Standard number three (MFCMA
Section 1851(b)(3)) requires an FMP, to the extent
practicable, to manage an individual fish stock "as a unit
throughout its range," and that interrelated stocks be
managed as a unit or in close coordination. NOAA
guidelines for interpreting the National Standards (50
C.F.R. Part 602)[8] encourage the councils to overlook
political boundaries, at least temporarily, during the
development of the FMP (Marine Law Institute 1982a). In
the planning process the councils are asked to seek
coordination among all management entities, including the
states. The guidelines strongly recommend that the FMP
specify conservation and management measures which should
be adopted everywhere, even though NOAA can only implement
them within the FCZ under ordinary circumstances. The FMP
should then identify what state action is necessary to
implement the measures within state waters to achieve the
plan's objectives. Councils are urged to include a
discussion of the interrelationship between state
regulations and the federal measures proposed for the
FCZ. If the state regulations applicable to FCZ fishing
conflict with the federal measures, the states would then
be given notice that these laws will be superseded.

NOAA probably assumed that, by requiring the FMP to
specify which existing state laws are incompatible with
the new federal measures and which new state laws are
required to achieve the FMP's objectives, the necessary
coordination of standards would occur. It did not,
however, give the councils any guidance on how to
determine the compatibility of existing state laws with
the new measures. Moreover, if NOAA anticipated using the
FMP as a source of objective criteria for determining
whether grounds existed for federal preemption in state
waters, it is likely that councils were uncomfortable with
the notion of assisting that process.

Federal officials had probably hoped that adoption of
certain regulatory provisions in the federal FMPs would at
least inspire states to adopt improved management measures
in state waters. This has occurred, but there are some
notable exceptions. For example, the American lobster
plan includes a prohibition against landing lobster
parts.[9] The New England Council adopted this
prohibition in an effort to ensure compliance with the
minimum size limit, which is the core of the lobster
management program. The states of New Jersey, Maryland,
and Virginia allow vessels to land lobster tails and

claws, effectively preventing any enforcement of the
minimum size. These states, however, have been reluctant
to ban the landing of parts. Due to limitations on the
federal preemption authority because the lobster fishery
occurs predominantly in state waters, there is little the
council or NOAA can do to override the inconsistent state
laws. A large potential loophole is thus created,
frustrating the application of the management program
throughout the range of the fishery. In fact, the
inconsistent state lobster laws were cited in the
Inspector General's 1985 report as an example of
conditions hampering the effectiveness of the regional
councils (U.S. Department of Commerce 1985).

The preemption authority has been used only twice; in
both instances the action was taken to overrule Oregon's
decision to extend its commercial chinook salmon season
beyond the closure date specified in the FMP. At the
second preemption proceeding, NOAA requested an emergency
closure of the state's waters and an indefinite preemption
of Oregon's authority to extend the salmon season, citing
the state's lack of commitment to regional decision-making
(Severance and Bubier 1985). This claim was eventually
dropped when Oregon adopted a policy to adopt regulations
for state waters that are consistent with the FMP and to
consult with the council when it believes new information
warrants changes in the regulatory regime.[10]

NOAA decided against using the preemption process in
1982 when actions by the New England states undermined the
federal quotas on Atlantic herring. Instead, finding that
an improvement in management coordination was unlikely to
occur, NMFS withdrew its approval of the herring FMP,
leaving management of the fishery to the states (Marine
Law Institute 1982b).

The Congress has also been aware for some time that
the state-federal system in the MFCMA has led to some
problems. For example, the 1981 House Subcommittee on
Fisheries and Wildlife Conservation and the Environment
found that the regional councils and the states needed to
make a greater effort at coordinating their regulations to
prevent potential harm to migratory fisheries (U.S.
Congress, Subcomm. on Fisheries 1981: 7). Congress has
tried to increase the coordination of interjurisdictional
management; however, it has done so primarily in the
context of anadromous species, such as Pacific salmon, or
in special emergency situations. For example, the Salmon
and Steelhead Conservation and Management Act of 1980 (16
U.S.C. 3301-3345) makes federal financial assistance for

hatchery and other enhancement programs contingent upon adoption and enforcement of measures recommended to the Secretary of Commerce by a special interjurisdictional commission established under the Act. Similarly, the Anadromous Fish Conservation Act (16 U.S.C. 757a-757g) provides for a 40% increase in the federal contribution toward cooperative programs with states for those that adopt interstate management plans.

The Chaffee bill, entitled the Coastal Migratory Fish Conservation Act (S. 2667), which failed to pass in the 98th Congress, proposed an institutional arrangement to encourage the coordinated management of inshore species in a manner similar to the MFCMA's system for offshore fisheries. States would have been required to implement the management measures adopted by the interstate compact commissions for particular species identified as priorities. They would have been free to adopt more stringent controls; the commission standards, however, were to be the minimum requirements. Failure to adopt these would have triggered imposition of federal emergency measures.

The only measure Congress has adopted that goes beyond financial incentives to promote intergovernment coordination has been the Atlantic Striped Bass Conservation Act of 1984 (P.L. 98-613, 98 Stat. 3187 (1984)). In that Act, the Congress recognized that the striped bass is at risk, but because no single management entity has authority over the entire range of the species, inconsistent and inadequate conservation measures are in effect (Section 2(a)(3)). To address the serious declines in the stocks, the Act requires each state within the migratory range to adopt management measures recommended by the Atlantic States Marine Fisheries Commission (ASMFC) or face a federally enforced moratorium on striped bass fishing within its waters. This was a temporary intervention and acceptable politically only because of the serious condition of the stocks (Bubier and Rieser 1984a).[11]

Congress has never seriously considered removing the states from the federal management program under the MFCMA. The oversight committees have in fact been distinctly nonfederal in their consistent support for the regional councils, even in the fact of large, proposed budget cuts to the council system. And amendments to the Act have only strengthened the councils' authority vis-a-vis the Secretary of Commerce in the review of fishery management plans (e.g., P.L. 97-453, 96 Stat. 2487, Jan. 12, 1983).

Proposed Alternatives for Interjurisdictional Management

Alternative institutional arrangements fall generally into three major categories: a federal model, involving more direct federal responsibility for policy formulation, implementation, and enforcement; a state model, where state governments are given greater responsibility for fishery research, policy development, and enforcement, either individually or through interstate compact commissions; and a hybrid state-federal model, one variation of which is in place currently.

There are numerous options under each category, including those described by NMFS (1983), such as the 0 to 200 or 3 to 200 miles regional commissions, and the expanded role of the states or interstate compact commissions (Buck and Sale 1985). For example, an individual state or a group of states could assume offshore responsibility through a delegation of authority from the federal government similar to the one authorized under the Marine Mammal Protection Act (16 U.S.C. 1379). Where vessels from more than one state engage in the fishery, the federal government could condition withdrawal of federal regulations on the involvement of an interstate commission and the assurance that residents of different states will be treated equitably.

Assessing the feasibility of such an approach will require examining several related questions, including whether state administrative law requirements are serious impediments to the expanded use of interstate compacts (Rieser and Ziegler 1982) and how they might be overcome through federal initiatives, such as the Atlantic Striped Bass Conservation Act of 1984. Also, where federal management has been deferred or withdrawn, as in the case of Atlantic herring, it should be determined whether the states, acting alone or through regional organizations, have responded and whether the fishery has improved without federal management.

The National Marine Fisheries Service (1985) prepared a policy statement on interjurisdictional fisheries management and planned to publish it in the Federal Register, but publication was held up by Office of Management and Budget (OMB) reviewers (Marine Fisheries Advisory Committee 1985). Development of the policy

statement was prompted by perceptions that states are
failing to adopt management measures that support
regulations implementing the fishery management plans and
failing to coordinate their measures among themselves
(Buck and Sale 1985: 31). The goal of the policy would be
to involve all governmental entities in the preparation of
fishery management plans, including those with
responsibility for habitat protection, research, product
quality, and interstate transportation. For strictly
interstate fisheries, NMFS envisions the federal role to
be one of mediator, to assist states in reaching
agreement. The policy also endorses transferring more
fiscal responsibility, research, and management authority
to the states. Critics of the proposed board of
conciliation and arbitration suggest this would only cause
further delay in implementation of controls (Buck and Sale
1985: 31). Delays are especially problemmatic in
fisheries management because the information basis of
proposed measures becomes out of date as conditions change
rapidly in the fishery (Rieser and Ziegler 1982). With
this approach NMFS seems to be encouraging more federal
involvement but less federal responsibility, perhaps one
reason OMB reviewers have been reluctant to release the
policy statement.

NOAA has undertaken a review of the basic approach to
federal isheries management with a view toward proposing
major amendments to the MFCMA in 1987. In light of the
state-federal relations in the past eight years, any
rethinking of fisheries intergovernmental relations must
begin with consideration of the capacity and willingness
of state governments to assume greater responsibility for
the management of marine fisheries. One must also inquire
whether increased state responsibility can ensure that
national interests in fishery resources are served.

Are states prepared fiscally, politically, and
administratively to adopt a greater role in fishery
management? Similar to the findings of Lester (1985) in
his study of the new federalism's impact on state funding
of environmental programs, an examination of state
management capacity will probably reveal considerable
variability in the degree of internal commitment to
fisheries management and of external dependence on federal
assistance for fisheries research and management
activities. Thus, the likely reaction of states to
federal pressure (through financial incentives or
otherwise) to assume more management responsibility will
differ. Unlike the pollution control field, however,

states have already assumed a significant role in the
development of federal policies and regulations for marine
fisheries through their participation on the regional
councils. Thus, a more successful transfer of authority
from the federal to state level may be possible in the
fisheries context, at least under carefully controlled
conditions (NMFS 1983 and 1985).

One must also ask how important uniformity is to the
system of fisheries management. As one commentator
suggests, there may be a tendency to "overemphasiz[e] the
need for and value of consistent management of a stock
throughout its full range, and [to] underempasiz[e] the
need to recognize regional variations in the nature of
fish populations and the fisheries that are directed on
them, as the Magnuson Act, the literature, and common
sense dictate" (McCallum 1985: 3). The recent report on
interjurisdictional fisheries prepared by the
Congressional Research Service (Buck and Sale 1985)
concludes that the existing legal framework sanctions
nonuniformity in the management of transboundary stocks,
but "whether the existing management regime should be
continued or modified appears ultimately to raise a policy
rather than a legal issue." If management of certain
resources can tolerate or even benefit from diverse
approaches, then new institutional arrangements should not
be designed to achieve uniformity, given the significant
political and administrative costs of such a goal.

Criteria against which any alternative institutional
approach must be measured include the extent to which
management costs are distributed equitably, in light of
the benefits which accrue from such efforts. Moreover,
before the state-federal relationship in marine fisheries
is redefined, a consensus should be reached as to what
extent there is national interest in fishery resources and
how much the nation is willing to spend to protect and
further these interests.

NOTES

Research for this chapter was supported in part by
grant NA81AA-D-0035 from the National Oceanic and
Atmospheric Administration to the University of
Maine/University of New Hampshire Sea Grant College
Program. The assistance of Jill Bubier and Beverly

Bayley-Smith of the Marine Law Institute is gratefully acknowledged.

   1. The relative distribution of harvests between state and federal waters has remained roughly the same since passage of the MFCMA. In 1975, the year before the MFCMA was passed, harvests from state waters were 59% by weight of the total U.S. fish and shellfish landings and 45% by value. Harvests from federal waters, which then extended from three to twelve miles, were only 18% by weight and 15% by value of the total U.S. landings. The remaining 23% was harvested in waters beyond U.S. jurisdiction. In 1983, harvests from state waters constituted 61% by weight and 47% by value of all U.S. landings, an increase of 2% in both weight and value. Landings in both areas have grown significantly, especially in federal waters, which now extend out to 200 nautical miles. State water harvests have increased 47% in weight (and 161% by value). Landings from federal waters have increased 158% by weight (and 629% by value), owing primarily to the displacement of foreign fishing fleets. Buck and Sale (1985: 25), citing NMFS, Fisheries of the United States, 1984.
   2. "Recruitment" as an ecological term means the influx of new members into a population by reproduction or immigration. Lincoln et al. (1982: 213).
   3. Under Amendment One to the Atlantic States Marine Fisheries Compact, and Section 10 of the Gulf States Marine Fisheries Compact, two or more states may agree to act on a regional basis to regulate an interstate fishery and to delegate authority to the commission to promulgate uniform regulations applicable to the waters of the agreeing states. States have not been eager to use this mechanism, and the joint regulatory process is only used for one fishery, Northern shrimp, and there only nominally. See Rieser and Ziegler (1982) for discussion of some of the legal questions surrounding this mechanism and Rieser and Taylor (1982) for description of model legislation designed to overcome these problems.
   4. In a 1984 amendment to the MFCMA, certain portions of the FCZ were placed under Alaska's fisheries jurisdiction. P.L. 98-623, section 404(4) (Oct. 1984). Irregularities in the southeastern coastline create pockets of federal waters surrounded by state waters. The amendment drew a closing line outside the archipelago and specified that Alaska regulations would now control fisheries in the included waters, with the exception of

the king, dungeness, and tanner crab fisheries. In a
previous action, Congress had placed the waters of
Nantucket Sound under the fisheries administration of
Massachusetts and all similar "enclaves" of federal waters
under the authority of the adjacent state. 16 U.S.C.
1856(a)(2)(A),(B).

5. The GAO found in 1979 that disagreements between
the states and the federal government were impeding
effective enforcement of FMP regulations. The Secretary
of Commerce was called upon to monitor the extent to which
jurisdictional problems were hindering FMP implementation
and to use the Act's preemption provision or to propose
additional legislation to extend federal management over
the territorial sea. (Comptroller General 1979a: 28;
1979b).

6. Maximum sustainable yield is defined as the
maximum yield or crop which may be harvested year after
year without damage to the system. Lincoln et al. (1982:
148).

7. Stipulated Settlement Agreement for Dismissal
Without Prejudice, Florida v. Baldrige I, No. TCA-83-7071
(N.D. Fla. 1985).

8. 50 C.F.R. 602, Guidelines for National Standards,
Subpart B, section 602.13; 48 Fed. Reg. 7402, Feb. 18,
1983. See "Proposed FMP Development Guidelines Encourage
Cooperation and Facilitate Preemption," Territorial Sea
Vol. 11, No. 2 (December 1982), p. 10.

9. 50 C.F.R. 649.7(a)(2); 649.20(c); 48 Fed. Reg.
36268, Aug. 10, 1983.

10. "Management of Ocean Fisheries," Oregon Fish and
Wildlife Policy No. 30, Nov. 16, 1984. For a discussion
of the first and second Oregon preemptions, see Marine Law
Institute (1982c) and Severance and Bubier (1985). The
first preemption action was taken in response to a
petition from the Washington Department of Fisheries.
Recognizing that the preemption proceedings require a
minimum of three weeks, the Congress has considered
amending the MFCMA to allow immediate preemption, followed
by the administrative proceedings. In Oregon, the state's
extended season was over by the time the administrative
law judge had made his findings. See Bubier (1985b).

11. Average landings in the years 1958-1976 were 9.5
million pounds. In 1979 landings were down by 3.1 million
pounds and 2.2 million in 1982, an 85% reduction. In
1984, state regulation differed considerably: Rhode Island
had a total moratorium, Delaware had not adopted any of
the ASMFC's 1981 plan, North Carolina had only partial

implementation in place. The Mid-Atlantic Council, in conjunction with the New England and South Atlantic councils, is preparing a striped bass FMP and hopes to "induce" adoption of the ASMFC plan by the member states. The FMP will apply the commission's minimum size limits to the FCZ. 50 Fed. Reg. 35105 (Aug. 29, 1985).

126

REFERENCES

Apollonio, Spencer. 1979. Migratory Species. In Janet
Caudle, ed., State and Interstate Fishery
Jurisdiction: Problems and Progress. Proceedings of a
Conference in Raleigh, N.C., UNC Sea Grant Program.

Bubier, Jill. 1985a. Florida and Alaska Courts Reach
Consensus on State Extraterritorial Fisheries
Jurisdiction, Territorial Sea, Vol. V, No. 2, Marine
Law Institute, Portland, ME.

_____. 1985b. FMCMA Reauthorization. Territorial Sea,
Vol. V, No. 4, Marine Law Institute, Portland, ME.

Bubier, Jill, and Alison Rieser. 1984a. Atlantic Striped
Bass Conservation Act: Unconstitutional Amendment of
an Interstate Compact? Territorial Sea, Vol. IV, No.
4, Marine Law Institute, Portland, ME.

_____. 1984b. Preemption or Supersession of State
Regulation in the Territorial Sea. Territorial Sea,
Vol. IV, No. 1, Marine Law Institute, Portland, ME.

Buck, Eugene H., and David M. Sale. 1985. Inter-
jurisdictional Fisheries Management: Issues and
Options. Report by the Congressional Research
Service, Library of Congress, for the House Committee
on Merchant Marine and Fisheries, Subcommittee on
Fisheries and Wildlife Conservation and the
Environment.

Comptroller General of the United States. 1979a.
Progress and Problems of Fisheries Management Under
the Fishery Conservation and Management Act. Report
to the U.S. Congress. CED-79-23.

_____. 1979b. Enforcement Problems Hinder Effective
Implementation of New Fishery Management Activities.
Report to the U.S. Congress. CED-79-120.

Congressional Research Service. 1976. A Legislative
history of the Magnuson Fishery Conservation and
Management Act of 1976. Prepared for the Senate
Commerce Committee. Committee Print. Washington, DC:
Government Printing Office.

Council of State Governments. 1975. To Stem the Tide:
    Effective State Marine Fisheries Management.
    Lexington, KY.

Jacobson, Jon, Daniel Conner, and Robert Tozer. 1985.
    Federal Fisheries Management: A Guidebook to the
    Magnuson Fishery Conservation and Management Act.
    University of Oregon School of Law, Publ. No.
    ORESU-H-85-001.

Leitzell, Terry C. 1979. State/Federal Management of
    Interjurisdictional Fisheries: Where Do We Go From
    Here? In Janet Caudle, ed., State and Interstate
    Fishery Jurisdiction: Problems and Progress.
    Proceedings of a Conference in Raleigh, N.C., UNC Sea
    Grant Program.

Lester, James P. 1985. New Federalism and Environmental
    Policy. Presented at the annual meeting of the
    American Political Science Association, New Orleans,
    LA.

Lincoln, Roger J., G.A. Boxall, and P.F. Clark. 1982. A
    Dictionary of Ecology, Evolution and Systematics.
    Cambridge Univ. Press.

McCallum, James. 1985. Comments of the Atlantic States
    Marine Fisheries Commission on NMFS Draft Policy on
    Interjurisdictional Fisheries.

Marine Fisheries Advisory Committee (MAFAC). 1985.
    Personal Communication with Ann Smith, Executive
    Secretary.

Marine Law Institute (MLI). 1982a. Proposed FMP
    Development Guidelines Encourage Cooperation and
    Facilitate Preemption. Territorial Sea, Vol. II, No.
    2, Portland, ME.

_____. 1982b. Withdrawal of Herring Plan Approval Due
    to Lack of State Cooperation. Territorial Sea, Vol.
    II, No. 2. Portland, ME.

_____. 1982c. Secretary of Commerce Preempts Oregon
    Salmon Regulations. Territorial Sea, Vol. II, No. 2.
    Portland, ME.

128

National Marine Fisheries Service (NMFS). 1983.
    Interjurisdictional Fishery Management: An Issue
    Paper. Distributed for discussion with the Atlantic
    States Marine Fisheries Commission, June 6, 1983.

_____. 1985. Policies for the Management of Inter-
    jurisdictional Fisheries. Draft, February 27, 1985.

NOAA. 1981. Formal Legal Opinion No. 93, Office of the
    General Counsel, NOAA. Supersession and Jurisdictional
    Operations Under Section 306 of the Magnuson Act.

_____. 1982. Administrator's Letter No. 37, Inter-
    relationship of the Magnuson Act and the Coastal Zone
    Management Act, Nov. 24, 1982.

Kieser, Alison, and Robert Taylor. 1982. ASMFC Develops
    Proposed Legislation to Implement Amendment One,
    Territorial Sea, 1982, Vol. III, No. 2, Marine Law
    Institute, Portland, ME.

Rieser, Alison, and Nancy Ziegler. 1982. Regional
    Fisheries Regulation Under the Atlantic States Marine
    Fisheries Compact: Promising Model or Unworkable
    Scheme? Territorial Sea, 1982, Vol. II, No. 1, Marine
    Law Institute, Portland, ME.

Rogalski, William R. 1980. The Unique Federalism of the
    Regional Councils Under the Fishery Conservation and
    Management Act of 1976. Boston College Env. L. Rev.
    9: 163.

Severance, David, and Jill Bubier. 1985. Preemption of
    Oregon's Extended Salmon Season, 1984. Territorial
    Sea, Vol V, No. 1, Marine Law Institute, Portland, ME.

Taylor, Robert A., and Alison Rieser. 1983. Federal
    Fisheries Management and State Coastal Zone Management
    Consistency: Florida Tests the Waters. Territorial
    Sea, Vol. III, No. 1, Marine Law Institute, Portland,
    ME.

U.S. Congress. House Committee on Merchant Marine and
    Fisheries. Subcommittee on Fisheries. 1981.
    Oversight Report on the MFCMA. Subcommittee on
    Fisheries and Wildlife Conservation and the
    Environment. 97th Congress, 1st Session.

U.S. Congress. Senate. Commerce Committee. 1975. Report
   on S. 961, Magnuson Fisheries Management and
   Conservation Act. Report No. 94-416. Washington,
   DC: Government Printing Office.

U.S. Department of Commerce. 1985. Office of Inspector
   General. Opportunities for Cost Reductions and
   Operational Efficiencies in Managing Fishery
   Resources.

5

Marine Mammals, Endangered Species, and Intergovernmental Relations

Stephen R. Kellert

INTRODUCTION

This chapter examines factors associated with the decline of most marine mammal species and the structure of· intergovernmental relations involved in the management and conservation of these animals today. Nine factors are identified as responsible for the historic depletion of many marine mammal species including: the common property characteristic of most marine mammal species, the "fugitive" quality of many species in the ocean environment, the biological vulnerability of many marine mammals as targets of exploitation, the presumed inexhaustibility of many species, widespread biological ignorance, large commercial benefits associated with harvesting certain species, the difficulty of developing effective international marine mammal conservation agreements, adverse impacts of various human activities on the habitats and behaviors of many marine mammals, and the historic lack of sympathetic attitudes toward marine mammals.

The chapter further describes how radical changes in the perception and uses of marine mammals provided the basis for major shifts in intergovernmental efforts to manage and protect these animals. The most dramatic change was the passage of the Marine Mammal Protection and Endangered Species Acts. The strengths and weaknesses of these legislative mandates are reviewed, particularly problems associated with administrative implementation and conflicts with a variety of commercial activities. The chapter finally indicates a variety of weaknesses still remaining in efforts to manage marine mammals in an effective and efficient manner.

The historic record of managing marine mammals is
sadly dismal and discouraging. No other group of higher
vertebrates so starkly reveals the cruel hand of human
society toward the animal world when motivated by
commercial greed and fueled by inadequate regulatory
mechanisms, biological ignorance, and human arrogance.
Conversely, no other contemporary conservation effort
illustrates how dramatically the management of a living
resource can change when confronted by fundamental shifts
in human attitudes and traditional exploitation patterns.
One of the greatest ironies of current marine mammal
protection efforts is despite a somber historical record,
these animals are now governed by the most ambitious and
visionary wildlife law ever enacted.

It would not be appropriate to detail the past
experience or present status of various marine mammal
species. As Norris (1978: 320) noted: "the marine
mammals, which include whales, porpoises, dolphins, seals,
sea lions, sirenians, the sea otter, and the polar bear,
have had a somber history. No other group of large
animals has had so many of its members driven to the brink
of extinction." Ehrenfeld (1970) relatedly indicates of
the three principal marine mammal orders 8 species of
cetacea (whales and dolphins), 10 species of pinnipedia
(seals and walrus), and 5 species of sirenia (manatees and
dugong)--representing respectively 9% (73% of the Baleen
whales), 32%, and 100% of each order's species--are
extinct or presently threatened with extinction.
Additionally, of two marine mustelids, the sea mink is
extinct, while the sea otter was driven to the brink of
extinction and is still regarded as highly endangered in
much of its range today (Scheffer 1981). Furthermore, the
polar bear (while perhaps not a "true" marine mammal) is
endangered despite the species' extraordinary geographic
isolation. Ironically, notwithstanding these grim
statistics, the great whales and northern fur seal were
among the first wildlife species to be the focus of
international conservation agreements--the 1911 Treaty for
the Preservation and Protection of Fur Seals, and the 1931
and '46 Conventions for the Regulation of Whaling (Bean
1983). Like most intergovernmental management efforts,
however, protective status typically occurred after the
species had been commercially depleted. As Peter
Matthiessen (1959: 107) perceptively noted: "As in the
case of the sea otter, the removal of financial incentives
[for the northern fur seal] made conservationists of one
and all."

An understanding of current intergovernmental efforts
at managing marine mammals is facilitated by a review of
factors associated with the decline of most of these
species. This review should identify structural
impediments which must be addressed if effective
conservation of marine mammals is to occur. Nine factors
responsible for the decimation of various marine mammal
species will be noted, followed by a discussion of current
management efforts and problems, particularly relating to
the Marine Mammal Protection and Endangered Species Acts,
the International Whaling Commission, and the Convention
on International Trade in Endangered Species of Fauna and
Flora.

FACTORS ASSOCIATED WITH THE DECLINE OF MARINE MAMMALS

A fundamentally important factor associated with the
decimation of many marine mammal species has been the
"common property" characteristic of most of the affected
species. Marine mammals in the open ocean have
historically been regarded as a resource owned in common
by all, with the subsequent difficulty of assigning
specific property rights to particular countries or groups
(Hardin 1968). This situation has been exacerbated by a
large number of harvesters operating independently of one
another, particularly regarding their access to the taking
of marine mammals. Little incentive existed for such
independent agents to limit levels of exploitation, beyond
the pressure of market forces, especially when reasonable
doubt prevailed that such restraint would be matched by
one's competitors. This problem was partially addressed
for the great whales by assigning access rights to
particular nations, but undermined by the absence, until
recently, of specific harvest quotas for individual
species (Allen 1980).

In contrast, one of the few marine mammal success
stories—management of the northern fur seal—was achieved
largely because this common property marine resource was
converted to a "privately" owned terrestrial resource with
fixed boundaries, assigned property rights, and specific
harvest quotas. Specifically, the northern fur seal
treaty eliminated pelagic harvesting of northern fur
seals, replacing this practice with the harvest of
bachelor males on the breeding grounds in the Pribilof and
Commander Islands.

A second factor associated with the decline of many marine mammal species is their "fugitive" character. Like many wildlife species, marine mammals possess the capacity to disrespect territorial boundaries, compounded by extraordinary mobility over much of the world's surface. Relatedly, the inability to render reliable observations of most marine mammals in the ocean environment and to identify distinct populations has exacerbated the "fugitive" character of many species (Bertrand 1975).

A third factor associated with marine mammal decline has been the particular biological characteristics of many species that historically have made them good targets of exploitation. One especially obvious example was the incredible bulk of the great whales which, once the technological problem of effective harvest in the open ocean had been solved, rendered these species particularly vulnerable to capture and highly profitable to exploit (McHugh 1974). The tendency of other marine mammal species toward extreme sociability, fidelity to breeding and feeding sites, large aggregations, and considerable sexual dimorphism, also facilitated capture and decimation.

A fourth factor associated with overexploitation of many marine mammal species was their presumed inexhaustibility (M'Gonigle 1980). The difficulty of detecting and monitoring particular populations in a marine environment, coupled with the arrogance of human presumption, compounded the problem. The assumption of unlimited mobility among many whale species rather than stationary individual stocks, for example, led to the elimination of one distinct population after another. The problem of presumed inexhaustibility was aggravated by the assumption that closely related species could be commercially substituted for species that became scarce or difficult to locate.

Biological ignorance and uncertainty have been endemic problems of marine mammal management efforts. One grievous expression was the application of fisheries harvest standards of "maximum sustainable yield" to the exploitation of various seal and whale species (Allen 1980). This harvesting regime, while sometimes appropriate for animals with "r-selected" breeding characteristics (e.g., short gestation periods, large numbers of offspring, little and brief socialization, marginal bonds between mother and offspring), was a disaster when applied to the "K-selected" reproductive strategy of most marine mammals who experienced considerable stress, disruption, and havoc (Bertrand 1975).

A sixth factor associated with the decline of various marine mammals was the large commercial gains obtained by their exploitation and harvest. Some of the first great American fortunes were, in fact, derived from the exploitation of whales, seals, and sea otters, and a highly romanticized history grew along with these pioneering exploits (Slijper 1979, Cart 1971). Various aspects of this highly profitable commercial activity encouraged the harvesters to defy the simplistic logic not to drive the targeted species to extinction. The slow reproductive capacity of most marine mammals made it more profitable to obtain maximum returns in the short-run and reinvest the surplus, than to disperse financial rewards so "thinly" over the long-term that little monetary incentive existed to support the cost of ongoing operations (Scarff 1977, Clark 1973). It made far more sense, in other words, to generate large capital returns immediately and to reinvest these profits than to sustain a long-term commercial harvest at marginal levels of financial reward. Large profits were also enhanced (at least during the early period of exploitation) by the considerable gap often existing between the financial costs borne by the capitalists who owned and financed the operations, and the minimal compensation paid to the actual harvesters (who were frequently indigenous peoples). Commercial overexploitation was additionally encouraged by the previously noted assumption of "substitutability"--that another closely related species could be used in place of a decimated species. Finally, various harvesters, especially in recent decades, became "locked into" their commercial operations because of large initial investments in sophisticated technology and equipment. The Japanese and Russians, for example, built expensive whaling ships and floating processing "factories", typically financed or highly subsidized by centralized governments, that created strong monetary pressures to maximize operations to justify investments and overhead costs (Schevill 1974).

A seventh factor in the decline of many marine mammal species was the inability of governments to generate effective international agreements in the marine environment. Among the problems encountered were the difficulty of eliciting international cooperation, development of an effective monitoring system, absence of enforcement procedures, and lack of an equitable distribution system for dispensing rewards (Nafzinger 1980). One major exception was the methodology developed

for managing northern fur seals. As previously noted, its
success was largely due to the "conversion" of a marine to
a terrestrial resource with associated jurisdictional and
territorial boundaries, a nation-related reward system,
and restriction of the harvest to specific, identifiable
individual animals on a land-based environment (Coggins
1980).

This relatively successful international marine mammal
agreement, however, has been undermined in recent years by
the decrease in northern fur seal populations due, in all
likelihood, to the emergence of an eighth factor
associated with the decline of marine mammals. Rather
than direct exploitation of the resource for commercial
gain, the culprit, in this case, appears to be the rapidly
increasing degradation of the marine environment
associated with the development of new fishing
technologies (e.g., use of nondegradable synthetic fishing
gear), as well as pollution resulting from oil and other
mineral extraction and industrial-related activities. In
this situation of indirect habitat and behavioral-related
impacts, it becomes exceedingly difficult to assign blame
to specific human agents or to identify simple remedial
responses to the problem.

A ninth and final factor associated with the decline
of many marine mammal species, particularly the great
whales, was the historical lack of a conservation-oriented
constituency, and the prevalence, until recently, of
relatively unsympathetic and negative attitudes.
Ironically, radical changes in public perceptions of
marine mammals in recent decades have been a critical
aspect in the emergence of a protective structure of
intergovernmental concern.

Prior to the twentieth century, however, many marine
mammal species were perceived in largely utilitarian,
dominionistic, and negativistic ways.* In Melville's Moby
Dick, for example, the great whale is portrayed in
monstrous terms, with its subjugation becoming the measure

*A typology of attitudes was devised to describe basic
perceptions of animals (Kellert 1980a). Definitions of
these attitudes with regard to marine mammals include:
aesthetic--primary interest in the artistic and symbolic
characteristics of marine mammals; dominionistic--primary
satisfaction derived from the mastery and control of
marine mammals; ecologistic--primary concern for the
interrelationships of marine mammals with other species
and their natural habitats; humanistic--strong affection

of the human capacity for conquest, mastery, and control
of the ocean environment. The contemporary willingness to
conserve and protect marine mammals, particularly the
large cetaceans, emerged only after a fundamental shift in
human attitudes (Holt 1977). The great whales, in
particular, became the recipients of moralistic,
humanistic, ecologistic, and naturalistic concern,
especially in the industrialized Western nations [in
contrast, in Japan, this animal continued to be regarded
as a large fish (Scarff 1980)]. Whales became viewed as
highly sentient, possessing a complex emotional life,
exceedingly intelligent, contributing important ecological
functions, and warranting ethical consideration (Lilly
1975, Scheffer 1969). The commercial exploitation of
whales was relatedly replaced by the historically
unprecedented development of a naturalistic appreciation
of whales in their natural habitats, with recent estimates
of whalewatching in the United States reported to yield
nearly one billion dollars per year (Tilt 1985a, Kaza
1982).

In effect, a conservation-oriented constituency
emerged, characterized by strong nonconsumptive interests
in marine mammals and motivated by fundamentally different
attitudes than prevailed in the past (Kellert 1985). This
historical evolution was, interestingly, somewhat similar
to the parallel development of the movement to conserve
terrestrial mammals and songbirds (Reiger 1975, Cart
1971). In the absence of these public pressures, however,
the combined effects of common property competition,
pressures towards the maximization of profits, a belief in
species product substitutability, and biological
vulnerability, led to the decimation of many marine mammal
species (Clark 1973, Scarff 1977, M'Gonigle 1980).

---

for individual marine mammals, with primary focus on
marine mammals with anthropomorphic associations;
moralistic--primary concern for the right and wrong
treatment of marine mammals with strong opposition to
exploitation and presumed cruelty toward marine mammals;
naturalistic--primary interest in recreational contact
with marine mammals in natural settings;
negativistic--primary orientation and avoidance of marine
mammals due to indifference, dislike or fear;
scientistic--primary interest in the physical attributes
and biological functioning of marine mammals;
utilitarian--primary concern for the practical and
material value of marine mammals.

THE CONTEMPORARY CONTEXT OF MARINE MAMMAL MANAGEMENT

Wilson (1980) hypothesized in the Politics of
Regulation that the emergence of regulatory structures can
often reflect the "entrepreneurial" activities of pressure
groups, particularly when the benefits of the policy are
dispersed while the costs are borne by a small segment of
society (Tilt 1985b). The enactment of the Marine Mammal
Protection and Endangered Species Acts (MMPA, ESA)--the
principal domestic means for regulating and managing
marine mammals--especially reflect the entrepreneurial
successes of a small group of dedicated conservationists.
The continued effectiveness of this entrepreneurial
activity is indicated by various reauthorizations of the
acts despite public support for the harvesting of
nonendangered cetaceans (Kellert 1980b), and a highly
unfavorable trade balance with Japan, America's principal
antagonist on international marine mammal policy. It is
also relevant to note that marine mammals are among the
only group of animals, aside from migratory birds, to
receive special protective legislation (Bean 1978).
    In addition to the MMPA and ESA, a variety of less
critical acts and international agreements affect the
conservation and management of marine mammals. In
general, three types of intergovernmental relationships
exist: legislation governing diverse federal agencies and
departments, laws affecting the relationship of federal
and state governments, and international treaties
involving American trade and commerce relationships with
other countries.
    The Marine Mammal Protection Act is certainly among
the most ambitious, comprehensive, and controversial
wildlife laws ever enacted. The MMPA was passed in 1972,
following the enactment of the first Endangered Species
Act of 1969; the MMPA's most recent congressional
reauthorization was in 1983. The critical elements of the
act include (GAO 1981):

1. A moratorium on the taking of marine mammals,
    although an exemption process exists in relation
    to the incidental impacts of commercial fishing
    activities, collecting for scientific research and
    display, and traditional subsistence activities of
    indigenous peoples.
2. The preemption by the federal government of state
    authority for managing marine mammals, although a
    procedure has been established for restoring

individual state control.
3. Dual management roles assigned to both the Departments of Commerce and Interior, with the former (through the National Marine Fisheries Service) responsible for the cetacea and pinnipedia (except the walrus), and the latter (through the Fish and Wildlife Service) assigned the management of the sirenia, walrus, sea otter, and polar bear.
4. A very broad definition of the "taking" notion, including not only direct effects of hunting, capturing, and killing, but also the indirect impacts of harassment and habitat degradation (including activities such as motorboat operation, oil well drilling, and a wide variety of acts adversely affecting the habitat or behavior of marine mammals).
5. Maintenance of marine mammal populations at "optimum sustainable" levels, including consideration of each species' contribution to the "health and stability" of marine ecosystems.
6. Creation of an independent Marine Mammal Commission, assisted by a Committee of Scientific Advisors, to provide information and recommendations to the Secretaries of Commerce and Interior regarding marine mammal management.
7. Authority to prohibit the importation of marine products from nations in violation of the policies of the MMPA and, relatedly, the right to rescind the fishing privileges of countries in violation of the act within the 200-mile American offshore economic zone.

The MMPA is, thus, an extraordinarily broad, comprehensive, and scientifically oriented act. It is also, in many respects, highly idealistic, somewhat naive, scientifically ambiguous, and politically contentious.
One of the more bitter intergovernmental conflicts associated with the act has stemmed from the problem of managing the incidental impacts of commercial fishing on marine mammals [e.g., the tuna-porpoise and sea otter-abalone controversies (Nafzinger and Armstrong 1977, Rich 1976, Scheffer 1981)]. The requirement of the MMPA to minimize or eliminate these impacts, while desirable in theory, has proved extremely difficult and costly to implement. More importantly, these conflicts have often pitted marine mammal protection against the economic needs

and political power of a major commercial maritime
industry (an economic sector often vulnerable to
competitive pressures from the commercial fishing
operations of other nations). While the MMPA has been a
relatively effective means for protecting various marine
mammals from the incidental impacts of commercial fishing,
the cost at times has been an erosion of public support
for the act. A partial recognition of this problem has
resulted in amendments to the act that allow a degree of
incidental take, while continuing to seek alternative
technological solutions to mitigating the adverse impacts
of commercial fishing operations.

The painful conflict associated with commercial
fishing activities and marine mammal protection may have
been exacerbated by problems stemming from the split
authority of the Departments of Commerce and Interior to
manage marine mammals. In this regard, the National
Marine Fisheries Service has been described as biased
toward the interests of commercial fishing, while the Fish
and Wildlife Service is perceived as more inclined to
promote the protection of marine mammals. Relatedly,
Yaffee (1982: 114) remarked: "the conflict between the
organizational goals of NMFS and FWS have led to
significant delays in implementation [of protective
measures]." Early recognition by Congress of this
potential for intergovernmental conflict was noted by the
House Committee on Merchant Marine and Fisheries:

> The committee is not satisfied that the jurisdictional
> split between agencies is helpful or useful. [The
> committee] retained the status quo largely upon the
> hope and expectation that a Department of Natural
> Resources would be forthcoming, at which point the two
> programs would be merged into one. If such a
> Department is not created within the reasonably near
> future, the Committee is prepared to re-examine the
> question and consider the virtues of consolidating the
> program within a single department. (U.S Congress
> 1971)

The creation of the Marine Mammal Commission and a
related Committee of Scientific Advisors it was hoped
would mitigate this potential intergovernmental conflict
by offering a presumably independent, objective, and
scientifically oriented basis for management
decision-making. Whether or not the Commission has
operated in this manner when confronted with considerable

socioeconomic and interagency conflict is subject to
debate. A less charitable view might argue that the
Commission has largely added one more layer of confusing
intergovernmental responsibility, tending to mask
sociopolitical decisions in a quasi-scientific expertise
governed more by biological uncertainty than definitive
empirical knowledge. On the other hand, a thorough
assessment by the General Accounting Office of the work of
the Marine Mammal Commission (MMC) concluded that, for the
most part, the MMC had substantially enhanced the
effectiveness and objectives of the Marine Mammal
Protection Act and had diminished the potential for
conflict between the Departments of Interior and
Commerce. The GAO report noted (GAO 1981: 16):

> MMC and its Committee of Scientific Advisors have
> played an active and constructive role in carrying out
> their responsibilities under MMPA. MMC has been
> instrumental not only in initiating action, such as
> coordinating research between Federal agencies, but
> has supported . . . a number of projects and
> activities pursuant to developing suitable management
> plans for marine mammals.

The potential for conflict may have been additionally
fostered by the broad definition of the "taking" notion as
indicated by the Marine Mammal Protection and Endangered
Species Acts and interpreted by the courts. The idea of
"harassment" as encompassing many indirect, incidental,
and habitat-related impacts has particularly encouraged
conflict between marine mammal conservation and an
extraordinary range of societal and governmental
activities (Coggins and Russell 1982). This situation is
rendered especially problematic by considerable
uncertainty regarding the effects of many marine
activities such as offshore oil drilling, dredging, or
even whalewatching on marine mammals (Reeves 1977).
Two recent controversies illustrate some of the
problems associated with a broad interpretation of the
"taking" notion, particularly involving indirect impacts
on habitat and "harassment." The first situation is the
case of Palilla v. the Hawaii Department of Land and
Natural Resources; a dispute not involving a marine mammal
(the Palilla is an endemic forest bird of Hawaii), but
relevant to the definition of "taking" as interpreted by
the ESA and MMPA (Dezendorf 1983). Briefly, the court
ruled that a significant modification of the Palilla's

habitat constituted a form of taking. The behavior in question resulted from the adverse foraging impacts on the Palilla's habitat by feral goats, animals ironically maintained by Hawaiian game officials for the benefit of resident hunters.

The second conflict involved the proposed oil development of Alaska's northern continental shelf in the Beaufort Sea. The possibility of direct mortality, significant habitat modification, and harassment of marine mammals were alleged by parties opposed to the development. The conflict involved considerable uncertainty and dispute regarding the extent and nature of such impacts on marine mammals. The courts have rendered varying opinions, although limitedly allowing the oil development to proceed. An additionally difficult aspect of this dispute was a bewildering jurisdictional involvement of diverse governmental agencies, resulting in near management paralysis from ambiguous and conflicting intergovernmental responsibilities. A partial listing, for example, of agencies and legislative acts involved in the Beaufort Sea dispute include (Bolze 1985):

Statutes/Treaties:
    Outer Continental Shelf Lands Act;
    Rivers and Harbors Act;
    Port and Tanker Safety Act;
    Clean Water Act;
    Marine Mammal Protection Act;
    Endangered Species Act;
    Marine Protection, Research and Sanctuaries Act;
    Coastal Zone Management Act;
    National Environmental Policy Act;
    Alaska Coastal Management Act;
    Fish and Wildlife Coordination Act;
    Alaska Native Claims Settlement Act.

Agencies:
    Minerals Management Service;
    Fish and Wildlife Service;
    Army Corps of Engineers;
    U.S. Geological Survey;
    National Oceanic and Atmospheric Administration;
    Office of Coastal Zone Management;
    National Marine Fisheries Service;
    Environmental Protection Agency;
    Various agencies of the State of Alaska.

The Alaskan oil development controversy was also
illustrative of another set of problems associated with
the MMPA--the rights and responsibilities of states versus
the federal government to manage marine mammals (Coggins
and Ward 1980). As previously indicated, the MMPA
initially preempted state authority to manage and regulate
marine mammals. A number of states vehemently protested
this usurpation of authority, the resulting conflict in
many ways mirroring the long struggle in American wildlife
law between local and national authorities regarding
federal encroachment on the traditional rights of states
to manage wildlife within state boundaries (Bean 1978).
The MMPA and ESA have involved major expansions of federal
control over wildlife and, thus, symbolized to many the
progressive assumption of proprietary rights over wildlife
by the central government. The states, particularly
Alaska, have strenuously objected to this aspect of the
MMPA (Gottschalk 1978). Alaska especially protested what
it regarded as an unwarranted interference with the
traditional harvesting of fur-bearing marine mammals,
decorative carving of walrus and narwhal tusks, and the
recreational enjoyment of marine mammals. Additionally,
Alaska asserted a superior ability to manage marine
mammals reflecting greater biological knowledge of local
conditions and a more sensitive understanding of citizenry
needs and traditional practices. The Reagan
administration has been sympathetic with the states'
rights position, particularly regarding the control of
wildlife within state boundaries (Goldman-Carter 1983).
Consequently, recent reauthorizations of the MMPA have
resulted in facilitation of the process for returning
management authority to the states through a three-step
procedure. Despite these new procedures, however, the
MMPA has resulted in the widespread adoption of relatively
uniform national standards for managing marine mammals.
    An additional dispute fostered by the MMPA has been
associated with the Act's requirement that marine mammals
be maintained at optimum sustainable population levels,
including consideration of each species' contribution to
ecosystem "health and stability." While a theoretically
worthwhile objective, the precise definition and
specification of optimal population levels are exceedingly
difficult to determine, inherently ambiguous and, thus,
subject to considerable debate (M'Gonigle 1980).
Long-lived, highly intelligent, and sociable marine mammal
species, with a low reproductive capacity, certainly
require a population buffer to accommodate mortality

impacts and changes in their environment. Additionally,
the ecological contribution of marine mammals species,
such as the sea otter in helping to maintain the
kelp-related ecosystem, requires understanding and
protection (Woodhouse, Cowen, Wilcoxen 1977). Once such
broad objectives of optimum sustainable population levels
have been identified, however, the precise specification
of particular populations for most marine mammals is
extremely difficult to determine or monitor. This
uncertainty has fostered considerable dispute in various
conflict situations involving the presumed impacts of
offshore oil activity, the entanglement of marine mammals
in fishing nets, or the adverse effects of oil spills and
other forms of water pollution (Risebrough 1979).

Still another source of intergovernmental dispute and
conflict stemming from the MMPA has been the hypothetical
ability to restrict the importation of marine products or
the harvesting activities of nations in violation of the
Act (GAO 1981). The most controversial example has been
the effort to limit Japanese fishing activities in
American waters resulting from continued whaling and the
killing of porpoises. Considerable dispute about the
wisdom of this policy has been linked to the United States
enormous trade imbalance with the Japanese, the economic
importance of the Japanese fishing harvest in American
(particularly Alaskan) waters, and the critical importance
of fish in the Japanese diet (occupying a niche similar to
beef consumption in the United States). As the recent
National Audubon Society Wildlife Report noted (Eno and
DiSilvestro 1985: 199): "the clash of federal marine
mammal policy with balance-of-trade concerns and the
increasingly close relationship between some American and
Japanese fishing industries have brought the issue of
commercial whaling to a point of explosiveness only dimly
foreseen even five years ago."

A number of conflicts involving marine mammal
protection have also stemmed from the Endangered Species
Act. Of particular concern has been the ESA's requirement
that all Federal agencies consult with the Secretaries of
Interior or Commerce when a government activity
potentially conflicts with the protection of an officially
listed threatened or endangered species or its habitat.
As a great many marine mammals are listed as endangered or
threatened, the ESA has been involved in a number of
disputes, most notably several major offshore oil and
coastal refinery development projects (Coggins and Russell
1982).

A final set of intergovernmental problems associated with marine mammal conservation have stemmed from the interaction of the United States with other nations, an issue briefly discussed with regards to the MMPA. Perhaps the most infamous example was the legacy of inadequate regulation associated with the International Convention on the Regulation of Whaling. The history of this tragic regulatory failure has been thoroughly described by others (cf., McHugh 1974, Scarff 1977, M'Gonigle 1980) and will not be discussed in detail here. As Norris summarized, the deficiencies of the International Whaling Commission (IWC) included:

> The veto whereby a member nation could ignore regulations it didn't like; the lack of observers to monitor the catch; the lack of enforcement power; an arrangement . . . in which . . . industrial parts could and did ignore the scientists; a nonbiological catch quota--the Blue Whale Unit--in which different species were lumped according to the yield of each to derive quotas and from which heavily affected species received no more protection than unexploited ones; and the setting of unrealistic quotas that reflected more the decline of available stocks than any attempt to regulate them. (Norris 1978: 329)

Perhaps the major accomplishment of the IWC, as McHugh (1974) noted, was to provide an international forum for the public scrutiny and debate of this classic "tragedy of the commons" situation. Eventually, this debate led, through the power of public opinion and changing attitudes, to the demise of whaling and profound alterations in IWC policies. While great battles were waged with often uncertain outcomes, the last of the major whaling nations had agreed by the mid-1980s to a moratorium on the continued commercial killing of whales.

The historic failure and radical change of IWC policies provides important insights regarding the conduct of international marine mammal agreements. As Bean (1983: 264) noted: "with no clear mandate for whale conservation, a directive to consider the needs of the whaling industry, and a regulatory structure that enabled individual nations to frustrate coordinated conservation actions by registering objections to them, the IWC for most of its life served as overseer of successive depletions of individual whale stocks." This international convention illustrates the ineffectiveness of any agreement which

inadequately provides for a mechanism to monitor harvest
levels, for enforcing sanctions when violations occur, for
equitably distributing penalties and rewards among
signatory nations, for providing an effective means for
the public to influence decision-making, or for ensuring
that the best scientific information is used to establish
management goals and standards.

The 1973 Convention on International Trade in
Endangered Species of Fauna and Flora (CITES), in
contrast, represented a far more effective international
agreement affecting marine mammal conservation. CITES has
been signed by approximately 90 nations and is probably
the most accepted international wildlife agreement in
existence. The convention incorporated a number of
important intergovernmental innovations including: the
requirement that each nation designate separate scientific
and management authorities, a methodology for regularly
assessing species listings, a means for nongovernmental
organizations to participate in member meetings, and a
procedure for differentiating species according to their
degree of threat and need for protection (King 1978).
CITES, nevertheless, is afflicted by a number of
fundamental regulatory problems including: the lack of
monitoring procedures, the right of individual nations to
register exemptions from formal rulings, the absence of a
means for punishing violators, an inability to prevent the
"laundering" of trade through noncooperating nations, and
a dearth of adequately trained government officials
(particularly in developing nations) capable of
implementing the terms of the convention (Inskipp and
Wells 1979). Like the IWC, the most important
contribution of CITES may have been the establishment of
an international forum helping to elevate governmental and
public awareness of the plight of endangered and
threatened species, including many marine mammals.

Dramatic changes in the management of various seal
species, particularly the Atlantic harp and Pacific
northern fur seals, have been indicative of the
considerable impact of changing public attitudes on the
management of marine mammals. The intense controversy
surrounding the harvest of newly born harp seals
especially reflects the pressures that can be exerted on
governmental agencies when the public becomes emotionally
involved (Lavigne 1978). As Tilt (1984: 1) noted: "If
wildlife issues were chosen on their merit as Madison
Avenue promotions, the advertising campaign against the
harp seal hunt would produce cries of unfair competition.

. . . . The combination of helpless, cute seal pups with coal black eyes and snow white fur together with the [seemingly] brutal nature of the harvest--i.e., clubbing--[were] forged into one of the strongest animal rights struggles." As a consequence, a marine mammal which had previously received very little governmental consideration became one of the most intensively managed creatures on earth. Various difficulties, nevertheless, continued to plague efforts to manage the harp seal adequately including (Lavigne 1979, Beddington and Williams 1980): an historically inappropriate use of maximum sustainable yield as a harvesting strategy, the difficulty of determining optimal sustainable population levels, the problem of reconciling harvest with conservation objectives, inadequate knowledge of harp seal biology, uncertainty regarding the harp seal's role in the northwest Atlantic ecosystem, and the difficulty of considering humane and ethical issues in the management of a marine species.

An additional problem encountered in the management of the harp seal, northern fur seal, bowhead whale, and walrus has been the nature and extent of traditional aboriginal Indian hunting. This difficulty has been particularly acute in situations where the species is endangered, such as the bowhead whale, and complicated by preexisting treaty obligations and the desire to respect traditional cultural practices (Mitchell and Reeves 1980). The courts and most government agencies have tended to defer to the perceived needs and demands of native peoples. This well-intentioned altruism has often provoked controversy, however, among those opposed to awarding superior rights to particular ethnic groups to harvest wildlife, as well as among groups concerned about impacts on marine mammals stemming from the use of modern harvesting technologies by native peoples. Moreover, the decision to allow a limited Eskimo harvest of bowhead whales may have undermined the American effort to promote a worldwide moratorium on the harvesting of large cetaceans (Allen 1980).

CONCLUSION

This paper has identified a number of factors implicated in the decline of many marine mammal species, among the most depleted of all groups of large animals. These factors will require understanding and consideration

if current efforts to conserve marine mammals are to be
effective. The nine factors cited included: the common
property characteristic of most marine mammal species, the
"fugitive" quality of many species in the ocean
environment, the biological vulnerability of many marine
mammals as targets of exploitation, the presumed
inexhaustibility of many species, widespread biological
ignorance, large commercial benefits associated with
harvesting certain species, the difficulty of developing
effective international marine mammal conservation
agreements, adverse impacts of various human activities on
the habitats and behaviors of many marine mammals, and the
historic lack of sympathetic attitudes toward marine
mammals.

On the other hand, radical changes in the perception
of marine mammals was cited as providing considerable
pressure toward the creation of new governmental
procedures to manage and protect these species. The most
dramatic result was the passage of the 1972 Marine Mammal
Protection Act, one of the most ambitious and visionary
wildlife management agreements ever enacted. Despite the
good intentions of this Act, major implementation problems
have at times rendered its effectiveness somewhat
questionable and uncertain. Particular difficulties have
included: conflicts with commercial fisheries, dual
regulatory roles assigned to the Departments of Interior
and Commerce, preemption of state management authority and
the related expansion of federal control over wildlife, an
ambiguous definition of "take" and "harassment", unclear
roles assigned to the Marine Mammal Commission and the
Committee of Scientific Advisors, difficulty of measuring
optimum population levels and the contribution of marine
mammals to ecosystem health and stability, and political
controversy concerning the right to limit the importation
of products or limit the fishing rights of nations in
violation of the MMPA. Despite these problems, the MMPA,
in conjunction with the ESA and CITES, has dramatically
improved the scope, effectiveness, and objectives of
marine mammal conservation and protection.

Several administrative and scientific problems,
nevertheless, remain and will continue to undermine
efforts to manage marine mammals adequately. Far better
monitoring and enforcement mechanisms will be needed, for
example, before international agreements can become
sufficiently effective. Additionally, the greatest
challenge will be to develop adequate procedures for
dealing with indirect, habitat and behavioral-related

impacts associated with various human activities in the ocean environment.

The future challenges of marine mammal management are considerable, but the progress of the past quarter century has been impressive and encouraging. Our society has begun to appreciate marine mammals as sources of wonder, beauty, and even spiritual inspiration, in addition to the more traditionally perceived providers of enhanced scientific knowledge and practical benefits. Our relationship has shifted markedly from one of exploiter to steward and even "student" of these species. Human attitudes toward marine mammals have, thus, become more gentle and benign and, in time, our regulatory responses may become cognizant of the limits of human knowledge and the need for maintaining not just future material options but for also seeking meaning and inspiration through a nurturing relationship with the nonhuman world.

150

REFERENCES

Allen, K.R. 1980. Conservation and Management of
    Whales. Seattle: University of Washington Press.

Bean, M.J. 1978. Federal Wildlife Law. In H.P. Broker,
    ed., Wildlife and America, p. 279-289. Washington:
    Government Printing Office.

_____. 1983. The Evolution of National Wildlife Law.
    New York: Praeger.

Beddington, J.R., and H.A. Williams. 1980. The Status
    and Management of the Harp Seal in the North-West
    Atlantic: A Review and Evaluation. Springfield,
    Virginia: National Technical Information Service.

Bertrand, G.A. 1975. The Management of Marine Mammals.
    Report to Marine Mammal Commission.

Bolze, D.A. 1985. Outer Continental Shelf Oil and Gas
    Development in the Alaskan Beaufort Sea. Yale School
    of Forestry & Enviornmental Studies.

Cart, T.W. 1971. The Struggle for Wildlife Protection in
    the U.S. 1870-1900: Attitudes and Events Leading to
    the Lacey Act. Ph.D. Dissertation. Raleigh:
    University of North Carolina.

Clark, C.W. 1973. The Economics of Overexploitation.
    Science, 181:630-634.

Coggins, G.C. 1980. Legal Protection for Marine
    Mammals: An Overview of Innovative Resource
    Conservation Legislation. Environmental Law, 6(1):
    1-59.

Coggins, G.C., and M.E. Ward. 1980. The Law of Wildlife
    Management on the Federal Public Lands. Oregon Law
    Review, 60(1&2): 59-155.

Coggins, G.C., and I.S. Russell. 1982. Beyond Shooting
    Snail Darters in Pork Barrels: Endangered Species and
    Land Use in America. Georgetown Law Journal, 70(6):
    1433-1525.

Dezendorf, B.E. 1983. Palilla v. Hawaii Department of Land and Natural Resources: A New Interpretation of "Taking" Under the Endangered Species Act of 1973. Idaho law Review, 19 (Winter): 157-176.

Ehrenfeld, D.W. 1970. Biological Conservation. New York: Holt, Rinehard and Winston.

Eno, A.S., and R.L. DiSilvestro. 1985. Audubon Wildlife Report. New York: National Audubon Society.

General Accounting Office (GAO). 1981. Congressional Guidance and Better Federal Coordination Would Improve Marine Mammal Management. Report by Comptroller General of the U.S.

Goldman-Carter, J. 1983. Federal Conservation of Threatened Species: By Administrative Discretion or by Legislative Standard? Boston College Env. Affairs Law Review, 11:63-104.

Gottschalk, J.S. 1978. The State-Federal Partnership in Wildlife Conservation. In H.P. Broker, ed., Wildlife and America. Washington: Government Printing Office.

Hardin, G. 1968. The Tragedy of the Commons. Science, 163(3859): 1243.

Holt, S.J. 1977. Commentary: Changing Attitudes Toward Marine Mammals. Oceanus, 21(2): 2-8.

Inskipp, T., and S. Wells. 1979. International Trade in Wildlife. London: Earthscan Press Briefing Document No. 16.

Kaza, S. 1982. Recreational Whalewatching in California: A Profile. Whalewatcher, 16(1): 6-8.

Kellert, S.R. 1980a Contemporary Values of Wildlife in American Society. In W.W. Shaw and E.H. Zube, eds., Wildlife Values. Fort Collins: U.S. Forestry Service.

_____. 1980b. Public Attitudes Toward Critical Wildlife and Natural Habitat Issues. New Haven: Yale University School of Forestry and Environmental Studies.

_____. 1985. Social and Perceptual Factors in Endangered Species Management. _Journal of Wildlife Management_, 49(2): 528-536.

King, F.W. 1978. The Wildlife Trade. In H.P. Brokaw, ed., _Wildlife and America_. Washington: Government Printing Office.

Lavigne, D.M. 1978. The Harp Seal Controversy Reconsidered. _Queen's Quarterly_, 85(3): 377-388.

_____. 1979. Management of Seals in the Northwest Atlantic Ocean. _Trans. North American Wildlife and Natural Resource Conference_, 44:488-497.

Lilly, J.C. 1975. _Lilly on Dolphins: Humans of the Sea_. New York: Anchor Press.

Matthiessen, P. 1959. _Wildlife in America._ New York: Viking Press.

Mchugh, J.L. 1974. The Role and History of the International Whaling Commission. In W.E. Schevill, ed., _The Whale Problem, A Status Report_. Cambridge: Harvard University Press.

M'Gonigle, R.M. 1980. The "Economizing" of Ecology: Why Big, Rare Whales Still Die. _Ecology Law Quarterly_, 9(1): 120-237.

Mitchell, E.D., and R.R. Reeves. 1980. The Alaska Bowhead Problem: A Commentary. _Arctic_, 33(4): 686-723.

Nafzinger, J.A. 1980. Global Conservation and Management of Marine Mammals. _San Diego Law Review_, 17(3): 591-615.

Nafzinger, J.A., and J.J. Armstrong. 1977. The Porpoise-Tuna Controversy: Management of Marine Resources after Committee for Humane Legislation v. Richardson. _Enviornmental Law_, 7:223-281.

Norris, K.S. 1978. Marine Mammals and Man. In H.P. Broker, ed., _Wildlife and America_. Washington: Government Printing Office.

Reeves, R.R. 1977. The Problem of Gray Whale Harassment: At the Breeding Lagoons and During Migration. Springfield, Virginia: National Technical Information Service.

Reiger, J. 1975. American Sportsman and the Origins of Conservation. New York: Winchester Press.

Rich, B. 1976. The Tuna-Porpoise Controversy. Harvard Environmental Law Review, 1:142-161.

Risebrough, R.W. 1979. Pollutants in Marine Mammals: A Literature Review and Recommendations for Research. Springfield, Virginia: National Technical Information Service.

Scarff, J.E. 1977. The International Management of Whales, Dolphins, and Porpoises: An Interdisciplinary Assessment. Ecology Law Quarterly, 6(2&3): 326-588.

_____. 1980. Ethical Issues in Whale and Small Cetacean Management. Environmental Ethics, 3:241-279.

Scheffer, V.B. 1969. The Year of the Whale. New York: Charles Scribner's Sons.

_____. 1981. The Amazing Sea Otter. New York: J.B. Lippincott Co.

Schevill, W.E. 1974. The Whale Problem: Preface and Reports of Working Groups. Cambridge: Harvard University Press.

Slijper, E.J. 1979. Whales. New York: Cornell University Press.

Tilt, W.C. 1984. The Harp Seal Controversy. Yale School of Forestry and Environmental Studies.

_____. 1985a. Whales and Whalewatching in North America. Yale School of Forestry and Environmental Studies.

_____. 1985b. The Endangered Species Act After the Snail Darter. Yale School of Forestry and Environmental Studies.

154

U.S. Congress, House of Representatives, Committee on
Merchant Marine and Fisheries. 1971. Marine Mammal
Protection Act of 1971. Washington: Government
Printing Office.

Wilson, J.Q., ed. 1980. The Politics of Regulation. New
York: Basic Books.

Woodhouse, C.D., R.K. Cowen, and L.R. Wilcoxen. 1977. A
Summary of Knowledge of the Sea Otter in California
and an Appraisal of the Completeness of the Biological
Understanding of the Species. Springfield, Virginia:
National Technical Information Service.

Yaffee, S. 1982. Prohibitive Policy. Cambridge: MIT
Press.

6

Ocean Resources and Intergovernmental Relations in the 1980s: Outer Continental Shelf Hydrocarbons and Minerals

Richard Hildreth

INTRODUCTION

This chapter utilizes the legal indicia, primarily court opinions, of federal-state conflict over outer continental shelf oil and gas development in the 1980s to support more general observations about intergovernmental relations offshore. The patterns derived from the offshore oil and gas experience are used to predict the probable course of intergovernmental relations in projected offshore hard minerals development and to evaluate proposed improvements in the current scheme.

In the thirty years between 1953 and 1983, the federal government received over $68 billion from outer continental shelf (OCS) oil and gas leases without sharing any with the adjacent coastal states. This fact alone perhaps explains why federal-state relations in the 1980s with respect to OCS oil and gas development generally have been adversarial in nature, despite elaborate statutory provisions for consultation between the federal Department of Interior and affected coastal states.

So far, the federal return from other OCS minerals is basically zero, and the intergovernmental relations track record for such minerals correspondingly is much shorter. However, recent discoveries of exploitable minerals within the U.S. 200-mile Exclusive Economic Zone (some on the inner continental shelf), coupled with the Interior Department's assumption of authority over such minerals, unfortunately suggests that the pattern of predominantly adversarial relations will extend to development of nonhydrocarbon minerals as well. This seems especially likely given Interior's approach and the fact that the coastal states have almost no statutory consultation rights with respect to such minerals in contrast to their extensive consultation rights in regard to oil and gas development.

While this paper emphasizes federal-state relations, it does not ignore the significant adversarial relations with both the federal and state governments concerning offshore oil and gas development that coastal local governments engaged in during the 1980s. See, e.g., Hammond v. North Slope Borough, 645 P.2d 750 (Alaska Sup. Ct. 1982); North Slope Borough v. Andrus, 642 F.2d 589 (D.C. Cir. 1980), reversing, 486 F. Supp. 326 (D.D.C. 1979), involving local government opposition to a combined federal-state oil and gas lease sale in the Beaufort Sea. Noteworthy also is the fact that national and regional environmental groups often have joined with state and local governments in the adversarial relations discussed in this paper. See, e.g., Conservation Law Foundation v. Watt, 560 F. Supp. 561 (D. Mass. 1983), involving Georges Bank Lease Sale 52 opposed by environmental groups, fishermen, and the State of Massachusetts.

Relying primarily on legal sources, this paper first documents the predominantly adversarial nature of intergovernmental relations concerning OCS oil and gas development in the 1980s. Those relations are examined in detail and applied to projected minerals development activities. The paper then reviews existing and proposed methods of reducing intergovernmental conflict over OCS hydrocarbon and minerals development, assessing their likelihood of implementation and success.

Underlying the author's rather pessimistic assessment are some fundamental features of U.S. intergovernmental relations concerning natural resources. These are examined in the paper's concluding section.

This paper also provides a data base of legal events in offshore intergovernmental relations for interpretation and analysis by other interested parties. Comments, especially from those with perspectives and disciplinary backgrounds different from the author's, are hereby solicited.

The federal government is not monolithic in its relations with state and local governments, so this analysis is divided between the three classic governmental branches, legislative, executive, and judicial. Initial emphasis is on the federal courts as resolvers of federal-state OCS disputes. In resolving such disputes the federal courts are interpreting and ruling on the legality of actions of the other two branches, so study of the court decisions is educational, regarding the intergovernmental relations roles played by the other two branches as well.

Immediately obvious is the very significant role of Congress in enacting federal statutes that provide state and local governments with various opportunities to challenge executive branch decision-makers. Without these statutory assists, state and local governments would be in a very weak position constitutionally to contest federal OCS oil and gas and minerals development decisions.

Generally, the continental shelf is treated by the federal courts as part of the federal public domain subject to disposition by Congress under the Property Clause (Art. IV section 3) of the Constitution. Congressional exercise of that power to convey the first three miles of seabed to the coastal states in 1953 is the ultimate illustration of Congressional sympathy for coastal state concerns to date. For reasons discussed later, in the 1980s Congress has continued to be the branch most sympathetic to coastal state concerns.

State and local governments have used the full panoply of federal environmental and ocean legislation (sometimes enacted over a presidential veto), e.g., Massachusetts v. Andrus, 594 F.2d 872 (1st Cir. 1979) (Fisheries Conservation and Management Act and Marine Sanctuaries Act); People of the Village of Gambell v. Clark, 746 F.2d 572 (9th Cir. 1984) (Alaska National Interest Lands Conservation Act); Village of False Pass v. Watt, 565 F. Supp. 1123 (D. Alaska 1983), affirmed, 733 F.2d 605 (9th Cir. 1984) (Endangered Species Act), to assert their positions. However, the three federal statutes most significant to OCS intergovernmental relations have been the National Environmental Policy Act (NEPA), Outer Continental Shelf Lands Act (OCSLA), and the Coastal Zone Management Act (CZMA). They are discussed in that order next, first in connection with oil and gas development, and then minerals development. This is followed by a discussion of other Congressional and administrative actions of special significance to OCS intergovernmental relations in the 1980s.

NATIONAL ENVIRONMENTAL POLICY ACT (NEPA)

Oil and Gas Development

Prior to the 1980s, NEPA was practically the only
statutory tool coastal state and local governments had
available for participating in the OCS oil and gas
development process. The OCS Lands Act was not amended
until 1978 to include extensive state consultation rights
with respect to oil and gas development. Furthermore,
most coastal states did not gain federal approval of their
coastal management programs developed under the 1972
federal Coastal Zone Management Act until the late 1970s,
at which time the CZMA's federal consistency obligations
applied to those programs as discussed further below.
Pending those significant changes in the OCS leasing
process, NEPA procedures became quite elaborate with
respect to OCS oil and gas development. The Interior
Department prepared and circulated draft and final
"programmatic" environmental impact statements (EISs) on
its nationwide program for accelerated OCS oil and gas
leasing. In addition, Interior prepared draft and final
EISs on specific sales pursuant to the program.
In connection with Lease Sale 35 off Southern
California, California state and local government agencies
responded to the multivolume Interior draft sale EIS with
lengthy "counter EISs" of their own, to which Interior
responded with an even lengthier final EIS. Several days
of public hearings, at which state and local government
representatives testified at length, were held as part of
the NEPA process as well. Dissatisfied with Interior's
subsequent decision to proceed with Sale 35 pursuant to
the nationwide accelerated leasing plan, the state and
Southern California local governments unsuccessfully
challenged both the nationwide program and Sale 35 in
California v. Morton, 404 F. Supp. 26 (C.D. Cal. 1975),
affirmed, 608 F.2d 1247 (9th Cir. 1979).
As Interior became more skilled at preparing EISs
which complied with NEPA's procedural mandates, the
ability of state and local governments to delay sales
which they opposed lessened significantly. See, e.g.,
Alaska v. Andrus, 580 F.2d 465 (D.C. Cir. 1978), in which
the court found the EIS inadequate after it allowed Gulf
of Alaska Sale 39 to proceed, and County of Suffolk v.
Interior, 62 F.2d 1368 (2d Cir. 1977), cert. denied, 434
U.S. 1064 (1978), rejecting on appeal state and local

government allegations of NEPA defects in Baltimore Canyon Sale 40.

Despite the major changes in the OCS Lands Act and the application of the CZMA consistency obligations referred to above, NEPA continues to play an important role in the 1980s in adversarial OCS intergovernmental relations. In the Village of False Pass case cited above, a Bering Sea lease sale was temporarily enjoined due to Interior's violation of the NEPA requirement that a worse-case analysis be performed where data gaps prevent a more certain analysis of potential environmental impacts. In this case, it was uncertain what impacts seismic exploration would have on endangered bowhead whales.

Similarly, in Massachusetts v. Watt, 716 F.2d 946 (1st Cir. 1983), Georges Bank Sale 52 was temporarily enjoined because Interior failed to revise the sale EIS to reflect significantly reduced oil and gas resource estimates. And in Massachusetts v. Clark, 594 F. Supp. 1373 (D. Mass. 1984), Georges Bank Sale 82 was enjoined because the EIS failed to present an adequate range of alternatives and covered too large a geographical area. Both Georges Bank sales ultimately were cancelled due to lack of industry interest.

Although Interior usually is able to correct such EIS defects and proceed with the sale, temporary injunctions based on NEPA violations decrease industry interest in the sale area. Further, they provide disenchanted state and local governments with time to negotiate with Interior about tracts to be excluded and sale conditions, or to seek a Congressionally imposed moratorium on the sale as discussed later.

Of course, the theory of NEPA is that decision-makers such as the Secretary of Interior will factor the EIS's environmental analysis into their decision by removing sensitive tracts from the sale, imposing environmentally protective conditions on lessee operations, etc. There is some evidence that EISs have such an effect, either on the secretary, or, if he responds inadequately, on Congress. If the June 1985 Congressional committee testimony of the American Petroleum Institute is accurate, more than 63 million acres have been withdrawn from lease sales either by Congress or the Interior Department after publication of the final sale EIS.

API's view was that these large withdrawals nullified the advantages of Interior's current "areawide" approach to lease sale offerings. Perhaps they also demonstrate the effects of EISs on OCS decision-making by both the

legislative and executive branches of the federal
government. Earlier availability of sale EISs has been
advocated as a way to help state and local governments,
and the public, participate even more effectively in the
OCS process.

State and local governments also may use NEPA to take
part in OCS development stages subsequent to lease sales.
In particular, section 25(e) of the OCS Lands Act requires
the Secretary of Interior to subject approval of a
lessee's development and production plan to the EIS
process at least once in all OCS areas other than the Gulf
of Mexico. With few major finds outside the Gulf of
Mexico to date, experience under this provision is quite
limited. One can predict that section 25(e) will yield
similar participation benefits to state and local
governments as do EISs prepared in connection with lease
sales. Principally, this participation provides
opportunities to suggest environmentally protective
conditions on oil field development and production
concerning such matters as transportation methods and
routes, e.g., pipelines vs. tankers. However, like the
other state consultation provisions added to the OCS Lands
Act in 1978, section 25(e) applies only to OCS oil and gas
development, not to OCS minerals development.

Minerals Development

In late 1983 Interior prepared a draft EIS for a
proposed polymetallic sulfide minerals lease offering in
the Gorda Ridge area offshore of Oregon and Northern
California. This draft EIS was thoroughly criticized at
public hearings held on the West Coast as being so legally
inadequate that its defects could not be repaired simply
by responding to the critical comments in a final EIS. In
part for that reason, Interior established a federal-state
task force to perform research and gather data for use in
an improved decision document, although the task force
would not be compiling an EIS. Use of such task forces
both in oil and gas and minerals development is discussed
further in connection with the OCS Lands Act below.

The Gorda Ridge process did not provide an auspicious
start for federal-state relations in OCS minerals
development. Without significant improvements in that
process, one can predict resort by disenchanted state and
local governments to the NEPA process (their only certain
tool) to litigate questions of EIS adequacy such as

inclusion of adequate worse-case analyses. NEPA will likely be used to create negotiating leverage and time to pursue legislative remedies with Congress, similar to the process followed in connection with oil and gas lease sales.

NEPA Conclusion

Milner Ball (1982: 623) aptly summarizes how the concept of federalism is buttressed by using the NEPA process in OCS development:

> One result of the EIS process has been the technical improvement of decisions. Another result has been the political improvement of the agencies, for impact statements also certify that official decisions have been politically [intergovernmentally] refracted. . . . The agency must prepare a sufficient impact statement before it can issue permits to others. The impact statement is thus a kind of permit, and like other permits it is in significant part a political instrument, an aid in making [federal] agencies more representative. . . . [Thus] it is possible to conclude that environmental impact statements are a type of permit that can be used to make [federal] agencies serve as political stages on which citizens [and state and local governments] take active roles.

OUTER CONTINENTAL SHELF LANDS ACT (OCSLA)

Oil and Gas Development

In 1978 Congress enacted significant amendments to the 1953 OCSLA. Many of those amendments were directed at increasing the involvement of state and local governments in the OCS oil and gas decision-making process. The changes wrought by those amendments are outlined in Table 1, drawn from the Office of Technology Assessment Report, Oil and Gas Technologies for the Arctic and Deepwater (U.S. Congress, OTA 1985: 141).

Table 1:   State Role in Offshore Oil and Gas Leasing

Subject	Action	Authority
Outer Continental Shelf Leasing Program	State and local government comments on proposed 5-year plan and on Secretary's annual review of the plan.	OCSLA Sec. 18
Environmental Impacts	Comments by the State on draft environmental impact statements at time of revisions in the 5-year leasing program and at submission of exploration and development and production plans.	NEPA Sec. 102(D) OCSLA Sec. 25
Proposed Lease Sale	Coordination and consultation with State and local officials concerning size, timing or location of proposed lease sale.	OCSLA Sec. 19
Leasing Within 3 Miles of State's Territorial Sea	Consultation with regard to development of shared oil pools.	OCSLA Sec. 8(g)
Geological and Geophysical Exploration Plans	Certification of consistency with State coastal zone management plans.	OCSLA Sec. 11(c) CZMA Sec. 307(c)(3)
Production and Development Plans	Coordination and consultation with State and local officials and certification of consistency of production and development plans with the State coastal zone management program.	OCSLA Sec. 25 CZMA Sec. 307(c)(3)
OCS Oil and Gas Information	Secretary directed to provide information on proposed plans, reports, environmental impact statements, tract nominations, and other information, including privileged information in the custody of the Secretary.	OCSLA Sec. 26

SOURCE: Office of Technology Assessment.

The 1978 amendments provided two major opportunities for state and local participation: (1) the development of a five-year OCS oil and gas lease sale plan under section 18, and (2) Interior consultation with state and local officials concerning individual sales and development and production plans under section 19.

From the state perspective, results under these modifications generally have been unsatisfactory and have led to calls for further changes in the OCSLA. Those experiences, and the amendments proposed in response to them, are discussed next. Also discussed are intergovernmental information sharing under the OCSLA, resolution of federal-state continental shelf boundary disputes, sharing of revenues from and state taxation of OCS development, and OCS air quality issues, all issues of major significance in OCS intergovernmental relations.

Section 18 Five-Year Plan Process. OCSLA section 18 requires the Secretary of Interior to develop and revise five-year schedules of "proposed lease sales indicating, as precisely as possible, the size, timing, and location of leasing activity." The secretary's decisions on size, timing, and location are to be based on several statutory factors, among them the "laws, goals and policies of affected states which have been specifically identified by the governors of such states as relevant matters for the Secretary's consideration." These include the state's federally approved coastal zone management program developed under the Coastal Zone Management Act discussed later. Furthermore, in developing this five-year plan of OCS lease sales, the secretary must invite, consider, and respond to suggestions from affected governors and local government executives.

California and Alaska successfully challenged Secretary Andrus's first five-year plan in California v. Watt, 668 F.2d 1290 (D.C. Cir. 1981). Secretary Watt's revised plan in response to the court's decision contained mostly minor changes and actually increased the acreage available for leasing from 885 million to slightly over a billion. The most significant change was the deletion of proposed Sale 75 in the North Aleutian Basin off Alaska. Although an Interior press release emphasized that this deletion was Alaska's "highest priority," Governor Hammond wrote the secretary that he was very disappointed that many of the state's other crucial concerns had been summarily rejected. However, California and Alaska's challenge to the legality of the revised plan supported by

several other coastal states was rejected in <u>California v.</u>
<u>Watt</u>, 712 F.2d 584 (D.C. Cir. 1983).

Since that court decision, legislation has been
introduced in several Congressional sessions which would:
(1) require the secretary to accept a governor's
recommendations unless he can show that they do not
provide a reasonable balance of state and federal
interests, i.e. place the burden on the secretary to show
why a state's recommendations are unreasonable; and, (2)
require the courts in reviewing secretarial five-year plan
decisions to apply the stricter "substantial evidence"
standard of review rather than the "arbitrary and
capricious" standard applied in the <u>California v. Watt</u>
litigation. Another suggestion would require specific
Congressional approval of each five-year plan.

These legislative proposals, even if adopted, are an
inadequate response to perceived problems with the
five-year plan process. The "substantial evidence"
standard of judicial review may not be sufficiently
different from the "arbitrary and capricious" standard to
guarantee meaningful judicial review of secretarial
five-year plan decisions, even when combined with a shift
of the burden of proof to the secretary. Congress
currently has given itself 60 days to review each
five-year plan under section 18(d)(2) prior to secretarial
approval and has imposed moratoria on specific sales as
discussed below, so requiring specific Congressional
approval of each five-year plan would not be as dramatic a
change from current procedures as it might appear.

Under section 18, lease sales may be held only in
areas included in the five-year plan, which provides up to
five years notice to affected state and local governments
adjacent to scheduled sale areas, and a minimum five year
respite to state and local governments adjacent to
unscheduled areas. However, only Washington and Oregon
benefited from this latter aspect under both the Andrus
and Watt version of the first five-year plan as sales were
scheduled in all areas except off Washington and Oregon.

More generally, Richard Burroughs (1986) of the
University of Rhode Island has questioned the ability of
the five-year plan process to mediate successfully, and
where possible avoid, conflicts between oil and gas
developers and other ocean resource users. Finally, both
sections 18 and 19, discussed next, may be unrealistic in
their assumptions about the ability of local governments,
especially in previously undeveloped "frontier" areas, to

meaningfully participate in the OCS decision-making
process.

Compared to the lower forty-eight states, Alaska faces
a dramatic increase in OCS exploitation under both the
first and proposed second five-year plans, which comprise
roughly one-half of the OCS leasing program. Yet Alaska
presents special operating difficulties related to seismic
activities, severe ice and storm conditions, and native
subsistence cultures dependent on endangered species.
Plus, it is thousands of miles from the ultimate markets
for any oil and gas produced.

Also, local planning capabilities in many Alaskan
coastal areas are very limited. As an extreme example,
the city of Yakutat, a potential staging area for Gulf of
Alaska OCS activity, had a 1973 population of
approximately 600, mostly Indians engaged in fishing,
timber, and tourism activities, and an annual city budget
of $95,000. Such a small total budget is certainly
inadequate to support a planning department capable of
dealing with the effects of OCS exploration and
development activities without major state or federal
assistance. However, federal funding to aid state and
local participation in the OCSLA process such as Coastal
Energy Impact Program grants pursuant to Coastal Zone
Management Act sections 308(c)(1) and (2) has been reduced
in the 1980s.

Section 19 Consultation Process. Under OCSLA section
19, the affected state's governor, and the executive of
any affected local government "may submit recommendations
to the Secretary regarding the size, timing, or location
of a proposed lease sale or with respect to a proposed
development and production plan." States with federally
approved coastal management programs also have the
opportunity to rule on the consistency with those programs
of development and production plans as discussed later.

Section 19 distinguishes between gubernatorial and
local government recommendations as to the obligation of
the Secretary to accept them. The Secretary must accept
recommendations of the governor and may accept local
government recommendations if "they provide for a
reasonable balance between the national interest and the
well-being of the citizens of the affected states." With
respect to gubernatorial recommendations only, the
Secretary must communicate in writing his reasons for
incorporating or disregarding the recommendations.

In reaching decisions under section 19, the Secretary
must provide the governor and local government executives

the opportunity for consultation. However, according to section 19, the Secretary's decision whether or not to incorporate recommendations is "final and shall not, alone, be a basis for [judicial] invalidation of a proposed lease sale . . . unless found to be arbitrary or capricious."

Despite the broad discretion accorded the secretary under section 19, state and local governments have sued to enforce section 19's requirements in situations where they have felt their recommendations have not been given sufficient weight. Of the five federal trial courts to rule on alleged section 19 violations to date, three have found the secretary violated section 19, California v. Watt, 17 ERC 1711 (C.D. Cal. 1982) (Southern California Sale 68); Conservation Law Foundation v. Watt, 560 F. Supp. 561 (D. Mass. 1983) (Georges Bank Sale 52); Massachusetts v. Clark, 594 F. Supp. 1373 (D. Mass. 1984) (Georges Bank Sale 82); and two have upheld the secretary's response to state and local recommendations, California v. Watt, 520 F. Supp. 1359 (C.D. Cal. 1982) (Central and Northern California Sale 53); Village of False Pass v. Watt, 565 F. Supp. 1123 (D. Alaska 1983) (Bering Sea Sale 70).

However, the only appellate court decision to date considering section 19 suggests that the secretary has wide discretion both substantively and procedurally in responding to state recommendations under section 19. In California's dispute with Interior over Sale 53, Secretary Watt consulted only very briefly with Governor Brown, and sent the Governor a letter explaining his reasons for rejecting most of the Governor's recommendations after deciding to proceed with the sale and after California had filed suit. Nevertheless, the Ninth Circuit Court of Appeals in California v. Watt, 683 F.2d 1253 (9th Cir. 1982), held that the secretary had complied sufficiently with what it characterized as the "technical" requirements of section 19.

For other sales, section 19 consultation appears to have produced results satisfactory to both Interior and affected states. For example, California's Governor Deukmejian successfully sought several environmentally protective conditions for Sale 73 off Central California, and several sales have proceeded in Alaskan waters without litigation after the negotiation of environmentally protective conditions between Alaska's governor and Interior.

But the overall experience to date has led the states and environmental groups to seek a statutory change in the standard of review under section 19 from the loose "arbitrary and capricious" standard to the "substantial evidence" standard discussed above in connection with the section 18 five-year plan process. They also seek to clarify the statutory criteria applicable to the secretary's lease sale decision. To be effective in meeting coastal state concerns, the new criteria would have to move beyond the usual unprioritized laundry list of factors to be balanced, ranging from serving national energy needs to avoiding pollution. Instead they should specify that the secretary must give greater weight to traditional state concerns such as the risk of oil spills, the lack of onshore support facilities, and conflicts with commercial fishing activities.

OCSLA section 5(a) authorizes the secretary to suspend or cancel a lease if environmental problems develop after issuing it to the highest qualified bidder. The secretary may do so with or without compensation to the lessee, depending on the circumstances. No explicit state or local government role is provided by section 5 other than a general mandate to the secretary to cooperate with affected states in the enforcement of safety, environmental, and conservation laws and regulations. However, judicial review of secretarial suspension and cancellation decisions is available under section 23, the OCSLA's "citizen suit" provision.

Congress has encouraged a litigious attitude by coastal state and local governments with respect to Interior compliance with sections 5, 18, and 19 and other aspects of the OCSLA. This encouragement results from section 23's authorization of "any person" (defined to include state and local governments) adversely affected to sue to compel compliance with the act. Section 23 further authorizes courts hearing such cases to award any party reasonable attorney and expert witness fees.

How likely the federal courts are to exercise their discretion to make such awards remains unclear. In Village of Kaktovik v. Watt, 689 F.2d 222 (D.C. Cir. 1982), the appeals court reversed a district court judgment, awarding the unsuccessful plaintiffs in the North Slope Borough litigation, cited above, $59,000 in attorney's fees under the OCSLA and the Endangered Species Act.

Intergovernmental Information Sharing. The OCSLA contains several general provisions regarding information sharing between the Interior Department and state and local governments. Like the consultation provisions just discussed, the information sharing provisions apply only to OCS oil and gas development, not the development of other OCS minerals.

OCSLA Section 20 requires Interior to conduct environmental studies of areas or regions included in oil and gas lease sales and share that information with affected state and local governments. As of September 1985, Interior had spent about $400 million under the environmental studies program since its inception in 1973, broken down by OCS areas as follows: Alaska (50%); Atlantic (22%); Gulf of Mexico (14%); Pacific (11%); and Washington, D.C. program administration (3%).

Pursuant to section 26, lessees and permittees must share all data and information gathered during exploration, development, and production with Interior. Interior must pass on summaries of such information to affected state and local governments, subject to conditions designed to protect the confidentiality of the lessee's or permittee's proprietary information. In United States v. Geophysical Corporation of Alaska, 732 F.2d 693 (9th Cir. 1984), permit conditions and regulations requiring exploration permit holders to disclose their data to Interior and authorizing Interior to disclose them publicly pursuant to section 26 were upheld.

More generally, section 19(e) authorizes Interior to enter into cooperative agreements with affected states regarding the sharing of information, the joint utilization of available expertise, and joint monitoring of OCS oil and gas operations.

A major problem with the foregoing information sharing regime is that Interior requests state and local governments to express their views on such matters as the environmental sensitivity of the area being considered prior to a lease sale. However, the act is oriented toward providing state and local governments with information at the lease sale stage and thereafter. Prior to the lease sale stage, Interior has in fact gathered geologic and environmental information on the general area to be leased but is not obligated to share it with state and local governments. One frustrated local government unsuccessfully challenged the lack of information sharing at stages preliminary to a lease sale in County of San

Diego v. Andrus, 10 ERC 1681 (S.D. Cir. 1977), claiming a violation of NEPA.

One partial remedy for the problem would be earlier circulation to state and local governments and the public of the draft EISs that Interior prepares in connection with proposed lease sales. Another would be to make industry submissions to the five-year plan process available to selected state and local planning officials from scheduled sale areas on a confidential basis. Interior currently protects such information from disclosure during the life of the plan.

Offshore Boundary Disputes, Revenue Sharing, and Taxation. No analysis of OCS intergovernmental relations would be complete without reference to the continuing litigation between the federal and coastal state governments over the exact location of the federal-state dividing line offshore (generally three miles). See, e.g., United States v. Maine (Rhode Island and New York Boundary Case), 105 S.Ct. 992 (1985). Difficulties in resolving federal-state offshore boundaries without litigation are due in large part to the potential oil and gas revenues which follow seabed ownership and the inability of the states to tax OCS oil and gas production.

Under the current system, any revenues derived from oil and gas leasing within the state's offshore boundary go to the coastal state's treasury, while revenues derived from beyond go to the federal treasury without any sharing with the adjacent coastal state. Furthermore, OCSLA section 4(a)(2)(A) makes state taxation laws inapplicable to the OCS. This contrasts with the revenue sharing and in-lieu of tax payments made to states by the federal government and state severance taxes imposed on federal land energy production onshore.

Legislation mandating federal sharing of OCS oil and gas revenues with the coastal states has been introduced in each recent session without passage by Congress. Lack of Congressional action is, in part, due to administration concerns about the federal deficit and the negative fiscal effects of sharing OCS revenue. The executive branch is very protective of OCS revenue, since the leasing of these lands is the second largest federal revenue producing program after the income tax. However, without meaningful OCS revenue sharing the generally adversarial nature of OCS intergovernmental relations will probably continue.

The original 1953 OCSLA anticipated disputes over oil and gas resources near the federal-state boundary. Therefore, section 7 authorizes the Secretary of Interior

to negotiate and enter into agreements with coastal states
concerning the continuance of oil and gas development and
production pending resolution of federal-state
jurisdictional controversies. Given the amounts of money
involved, it is not surprising that disputes have arisen
over the interpretation of federal-state agreements
reached under section 7. See, United States v. Louisiana
448 U.S. 253, rehearing denied, 447 U.S. 930 (1980).

Section 8(g) added in 1978 requires the sharing of
revenues from OCS leases which include oil and gas pools
spanning the federal-state boundary. Such revenue sharing
must be based on case-by-case agreements negotiated by the
secretary and the relevant coastal state governor.
Failing agreement, the federal district courts are to make
a "fair and equitable disposition" of the revenues. Five
coastal states and Interior so far have been unable to
reach agreement on the division of $5.8 billion held in
escrow pursuant to section 8(g). Since the escrow account
was established in 1978, only one federal-state allocation
agreement had been reached, while Texas and Louisiana sued
to force distribution of the funds and received favorable
rulings from the district courts. These rulings have been
appealed to the Fifth Circuit Court of Appeals. See Texas
v. Interior, 580 F. Supp. 1197 (E.D. Texas 1984) (disputed
revenues split 50-50).

The sympathetic treatment of the coastal states by the
courts regarding section 8(g) revenues contrasts with the
results in the boundary dispute cases decided by the
United State Supreme Court. Exercising its original
jurisdiction, the Supreme Court has tended to side with
the federal government going back all the way to its 1947
decision United States v. California, 332 U.S. 19 (1947),
in awarding the entire continental shelf to the federal
government vis-a-vis the states. Congress modified this
decision by returning the first three miles to the coastal
states under the 1953 Submerged Lands Act.

Regarding disposition of the 8(g) revenues remaining
in escrow, the fall 1985 budget reconciliation package
passed by both houses and sent to conference called for
awarding the states 27% of bonus bids, interest, and rents
from the $5.8 billion then held in escrow. Under the
proposal, which reportedly had administration support, the
federal government would receive over $4.4 billion. The
remaining $1.4 billion would be divided among the seven
affected coastal states as follows: Alabama, $70 million;
Alaska, $44 million; California, $375 million; Florida,

$ .03 million; Louisiana, $485 million; Mississippi, $14 million; and Texas, $375 million.

If implemented, this proposal would provide not only a legislative model for disposition of future 8(g) revenues, but also one for federal-state division of OCS revenues generally. Left out of such a split, of course, are the inland states who only benefit indirectly from the portion going into the federal treasury. To gain their political support, proposals like Senate Bill 130, 94th Cong., 1st Sess. 1975, which would have split revenues 50/25/25% among the federal government, the coastal states adjacent to OCS development, and the other states, should be reexamined.

For the special problem of developing common pools spanning the federal-state line, one approach is joint federal-state lease sales such as the Beaufort Sea Sale recently conducted with Alaska. Alternatively, the pool could be leased separately, but by closely-timed federal and state lease sales on either side of the line, such as in the Santa Barbara Channel. In similar situations, Canada and Australia have used joint management and revenue sharing agreements negotiated with the relevant province or state successfully.

Whether such an approach would work in the United States remains to be seen. Expansion of the territorial sea claimed by the United States from three to twelve miles would provide an opportunity for a major Congressional reassessment of intergovernmental relations offshore. For example, legislation amending the Submerged Lands Act to expand state ownership an additional nine miles based on the judicially resolved three-mile boundary line would relieve some but not all of the tensions currently hindering resolution of offshore boundary and revenue sharing questions.

OCS Air Quality Issues. OCSLA section 5(a)(8) authorizes the Secretary of Interior to regulate OCS development activities which significantly affect coastal state air quality. California v. Kleppe, 605 F.2d 1187, 1199 (9th Cir. 1979), held that this section gave the secretary primary jurisdiction to regulate air emissions from OCS facilities vis-a-vis the federal Environmental Protection Agency under the federal Clean Air Act. Through the lease sale process and the federal Coastal Zone Management Act consistency process discussed next California has continued to question and litigate the adequacy of the OCS air quality regulations adopted by

Interior to protect onshore air quality (Selmi 1985:
9-16). The Interior-California air quality dispute
illustrates the breadth of the state-federal issues raised
by OCS oil and gas development and suggests similar
breadth can be expected in connection with the development
of other OCS minerals pursuant to the OCSLA.

Minerals Development

The legal regime under the OCSLA governing minerals
development is remarkably simple compared to the
relatively elaborate one governing oil and gas
development, especially with respect to intergovernmental
relations. Under section 8(k), the Secretary of Interior
is authorized to lease minerals other than oil, gas and
sulfur to the highest cash bonus bidder upon such terms
and conditions as he may prescribe. Of the several
federal-state interactions listed in Table 1 for oil and
gas leasing, only the NEPA EIS process previously
discussed, and, arguably, the Coastal Zone Management Act
consistency process discussed below are applicable to
minerals development.

In addition, OCSLA section 7 would support
federal-state minerals development agreements pending
resolution of jurisdictional controversies. At this time,
resolution of federal-state boundary disputes seems less
relevant to OCS minerals development because exploration
and recent discoveries have been in deeper waters
relatively far offshore.

However, Interior has reported some significant
concentrations of minerals in seabed deposits on the inner
continental shelf 10-50 miles off Virginia and Georgia.
Also, Interior has proposed leasing Alaska sand and gravel
deposits and Atlantic Coast phosphorite deposits closer to
shore without revenue sharing. Depending on the extent
and location of the resource, these proposals could
generate federal-state boundary disputes and increase
intergovernmental tensions generally. One simple
legislative response would be to extend the OCSLA oil and
gas intergovernmental consultation provisions to OCS
minerals development. It is questionable how satisfactory
such a response would be from the coastal states'
perspective, given their experiences with OCS oil and gas
intergovernmental relations to date.

An alternative approach to reducing federal-state
conflicts and litigation would be expanded use of the

regional task forces first created by Interior in connection with offshore oil and gas development. More recently, this approach was used as a federal-state coordination device in connection with Interior's investigation of seabed cobalt-rich manganese crusts near Hawaii and the Gorda Ridge polymetallic sulfide mineral lease sale off Southern Oregon/Northern California. The 15-member Gorda Ridge Technical Task Force, composed of scientists and state and local government representatives from Oregon and California, was the product of discussions between Governor Atiyeh of Oregon and then Secretary of Interior Clark.

The Gorda Ridge task force's principal purpose was to help fill data gaps concerning exploitation of mineral resources on the Gorda Ridge. The intention was not that it compile an EIS-type document or engage in multiple-use planning; instead, it identified areas of concern to be investigated and considered in Interior's decision-making process. Creation of the Gorda Ridge task force has made available federal funds for researchers from state government and state universities to begin filling major data gaps concerning both the mineral resources and the potential environmental impacts of mineral exploration and exploitation of the Gorda Ridge.

More generally, OCS-regional task forces such as that assembled for Gorda Ridge can serve the useful purpose of assuring the consideration of state and local concerns with offshore activities before the decision-making process has progressed significantly. It must be emphasized, however, that the task force is primarily a nonstatutory advisory group. Its effectiveness ultimately depends on the willingness of the Interior Department to consider seriously the advice offered. The Department's consideration of such advice in its decision-making process is not subject to judicial review, even under the loose arbitrary and capricious standard.

OCSLA Conclusion.

Milner Ball pointed to the 1978 OCSLA amendments as offering the potential for revitalizing federalism offshore. After remarking that evidence of federalism could not be found in the old systems of continental shelf leasing (Ball 1982: 663), he then notes the changes made (p. 677):

A formerly closed operation has been opened a little
to states, local governments, environmentalists,
fishermen, and others so that they may begin to play
the superintending, governing parts intended for them
by federalism. Moreover, the activities now permitted
on the continental shelf do not necessarily represent
a one-time, once-and-for-all decision. There is a
continuous series of decisions, and its increments are
marked by permits. The government of marine and
coastal affairs is becoming more of a rolling judgment
containing Secretarial approval, state and local
government consultation, and judicial review.

Ball also points out that true Madisonian federalism
requires not only the spirit and form of popular
government but also the assurance of protection for the
powerless (Ball 1982: 660). He bravely suggests the
treatment of Alaskan Eskimos in the oil and gas
development decision-making process will be the ultimate
test of the OCSLA as true federalism: "Were the Eskimos
to be forced on the scales and weighed against oil, the
permit system for offshore oil and gas development would
fail absolutely to realize the Madisonian desideratum"
(pp. 673-74).
    Unfortunately, the results to date in the North Slope
Borough, Village of Kaktovic, Village of False Pass, and
People of Gambell cases cited above suggests that the
process may be failing from this Madisonian perspective.
In each case, the courts have refused to rule that Alaskan
Eskimos and their subsistence lifestyle must be guaranteed
survival in the context of Arctic OCS oil and gas resource
development. However, in an October 1985 decision, the
U.S. Ninth Circuit Court of Appeals did enjoin further
exploratory drilling by OCS lessees in Norton Sound and
the Navarin Basin pending further consideration by
Interior of potential impacts on native subsistence
hunting and fishing, stating that "the uses and needs of
the Alaskan natives, and our national concern over
survival of their culture, must prevail over possible
energy needs" (People of Gambell v. Hodel, 774 F.2d 1414,
9th Cir. 1985, petition for Supreme Court Review
pending.) See also Inupiat Community of the Arctic Slope
v. United States, 746 F.2d 570 (9th Cir. 1984), certiorari
denied, 54 USLW 3223 (Oct. 7, 1985), holding that there
are no aboriginal property rights offshore Alaska that
must be accounted for in Arctic OCS oil and gas
development.

Several coastal states including Massachusetts, California, and Alaska, probably would agree with the assessment that the OCSLA is insufficiently federalist in structure and operation despite the extensive consultation provisions. The Coastal Zone Management Act discussed next goes beyond consultation in structuring intergovernmental relations, especially in its provisions requiring federal agencies to act consistently with federally approved state coastal management programs. These coastal management programs frequently provide substantive policies against which federal decisions such as those concerning OCS development can be measured for consistency. This aspect of the Coastal Zone Management Act led this author to comment in an earlier article that it emphasized the role of the states as mediator between the national and local levels of government, thus preserving federalism in energy decisions. This author further noted that use of the CZMA process for coastal energy questions would test the viability of federalism in energy decisions generally, while others were criticizing the act's scheme as unworkable. (Hildreth 1976)

COASTAL ZONE MANAGEMENT ACT (CZMA)

Oil and Gas Development

Two incentives are offered under the CZMA for increased state attention to coastal zone management: federal funds for program development and administration, and a federal commitment to act consistently with state coastal zone management programs. The CZMA's consistency aspects have assumed greater importance in the 1980s, while the flow of federal funds has been reduced.

The CZMA consistency provisions have played a large ·role in the predominantly adversarial intergovernmental relations with respect to OCS oil and gas development. Three separate consistency provisions are relevant to oil and gas development: (a) section 307(c)(1), which was applied to lease sale consistency questions; (b) section 307(c)(3)(B), applicable to exploration, development, and production plans; (c) section 307(c)(3)(A), applicable to OCS-related permits not encompassed by exploration, development, and production plans.

Lease Sale Consistency Under Section 307(c)(1). Section 307(c)(1) states "each Federal agency conducting

or supporting activities directly affecting the coastal
zone shall conduct or support those activities in a manner
which is, to the maximum extent practicable, consistent
with [federally] approved state [coastal] management
programs." During the 1980s much attention has been
focused on the interpretive question of whether section
307(c)(1) applies to Interior's lease sale decisions. The
question was answered in the negative by the United States
Supreme Court in Interior v. California, 104 S.Ct. 656
(1984).

That decision has been much discussed and criticized
elsewhere so it will not be dwelt on here, other than to
point out that after an initial flurry of mostly adverse
reaction, proposed legislative and administrative
corrections to the decision have not made significant
progress. In addition, the Supreme Court's reversal of
the Ninth Circuit Court of Appeals' decision (683 F.2d
1253) failed to deal with three important issues addressed
by the Ninth Circuit. First, the Ninth Circuit's decision
contained disturbing loose interpretations of section
307(c)(1)'s "maximum extent practicable" language.
Second, it incorrectly applied the 307(c)(3) secretarial
override process discussed below to 307(c)(1) questions.
Third, it held that environmental groups have standing to
enforce the CZMA's consistency requirements. Finally, the
decision has major ramifications for the consistency
process outside of OCS oil and gas development, especially
the consistency process for OCS minerals lease sales as
discussed below.

Prior to the Supreme Court's decision, four federal
trial courts had sided with state claims that OCS lease
sales "directly affect" state coastal zones within the
meaning of section 307(c)(1). These courts held,
therefore, that OCS lease sales must be consistent with
the coastal management programs of adjacent states before
they proceed. See the Conservation Law Foundation v. Watt
case cited above; Kean v. Watt, 18 ERC 1921 (D.N.J. 1982),
reversed and dismissed as moot, Nos. 82-5679 and 82-5752
(3rd Cir., opinion filed March 21, 1984); California v.
Watt, 520 F. Supp. 1359 (C.D. Cal. 1982) (Sale 53);
California v. Watt, 17 ERC 1711 (C.D. Cal. 1982) (Sale
68).

The one attempt to mediate rather than litigate the
section 307(c)(1) interpretive question occurred between
California and Interior in connection with Lease Sale 48.
However, this failed when Interior rejected the federal

mediator's nonbinding decision which sided with California's interpretation of 307(c)(1).

That failed mediation is one of the two unsuccessful uses to date of CZMA section 307(h)(2). This section provides for voluntary, nonbinding mediation by the Secretary of Commerce (who administers the CZMA) of disputes arising between federal agencies and coastal states in connection with state's administration of its federally approved coastal management program. In five other situations, federal agencies have refused state requests to engage in such mediation.

Even against a highly charged, litigation oriented background, the author contends that the results of applying section 307(c)(1) consistency to OCS lease sales were mostly positive, both from a national interest and a state perspective. Prior to the Interior v. California decision removing lease sales from that process, the states appeared to have been reasonable in litigating specific consistency disputes with Interior. Even in the hotly contested Sale 53 dispute, the California Coastal Commission's recommendations would have allowed leasing of over 80% of the oil and gas resources included in the proposed sale which was otherwise alleged to be inconsistent with California's coastal management program. Oregon joined California and Alaska's challenge to Interior's first five-year OCS sale plan, discussed above, in part because the state had asked Interior to specify at which stage in Interior's proposed streamlined sale process consistency determinations would be made, and because Interior did not respond.

Furthermore, the states did not oppose all OCS sales in all areas, and expedited consistency reviews in many sale areas. Early court decisions favoring the states on the consistency issue appeared to promote settlement of subsequent Interior-state disputes about lease sales. For example, Alaska and Interior reached agreement quickly on changes to OCS Sale 71 stimulated in part by the Ninth Circuit's decision in California v. Watt (Sale 53) favoring California's position on the consistency issue.

Quite appropriately, Charles Colgan, of Maine's State Planning Office in the Executive Office of the Governor, has suggested that many of these controversies should not be viewed as clashes of state interests with national interests, but as situations of conflicting national interests in ocean development. For example, the continued productivity of the Georges Bank fishery and its development for oil and gas resources are each potentially

conflicting national interests. However, the
responsibility to attempt their resolution is forced upon
the state by default through the consistency process.

According to the April 1985 Office of Ocean and
Coastal Resource Management's Federal Consistency Study
Draft (U.S. Department of Commerce 1985), the pattern of
reasonable accommodation of state and federal interests in
OCS lease sales continued during the 17 months the
Interior v. California case was pending before the Supreme
Court. During that time Interior prepared 28 consistency
determinations for nine lease sales involving 18 coastal
states. The affected states concurred with 18 of those 28
Interior consistency determinations. Of the ten state
inconsistency objections, five were resolved through
Memoranda of Understanding negotiated between coastal
state governors and Interior pursuant to the consultation
provisions of OCSLA section 19.

The states filed suit with respect to the remaining
five objections, but four of the suits were dismissed and
the sales took place either as scheduled, or with a one or
two month delay. In the fifth case, involving Georges
Bank Sale 52, the sale was temporarily enjoined and then
cancelled by Interior due to lack of industry interest.

Exploration, Development, and Production Plan
Consistency Under Section 307(c)(3)(B). Added to the
original 1972 CZMA in 1976, section 307(c)(3)(B) requires
OCS lessees submitting exploration, development, and
production plans to Interior to certify that all
activities described in those plans "affecting any land
use or water use in the coastal zone" comply with the
state's federally approved coastal management program and
will be carried out in a manner consistent with the
program. No federal licenses or permits for such
activities may be issued until the state concurs in the
applicant's consistency certification, or, the Secretary
of Commerce overrides the state's inconsistency objection
by finding either that the activity is consistent with the
objectives of the CZMA or "is otherwise necessary in the
interest of national security." The section 307(c)(3)(B)
consistency obligation is specifically reinforced and
repeated in OCSLA sections 11 and 25 regarding Interior
approval of lessee exploration, development, and
production plans.

With expansion of the OCS oil and gas program
continuing in the 1980s, federal approval of coastal
management programs in most states adjacent to significant
OCS leasing activity, and the termination of section

307(c)(1) review of lease sales, section 307(c)(3)(B) consistency reviews have assumed central importance in OCS intergovernmental relations. In fiscal year 1983 alone, OCS lessees submitted 432 consistency certifications on exploration, development, and production plans to coastal states. The states concurred with 97% of those certifications.

The most contentious geographic area has been the Santa Barbara Channel. There, conflicting national interests in navigation, defense, commercial fishing, marine mammal habitat, a national marine sanctuary, and greatly expanded oil and gas activity in both federal and state waters have been sorted out through the section 307(c)(3)(B) consistency process. Four appeals to the Secretary of Commerce for override of state inconsistency determinations have been filed in connection with Santa Barbara Channel oil and gas development as discussed below. Even there, the section 307(c)(3)(B) process has provided a vehicle for state-lessee negotiated agreements allowing operations to proceed without litigation or an appeal to the Secretary of Commerce.

The Supreme Court in Interior v. California placed great weight on state review of exploration, development, and production plan consistency in deciding Congress had not intended to subject lease sales to section 307(c)(1) consistency review. In fact, the court went so far as to state that under section 307(c)(3)(B) states can "veto" inconsistent lessee plans submitted to Interior. Although the designated state coastal agency manages the consistency process, local government concerns can be expressed through that agency and come into play through local land use plans formally incorporated into state coastal management programs. Lower federal courts ruling both prior to and subsequent to Interior v. California have placed great weight on the availability of post-lease consistency reviews in rejecting state and local government attempts to enjoin lease sales.

Given the great weight being placed on the 307 (c)(3)(B) consistency process by the courts, is there adequate respect for state and local interests, and the interests of special groups like Alaskan natives, in that process? Arguably not, given the statutory power of the Secretary of Commerce to override state inconsistency objections which the Supreme court failed to recognize in stating that states can "veto" inconsistent lessee plans. The limited nature of any judicial review of secretarial override decisions based on the arbitrary and capricious standard suggests that secretarial administration of the override process will be a key component of section 307(c)(3)(B)'s overall operation.

Three secretarial decisions have been rendered in the four Santa Barbara Channel override appeals filed to date, one of which has been challenged in the courts. That decision sustained California's inconsistency objection to protect the thresher shark fishery through seasonal drilling restrictions, but a federal district court held the 307(c)(3)(B) consistency process inapplicable to impacts on resources located beyond the three-mile coastal zone like the thresher shark fishery at issue. See Exxon v. Fischer, Civ. No. 84-2362, C.D., filed Oct. 11, 1985, 9th Cir. appeal pending. See also Granite Rock Co. v. California Coastal Commission, 23 ERC 1075 (9th Cir. 1985), reversing, 590 F. Supp. 1361 (N.D. Cal. 1984 Supreme Court Review granted), holding California Coastal Act permit requirements inapplicable to private mining activities in a national forest. Another secretarial decision overrode California's objection to exploratory drilling near a vessel traffic lane partially within the boundaries of the Channel Islands National Marine Sanctuary and near breeding colonies of the endangered California brown pelican. In the third decision, the secretary ruled preliminarily in favor of expanded use of an anchored vessel to store and treat produced oil to which California objected based on the risk of oil spills and adverse affects on coastal zone air quality.

Although the CZMA's legislative history indicates that secretarial overrides based on "national security" were to be tied to national defense needs, both the regulations implementing the override process (see 15 C.F.R. 930.121 and .122) and the three secretarial decisions to date almost inevitably tend to equate "national security" with broader national interests such as energy supply. This view raises the possibility of secretarial override any time a state inconsistency objection significantly interferes with energy development and production. Such overrides in the alleged national interest contradict the Commerce Secretary's original approval of the state's coastal management program (upon which the state's inconsistency objection is based). To approve a state's program, the secretary must find that it adequately balanced state and national interests, including national interests in energy facility planning and siting.

Another problem hampering effective state use of the section 307(c)(3)(B) process is that the states usually

make their consistency rulings prior to the availabiity of
EISs evaluating the environmental impacts of the proposed
exploration, development, or production activities.
Correcting this problem probably would necessitate
legislation revising and coordinating decision timetables
under NEPA, the CZMA, and the OCSLA.

Consistency of Other OCS-Related Permits Under Section
307(c)(3)(A). For Federal OCS related licenses and
permits not included in an exploration, development, or
production plan under section 307(c)(3)(B), section
307(c)(3)(A) applies. This section provides that the
permit applicant shall certify to the federal permitting
agency that the proposed activity complies with the
state's coastal management program and will be conducted
consistent with it, and that the state must concur in the
certification or the Secretary of Commerce must override
the state's inconsistency objection before the permit may
be issued. The two principal permits issued by Interior
under the OCSLA, affected by section 307(c)(3)(A), are
pipeline rights of way issued pursuant to OCSLA section
5(e) and pre-lease geophysical exploration permits issued
pursuant to section 11(a). During fiscal year 1983 the
coastal states concurred in forty such permits processed
by Interior pursuant to section 307(c)(3)(A).

Perhaps the most notable and successful use of section
307(c)(3)(A) with respect to Interior permits occurred
following the December 1980 destruction of over 1200
crabpots by a seismic survey vessel. This vessel was
operating off the Oregon and Washington coasts pursuant to
an Interior-issued geophysical exploration permit.
Subsequently, Oregon and Washington successfully invoked
the consistency process and negotiated Memoranda of
Agreement [which Interior entered pursuant to OCSLA
section 19(e)] to protect their crab fishermen from such
incidents in the future. These memoranda scheduled
seismic survey operations to coincide with periods of low
fishing activity and provided early notification to the
states' fishermen of the time, extent, and nature of
permitted operations. Pursuant to them, repetition of the
December 1980 incident so far has been avoided.

Section 307(c)(3)(A) also provides states with very
important rights regarding OCS-related permits issued by
federal agencies other than Interior. Most significant
here are the so-called "general" permits issued by the
federal Environmental Protection Agency (EPA) for various
OCS areas for discharges from OCS oil and gas operations
(such as drilling muds) pursuant to section 402 of the

Clean Water Act. During fiscal year 1983, EPA issued such
general permits for OCS oil and gas operations off
Louisiana, California, and Alaska. These states concurred
in their issuance pursuant to section 307(c)(3)(A).
However, prior to concurring in their consistency, Alaska
and California engaged in significant negotiations with
EPA over the terms and conditions of the permits, and EPA
subsequently included important permit conditions sought
by those states. For example, one condition subjected all
new oil and gas facilities within 1,000 meters of
California waters to an individual discharge permit
process, rather than extending the general permit's
blanket coverage to them.

No appeals have yet been made to the Secretary of
Commerce for override of a state inconsistency objection
to issuance of an OCS-related permit under section
307(c)(3)(A). In the two appeals to date unrelated to OCS
development, the secretary overrode California's
inconsistency objection concerning proposed rehabilitation
of a coastal railroad bridge (see 50 Federal Register
41722, Oct. 15, 1985) and upheld North Carolina's
objection to the potential water quality impacts of a
proposed marina project (see 49 Federal Register 23906,
June 8, 1984; 48 Federal Register 51677, Nov. 10, 1983).

Minerals Development

Similar to the situation under the OCSLA, the CZMA
consistency regime for OCS minerals development is less
elaborate than the consistency regime for oil and gas
development. As discussed above, the OCSLA does not
require exploration, development, and production plans for
OCS minerals development. Therefore, CZMA section
307(c)(3)(B), requiring such plans to be consistent with
state coastal management programs, probably does not apply
to OCS minerals development. However, section
307(c)(3)(B) is not expressly limited to oil and gas
exploration, development, and production plans, and
Interior has considered using the exploration plan process
for OCS minerals development.

More likely, Interior-approved exploration plans and
Interior-issued permits for OCS minerals development will
be subjected to the very similar section 307(c)(3)(A)
process just discussed in connection with oil and gas
development. As with oil and gas development, section
307(c)(3)(A) also would apply to OCS minerals-related

permits issued by other federal agencies such as the Environmental Protection Agency.

In perhaps the only use of section 307(c)(3)(A) consistency in connection with seabed minerals mining activities to date, EPA initially contended that its proposed Clean Water Act general permit for deep seabed mining and exploration activities would not affect Hawaii's coastal zone and therefore no consistency determination was necessary. When Hawaii expressed concern about possible negative effects on certain atolls and inter-island channel waters, EPA agreed to certify the consistency of the permitted discharges (which included vessel deck drainage, sanitary wastes, uncontaminated bilge water, and cooling water) as consistent with Hawaii's coastal program. Hawaii then concurred with EPA's consistency certification upon the condition that the permittees inform the state of any anticipated or unanticipated discharges that would bypass the treatment system and therefore technically violate the EPA permit. The permitted deep seabed mining and exploration activities at issue were being carried out under the United States Deep Seabed Hard Minerals Resources Mining Act, rather than the OCSLA.

The Interior v. California decision has raised a large question as to whether CZMA section 307(c)(1) applies to OCSLA minerals lease sales as contrasted with oil and gas lease sales which the court clearly held it did not. As mentioned above, the court relied heavily upon post-lease consistency review of exploration, development, and production plans under section 307(c)(3)(B) in deciding that Congress did not intend 307(c)(1) to apply to the lease sale stage. However, as just discussed, 307(c)(3)(B) probably does not apply to exploration, development, and production plans for mineral leases. If so, an important point is thereby removed from the foundation upon which the Court built its conclusions. On the other hand, throughout the opinion the Court referred to oil and gas lease sales and OCS lease sales indiscriminately, without clearly indicating whether it was limiting its ruling to oil and gas lease sales.

In April 23, 1985 letter opinions, the Justice Department and the National Oceanic and Atmospheric Administration (NOAA, the agency within the Commerce Department administering the CZMA) disagreed on this very issue. The Justice Department contended that the Court intended to exclude all OCS lease sales from 307(c)(1) consistency, but NOAA contended that mineral lease sales remained subject to 307(c)(1) and incorporated that view in a consistency regulation revision (see 50 Federal Register 35120, Aug. 30, 1985).

Factors supporting the NOAA view include: (1) the lack of mandatory preparation of consistent exploration, development, and production plans under the OCSLA minerals regime previously discussed; (2) the fact that critical cumulative impacts of a lease sale are best reviewed at the sale stage rather than tract-by-tract, permit-by-permit after the lease sale; and (3) the fact that sunk investment costs tend to tilt post-lease sale decisions [such as secretarial override decisions under CZMA 307(c)(3)(A)] toward allowing operations to continue despite environmental risks.

A simple legislative correction to the problems of mineral lease sale consistency would be a clarification that section 307(c)(1) applies to mineral lease sales under the OCSLA (and perhaps oil and gas lease sales too'.). Another improvement would be to apply section 307(c)(3)(B) to a sequence of exploration, development, and mining plans required by corresponding changes in the OCSLA minerals development regime discussed above.

Conclusion

Some commentators have objected to the CZMA consistency provisions as allowing the states to block plans in the courts, instead of joining in the original development of plans as part of the federal agency administrative process. But, from the data reviewed above, the predominant mode of consistency operation has been one of negotiation and collaboration among OCS lessees and permittees, the Interior Department and other federal agencies, and state coastal management agencies.

Unfortunately, the CZMA consistency era in offshore federalism may be on the wane. This is due to: (1) expanded use of the secretarial override process under section 307(c)(3)(A) and (B); (2) reduced federal funding for state coastal management programs which could result in the programs being disapproved by the Secretary of Commerce for failing to continue to comply with the CZMA's minimum program requirements (thereby ending the applicability of the consistency provisions); (3) and blatant federal disregard of state coastal management programs in federal energy and economic development decision-making as has recently occurred in Delaware in connection with a proposed offshore coal loading facility.

The departments of Commerce and Justice have filed amicus curiae briefs supporting litigation challenging the validity of Delaware's Coastal Zone Act which prohibits offshore bulk transfer operations in order to protect the Delaware Bay ecosystem. The irony is that the Delaware Coastal Zone Act, including its prohibition on offshore bulk transfer operations, was specifically included in Delaware's coastal management program. The program was approved by the Secretary of Commerce under the CZMA as adequately balancing state and national interests in energy development (coal transshipment) and environmental quality (concerns about coal dust impacts on air and water quality and secondary shoreline development).

Such deliberate federal disregard of state coastal management programs is particularly discouraging given almost 15 years of federal, state and local government effort to develop state coastal management programs containing meaningful coastal development policies based on sound scientific information. The scientific and policy basis for decision-making under the CZMA contrasts dramatically with the mostly political decision-making that has occurred in connection with OCS oil and gas development. Frustrated in their dealings with the Interior Department over oil and gas development, the coastal states successfully sought Congressional moratoria on oil and gas development in particularly sensitive offshore areas as discussed next.

CONGRESSIONAL INTERVENTION ON BEHALF OF THE STATES

After enacting NEPA, the CZMA, and significant amendments to the OCSLA in the 1970s, Congress remained sensitive to coastal state concerns about OCS development in the 1980s by enacting moratoria on oil and gas lease sales in specific areas. These sometimes formed the basis for subsequent negotiated settlements between the states and the Interior Department. Generally acting through appropriations legislation, at various times Congress has protected areas off Massachusetts, Florida, and California from OCS oil and gas development for the duration of the next budget cycle. On a more permanent basis OCSLA section 11(h) prohibits the issuance of leases or exploration permits within 15 miles of the Point Reyes, California National Seashore unless California allows the exploration and development of adjacent state submerged lands.

These enactments reflect national political recognition of coastal state dissatisfaction with Interior Department decisions reached under the NEPA, CZMA, OCSLA statutory framework discussed above. Interestingly, the areas excluded from leasing pursuant to Congressional moratoria often have coincided with the 40 to 55 million acres in various areas of the OCS which the Department of Defense has requested be excluded from leasing. Interior Secretary Hodel has stated that potentially one billion barrels of oil are recoverable in areas covered by Congressional moratoria.

Similar to the threat of litigation on the consistency of lease sales, the threat of Congressional moratoria has increased Interior willingness to negotiate with coastal state representatives, especially their Congressional delegations, about the size, location, and timing of OCS oil and gas lease sales adjacent to their coasts. A subsequently abandoned July 1985 tentative agreement between Secretary Hodel and some members of the California Congressional delegation illustrates the political nature of the results reached. Under the tentative agreement, OCS oil and gas development adjacent to California would have been shifted north off the more sparsely populated Central and Northern California coasts where public opposition is more muted than in the Santa Barbara Channel, Santa Monica Bay, and San Diego areas where leasing is most vigorously opposed. Following the announcement of the tentative agreement, and again after its abandonment, the House Appropriations Committee voted not to extend the California moratorium, limiting the 1986 moratorium to Georges Bank and other areas off Massachusetts.

The continued viability of the Congressional moratoria process has been questioned by several knowledgeable individuals in state government, the oil industry, and the federal government. They point out that the 1985 moratorium legislation passed by only one vote in the House Appropriations Committee, that Alaska's summer 1985 effort to have Bristol Bay included in a moratorium failed before the House Interior Appropriations Subcommittee, and that some coastal states now are more receptive to a second round of exploratory drilling in some frontier areas where the first round of drilling provided no major discoveries.

Use of the Congressional moratoria process seems less likely for OCS mineral lease sales given the greater distance of most known mineral resources from state coastlines. However, use of the moratorium process, principally as a political weapon, should not be ruled out, given the sometimes highly visible, rhetoric-filled approach Interior has taken to OCS minerals development, discussed next.

ADMINISTRATIVE ACTIONS OFFENSIVE TO MANY COASTAL STATES

In a January 1985 address to the California Senate Committee on Natural Resources and Wildlife, the California Attorney General stated, "Regardless of what Congress has decided . . ., there lurks in these great federal agencies a vestigial will to fight fiercely to retain what they have come to think of as their lands, their revenues, and their plenary power over both of them." During the 1980s the generally adversarial nature of OCS intergovernmental relations has been significantly affected by Reagan administration positions and executive branch agency actions. These administrative actions weaken state and local government roles offshore, and run contrary to the commonly understood tenets of the "new federalism." So long as they are maintained, one can safely predict that the pattern of adversarial intergovernmental relations for OCS oil and gas development will continue and extend into OCS mineral development as well.

With respect to adversarial relations over oil and gas development, the more significant administration actions include: opposition to OCS oil and gas revenue sharing with the coastal states; failure to agree on distribution of OCSLA section 8(g) revenues held in escrow; continuation of the areawide leasing program opposed by many states and environmental groups; opposition to expansion of the territorial sea from three to twelve miles and the use of straight baselines to measure the territorial sea where appropriate under international law; proposed elimination of federal funding for state coastal management programs; and Commerce Secretary overrides of state objections to activities inconsistent with their coastal management programs.

With respect to projected adversarial intergovernmental relations over OCS minerals development, significant administration actions have included the

Justice Department opinion interpreting the <u>Interior v.
California</u> decision as excluding OCS mineral lease sales
from the CZMA 307(c)(1) consistency process, and the
Interior Department's hasty assertion of jurisdiction over
seabed mineral deposits beyond the geographic continental
shelf but within the 200-mile Exclusive Economic Zone
(EEZ). Establishing national jurisdiction over such
mineral deposits clearly was a primary motivation for
President Reagan's March 1983 EEZ Proclamation, but many
coastal states and mining industry representatives would
prefer to see their mining administered by NOAA pursuant
to the Deep Seabed Mining Act rather than Interior under
the OCSLA.

In its eagerness to establish jurisdiction vis-a-vis
NOAA, Interior has offended coastal states by: (1)
unilaterally and prematurely claiming jurisdiction over
polymetallic sulfide deposits on the Juan de Fuca Ridge,
an action which also offended Canada due to its
overlapping jurisdictional claim; (2) giving very shallow
treatment of the jurisdictional question in the draft EIS
for its proposed Gorda Ridge Polymetallic Sulfide Lease
Offering in December 1983; (3) releasing in May 1985 an
Interior Solicitor's opinion supporting Interior's Gorda
Ridge jurisdiction which is an advocacy document rather
than a reasoned analysis effectively dealing with
arguments contrary to Interior's predetermined position;
(4) proposing OCS minerals leasing regulations prior to
resolution of the jurisdictional question; and (5) issuing
in January 1985 a nationwide call for information on
non-energy minerals.

The call for information extended to the entire United
States' EEZ and OCS and covered minerals ranging from
phosphorites to cobalt-manganese minerals. Study areas
delineated pursuant to the call would be reviewed by
Interior for possible leasing. Interested parties were
asked to identify areas that should be excluded from
leasing and to provide the rationale for such exclusion.
Thus coastal states were faced with reviewing the entire
EEZ and OCS adjacent to their coasts in order to be able
to participate meaningfully in Interior's approach to OCS
and EEZ minerals development.

CLOSING

As the ultimate example of adversarial OCS
intergovernmental relations, the litigation concerning the

three oil and gas lease sales that the Interior Department attempted to conduct on Georges Bank resulted in at least thirteen federal court decisions. To date, the exploration that has taken place on Georges Bank has resulted in no significant finds of oil and gas resources. Such results raise the question whether the costs of Interior's adversarial approach are worth the benefits.

Obviously, this is a difficult question to answer, but from the perspective of those willing to litigate to prevent leasing in special areas like Georges Bank, the Santa Barbara Channel, Bristol Bay, and Alaskan Arctic areas, very large costs are worth incurring to avoid irreversible impacts on irreplaceable resources. If the uniqueness of those areas is accepted, a further question arises as to whether state and local governments, environmental and fishermen's groups, and Alaskan natives are suitably equipped or should be entrusted with making the factual case for their special treatment under existing procedures. This question is especially critical because Congressional intervention in the form of moratoria is available only as an uncertain back-up.

The major exception to the pattern of adversarial relations to date is the Gulf of Mexico where there has been very little litigation and a great deal of oil and gas production. Active leases and total acres under lease in the Gulf outweigh the totals for the other three OCS regions (Alaska, Atlantic, and Pacific) combined roughly 4 to 1. Even there, however, Florida was forced to resort to the Congressional moratorium process in order to get the Flower Garden Banks area excluded from recent sales and Texas and Louisiana filed unsuccessful suits to block sales carried out by the areawide leasing method.

Barring a radical restructuring of the offshore ownership and jurisdiction rules, a certain irreducible amount of intergovernmental conflict over OCS development can be expected. This appears inevitable due to differing federal, state, and local perceptions as to the allocation of benefits and costs from OCS development. When consultations between federal administrative agencies and state and local governments are exhausted regarding such key decisions as whether to allow OCS oil and gas development in Bristol Bay, our constitutional structure currently provides two avenues of relief, the federal courts and Congress.

Many commentators agree that recent federal appellate court decisions such as <u>Interior v. California</u> incorrectly

have supported central national authorities and
policy-makers who often are insulated from the practical
implications of their decisions. They feel the courts may
be placing too high a value on predicable results (e.g.,
"in case of alleged conflict, the national government
wins") instead of taking a more neutral (or Madisonian
federalist) position, utilizing intergovernmental conflict
to expose clearly for political accountability purposes
the goals and values of the respective governments who are
in conflict.

Without more judicial sensitivity to the values of
federalism regarding offshore resources, federal
administrative decisions routine in appearance may escape
meaningful judicial and legislative-political review. Yet
these "routine" decisions may have significant
consequences for OCS intergovernmental relations, e.g.,
Commerce Secretary inconsistency overrides, Commerce
Secretary disapprovals of state and local coastal
management programs, and federal agency disregard of key
elements of federally approved state coastal management
programs (as occurred in Delaware).

Given their political connection to state electorates,
it is not surprising that coastal state Congressional
delegations are more sensitive to coastal state concerns
than either the judicial or executive branches. The state
roles created by Congress in NEPA, the CZMA, and the OCSLA
have been the principal focus of this paper. Some may
view those provisions as an unacceptable transfer of
responsibility to state governments. However, along with
those relatively modest enactments built around
consultation and coordination, Congress also has delegated
significant responsibilities offshore to coastal states.
These delegations of responsibility began with the 1953
Submerged Lands Act awarding the states the first three
miles of ocean seabed. They are exemplified to the
fullest under the Deepwater Ports Act by the granting of
veto power to coastal states over federally licensed
deepwater ports located more than three miles off their
coasts.

Some of the techniques Congress has used to create
coastal state offshore roles are preferable to others.
The current complex of federal statutes governing oil
spill liability is unsatisfactory in merely providing that
the states are not preempted from enacting similar laws.
Such provisions merely entrust exact delineation of
federal-state responsibilities to the same federal courts
whose recent decisions in this area were criticized

above. Also, jurisdictional lines drawn on water, like
the Submerged Lands Act, ignore the fluidity of the ocean
environment, important national interests in territorial
sea management, and legitimate state environmental and
economic interests that extend beyond three miles. (Over
30 years after passage of the SLA, a comprehensive
evaluation of state territorial sea management efforts
seems long overdue.) When compared to management
decisions based on science and policy, the temporary,
inconsistent, and excessively political nature of
Congressional OCS oil and gas drilling moratoria makes
them an unsatisfactory tool over the long term.

Instead, the goal to be achieved is better statutory
articulation of decision formulas which are sensitive to
intergovernmental concerns. The author previously has
advocated explicit recognition and weighing in federal
decision-making processes of individual state
contributions to the national interest, fully recognizing
the difficulties of calculating such individual state
contributions. In any case, Congressional delineation of
the respective federal and coastal state roles offshore
will continue to be a difficult process, which is not
surprising given the resources at stake.

As fiscal year 1985 drew to a close, states rights
with respect to ocean resource matters in general and OCS
hydrocarbon and minerals development in particular were at
a low ebb. Paradoxically, this ran counter to the tenets
of the "new federalism," which meant the return of
considerable power and responsibility to the states in
other functional areas. The federal government
consciously had strengthened its hand vis-a-vis the states
offshore, basically viewing concerned coastal state and
local governments as obstructing the national ("security")
interest in oil and gas and strategic minerals
development.

This trend can be expected to extend at least through
the balance of President Reagan's second term, and
probably would be continued by a succeeding Republican
administration. However, over the longer term, the
Congressional enactments and court decisions interpreting
them will be quite significant in comparison to the
policies of individual administrations. After all, oil
and gas development from leasing through production takes
from 8 to 15 years, thereby spanning at least two
presidential administrations. The timetable for minerals
development is expected to be even longer.

However, even at low ebb, there is more natural resources federalism offshore than onshore. The onshore situation has been described as one of co-optive federalism or managerial federalism built around a strongly dominant federal government. Thus, important participants in onshore intergovernmental relations, such as Arizona's Governor Babbitt, have yearned for something akin to the CZMA consistency process to apply to federal public lands management decisions onshore, despite the fact that there is revenue sharing with affected states onshore but not offshore! This suggests that the state participation, consultation, and consistency rights discussed in this paper are and should be highly valued by the states, taken seriously by the federal government and industry, and not viewed cynically as state leverage for gaining access to the substantial OCS oil and gas revenues currently flowing into the federal treasury.

REFERENCES

Ball, M. S. 1978. Law of the sea: Federal-state
   relations. University of Georgia Dean Rusk Center
   Monograph no. 1. Athens, Ga.: Dean Rusk Center for
   International and Comparative Law, School of Law,
   University of Georgia.

Ball, M. 1982. Good Old American Permits: Madisonian
   Federalism on the Territorial Sea and Continental
   Shelf. Environmental Law 12.

Berger, T., and Saurenman, J. A. 1983. The role of
   coastal states in outer continental shelf oil and gas
   leasing: A litigation perspective. Virginia Journal
   of Natural Resources Law, 3:35.

Bergerbest, N. 1985. Consistency Appeals-recent
   developments. Coastal Zone '85 Proceedings, 1:223.

Botzum, J. Coastal Zone Management Newsletter (various
   issues).

Botzum, J. Ocean Science News (various issues).

Breeden, R. 1978. Federalism and the development of
   outer continental shelf mineral resources. Stanford
   Law Review, 28:1107.

Briscoe, J. 1984. Federal-State Offshore Boundary
   Disputes: The State Perspective. Presented at the
   1984 Law of the Sea Institute, San Francisco, CA.

Brown, A. 1985. Bristol Bay regional planning: An oil
   industry perspective. Coastal Zone '85 Proceedings,
   1:1257.

Burroughs, R. 1986. "Interests and the U.S.
   Jurisdictional History." In Thomas A. Grigalunas and
   Lynne C. Hanson, eds., The Continental Shelf:
   Resources, Boundaries, and Management. Kingston,
   R.I.: Ninth Annual Conference, Center for Ocean
   Management Studies, University of Rhode Island, pp.
   83-50.

Charney, J. 1981. The Delimitation of Lateral Seaward Boundaries Between States in a Domestic Context. The American Journal of International Law, 75:28.

Charney, J. 1974. Judicial deference in Submerged Lands Act Cases. Vanderbilt Journal of Transnational Law, 2:383.

Christie, D. 1979. Coastal Energy Impact Program Boundaries on the Atlantic Coast: A Case Study of the Law Applicable to Lateral Seaward Boundaries. Virginia Journal of International Law, 19:841.

Claiborne, L. 1984. Federal-State Offshore Boundary Disputes: The Federal Perspective. Presented at the 1984 Law of the Sea Institute, San Francisco, CA.

Comment. 1980. Achieving federalism in the regulation of coastal energy facility siting. Ecology Law Quarterly, 8:533.

Comment. 1983. Outer continental shelf revenue sharing for coastal states. Virginia Journal of Natural Resources Law, 3:131.

Corwin, E. 1984. Prospects for increased state and public control over OCS leasing: The timing of the environmental impact statement. San Diego Law Review, 21:709-731.

Evans, N. 1985. What's going on with federal consistency? Coastal Zone '85 Proceedings, 1:194.

Goldstein, J., ed. 1982. The politics of offshore oil. New York: Praeger.

Gross, A. M. 1966. The Maritime Boundaries of the States. Michigan Law Review, 64:639.

Hildreth, R. G. 1976. The coast: Where energy meets the environment. San Diego Law Review, 13:253.

Miller, D. S. 1984. Shore federalism: Evolving federal-state relations in offshore oil and gas development. Ecology Law Quarterly, 11:401-450.

Monteferrante, F. and Lindstedt, D. 1985. Interagency coordination in Louisiana's coastal zone. Coastal Zone '85 Proceedings, 1:214, 218-219.

Noonan, D. 1985. Permitting for oil and gas activities in the OCS Mukluk Island-Beaufort Sea, Alaska 1983. Coastal Zone '85 Proceedings, 2:1691.

Perkins, S. 1985. Splitting common-pool offshore oil and gas revenues. Coastal Zone '85 Proceedings, 2:1686.

Selmi, D. 1985. The Controversy over Regulation of Air Pollution from Outer Continental Shelf Leasing. Western Natural Resources Law Digest (Winter).

Shapiro, M. E. 1985. Sagebrush and Seaweed Robbery: State Revenue Losses from Onshore and Offshore Federal Land. Ecology Law Quarterly, 12:481.

Stewart, R. 1977. Pyramids of sacrifice?: Problems of federalism in mandating state implementation of national environmental policy. Yale Law Journal, 86:1196.

Symposium. 1982. Federalism and the environment: A change in direction. Environmental Law, 12:847.

Symposium. 1982. The new federalism in environmental law: Taking stock. Environmental Law Reporter, 12:15065.

Tarlock, D. 1983. National power, state resources sovereignty and federalism in the 1980's: Scaling America's magic mountain. Kansas Law Review, 32:111.

U.S. Congress. Office of Technology Assessment (OTA). 1985. Oil and Gas Technologies for the Arctic and Deepwater. Washington, D.C.: U.S. Congress, Office of Technology Assessment, May.

U.S. Department of Commerce. 1985. National Oceanic and Atmospheric Administration, Office of Ocean and Coastal Resource Management. Federal Consistency Study, Draft. 3 volumes.

Wulf, N. 1971. Freezing the boundary dividing federal and state interests in offshore submerged lands. San Diego Law Review, 8:584.

7

Intergovernmental Relations and Marine Policy Change: Ocean Dumping and At-Sea Incineration of Hazardous Waste

James P. Lester
and Michael S. Hamilton

INTRODUCTION

Changes in federal marine policy and the role of intergovernmental participants are the subject of this chapter. Specifically, it analyzes marine policy change in two key areas during 1971-1985 by utilizing a framework that accounts for the role of intergovernmental participants in policy change.

The findings suggest several considerations in the politics of policy change. First, they illustrate the ability of intergovernmental coalitions ultimately to achieve their policy objectives and, in doing so, bring about significant policy-oriented learning on the part of executive branch participants. Second, these findings suggest that drastic marine policy changes are unlikely in the absence of macropolitical (or system-wide) influences. Finally, they point out the growing role of intergovernmental participants in two marine policy subsystems.

Federal ocean policy, according to many analysts, is in transition. A debate has now developed between those who argue on the one hand that "the oceans are sacrosanct and that any entry of polluting substances is undesirable" and, on the other hand, "that the oceans do have a finite capacity to receive some societal wastes" (Goldberg 1981: 4). Moreover, it is the position of the current President that, in general, our environmental laws and regulations need careful review and modification. The Reagan administration is concerned that benefits to be derived from rigid environmental regulation may not be justified in terms of economic costs (Swanson and Devine 1982: 16).

These recent developments have led some observers
(Lahey 1982, Curlin 1980) to believe that we are
undergoing a policy change from an "ocean protection"
strategy (characteristic of the 1970s) to an "ocean
management" strategy (characteristic of the 1980s):

> . . . it is likely that we will see the development
> of an overarching philosophy for the management of
> ocean space and resources, not unlike the principles
> of management which have evolved for our public lands
> since the turn of the century. The strong
> environmental and conservation programs which were
> implemented in the 1970s will be melded with
> provisions for encouraging the responsible development
> of marine resources. A system of ocean management
> will mature. (Curlin 1980: 28).

Use of the oceans as a sink for solid waste and as a
location for incineration of liquid wastes has generated
considerable conflict and some cooperation in
intergovernmental relations in the United States. Results
have included litigation, rancorous public hearings, and
some modification of public policy.

Proposals to move materials dredged from one local
jurisdiction and dump them in another jurisdiction have
pitted some local governments against each other and
against federal decision-makers, on the one hand, while
allying other local officials with the same federal
agency, on the other hand (Manatee County, City of Holmes
Beach and City of Anna Maria, Florida v. Anne Gorsuch,
EPA, and Tampa Port Authority, Case No. 82-248-Civ.-T-GC,
U.S. District Court, Middle District, Florida, 1982, in
U.S. Congress, House, 1983c: 703). Attempts to terminate
sewage sludge dumping in the New York Bight, discussed
below, arrayed municipal governments and a federal agency
against other city and county governments in several
states during administrative proceedings, federal court
litigation, and Congressional hearings (City of New York
v. EPA, 543 F.Supp. 1084, 1981; U.S. Congress, House,
1981a, 1981b, 1982, 1983a: 299, 1983b, 1983c, 1984). This
resulted in a three-year delay in reauthorization of the
Marine Protection, Research, and Sanctuaries Act of 1972
(Congressional Quarterly 1984: 3). A recent proposal to
permit incineration of liquid hazardous wastes off the
coast of Texas, discussed below, pitted local and state
governments in opposition to federal agency
decision-makers (Technology Review 1984; Schneider 1984a,

1984b). Virtually every conceivable combination of intergovernmental relations has been apparent in ocean policy discussions since 1971.

Consequently, some researchers have pointed out the growing role of intergovernmental actors in ocean policy (Spirer 1982). As one analyst noted, "the phenomenon of national ocean policy formulation should be visualized as another, however somewhat distinct, public policy process in the intergovernmental arena" (Cannon 1985: 50). That is, "there is a unique and diverse range of groups and institutions in the intergovernmental public policy arena whose claims, counterclaims, and concerns are factored into any policy equation or strategy being considered by governmental or ocean industry corporate decision-makers" (Cannon 1985: 50).

Thus, in order to analyze changes in ocean policy over the past fourteen years, it is necessary to utilize a framework which accounts for involvement by many diverse intergovernmental actors, including state, regional, and local public interest groups; the national executive branch of government; state and local governments; national advisory groups, and the judicial branch at state and federal levels. The purpose of this chapter is to analyze changes in two key areas of marine policy: ocean dumping and at-sea incineration of hazardous waste. To do so, we utilize the "advocacy coalition" model of policy change developed by Paul Sabatier (1985).

The chapter is divided into four parts. First, we describe a conceptual framework for analyzing public policy change in which a multiplicity of actors at each level of government may exert significant influence upon public policy outputs. Next, we apply this framework to ocean dumping and at-sea incineration of hazardous waste. Both of these areas have undergone (or are now undergoing) significant policy change. Finally, we suggest a number of conclusions and implications for "policy learning" drawn from these two case studies of marine policy change.

PUBLIC POLICY CHANGE: A CONCEPTUAL FRAMEWORK

The conceptual framework for analyzing ocean policy change used here is based on a conceptualization developed by Paul Sabatier. Figure 1 presents an illustration of his framework and the factors that condition public policy change (Sabatier 1985: 4-8).

200

FIGURE 1. General Overview of Conceptual Framework of Policy Change.

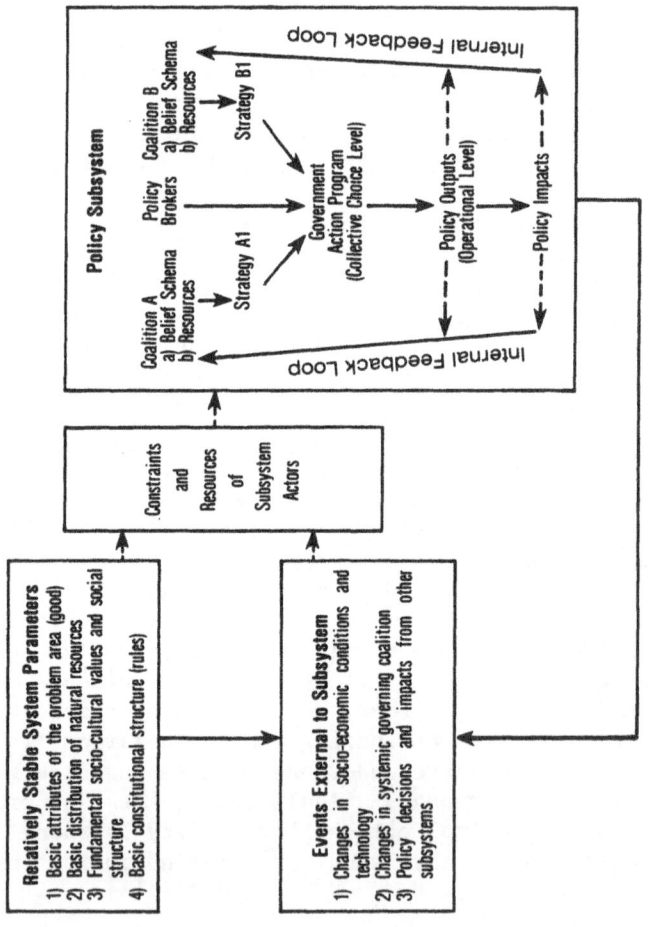

SOURCE: Sabatier (1985).

In his model, Sabatier suggests that "policy subsystems" constitute the most useful aggregate unit of analysis for understanding policy change over periods of a decade or more. Policy change is viewed as the product of both (1) changes in system-wide events, such as socioeconomic perturbations or outputs from other subsystems, and (2) the striving of competing advocacy coalitions within the subsystem to realize their core beliefs over time as they seek to increase their resource bases, to respond to opportunities provided by external events, and to learn more about the policy problem(s) of interest to them (Sabatier 1985).

More specifically, it is assumed that actors concerned with a policy problem can be aggregated into one or more advocacy coalitions which share a set of normative and causal beliefs and which dispose of certain resources. At any particular point in time, each coalition adopts a strategy envisaging institutional innovations which it feels will further its policy objectives. Conflicting strategies from various coalitions are normally mediated by a third group of actors, termed "policy brokers," whose principal concern is to find some reasonable compromise which will reduce intense conflict. The end result is one or more government action programs, which in turn produce policy outputs at the operational level (e.g., regulations or agency permit decisions). These outputs eventually result in a number of impacts on targeted problem parameters (e.g., ocean or air quality), as well as side effects (Sabatier 1985: 5).

On the basis of perceptions of the adequacy of governmental decisions and/or the resultant impacts, as well as new information arising from search processes and external dynamics, each advocacy coalition may revise its beliefs and/or alter its strategy. The latter may involve the seeking of major institutional revisions at the level of collective choice, minor revisions at the operational level, or even going outside the subsystem e.g., by seeking changes in the dominant electoral coalition at the systemic level (Sabatier 1985: 5). Moreover, this framework has special significance for the study of policy-oriented learning, i.e., relatively enduring alterations of thought or behavioral intentions which result from experience and which are concerned with the attainment or revison of public policy (Heclo 1974: 306).

In the following sections, we use Sabatier's advocacy coalition framework to analyze emerging changes in two key areas of marine policy. We are particu- larly interested

in understanding the extent of (and the reasons for)
policy change in these two areas. In carrying out this
analysis, we also examine the following hypothesis
suggested by Sabatier:

> Proposition: The core (basic attributes) of a
> governmental action program are unlikely to be changed
> in the absence of significant perturbations external
> to the subsystem, i.e. changes in socioeconomic
> conditions, system-wide governing coalitions, or
> policy outputs from other subsystems.

This hypothesis (or "plausibility probe") is first
examined in the area of ocean dumping policy and next in
the area of at-sea waste incineration policy.

OCEAN DUMPING POLICY: FROM STRICT PROTECTION TO
MANAGEMENT FLEXIBILITY

The Ocean Dumping Policy Subsystem

The ocean dumping subsystem contains a large and
diverse set of actors. Essentially two coalitions have
developed which we label as "the pro-dumping coalition"
and "the anti-dumping coalition." The pro-dumping
coalition is composed of some members of the scientific
community (e.g., Edward D. Goldberg), the Council of
Coastal Agencies of the Association of Metropolitan
Sewerage Agencies, the American Association of Port
Authorities, the National Advisory Committee on Oceans and
the Atmosphere (1981), the National Academy of Sciences
(1978), the National Oceanic and Atmospheric
Administration (NOAA), the New York City Department of
Environmental Protection, the Army Corps of Engineers, the
Passaic Valley (New Jersey) Sewerage Commission, Chemical
Waste Management, N.L. Industries, Inc., and several
politicians including former representative John Murphy,
representatives John Scheuer and Norman Lent of New York,
Mayor Ed Koch of New York (U.S. Congress, House 1982,
1983a, 1983b, 1983c, 1984), and perhaps President Reagan
himself among others. It has a belief system which
stresses that (1) the ocean has a significant
self-cleansing ability which enables it to absorb some
wastes without unacceptable consequences, (2) ocean
dumping is less hazardous than land disposal (Goldberg

1981), and (3) ocean dumping is the least expensive
disposal alternative for some coastal communities (U.S.
Congress, House 1982: 198, 389; 1984: 252).

The competing anti-dumping coalition is largely
dominated by environmental groups, such as the American
Littoral Society, Greenpeace, the Jersey Shore Audubon
Society, the Center for Law and Social Policy, the Sierra
Club, the New Jersey Conservation Foundation, the Clean
Ocean Action Project, the National Wildlife Federation,
the Ocean Dumping Task Force, and the Cousteau Society.
Its members also include civic organizations (e.g., local
chapters of the American Association of University Women,
the League of Women Voters, the Girl Scouts, the National
Council of Jewish Women, the New Jersey Academy of Family
Physicians, and the Public Interest Research Group),
business associations such as Marine Underwriters, Inc.,
and South Monmouth (New Jersey) Board of Realtors,
commercial and sport fishing organizations (e.g., the
Jersey Coast Anglers Association, the Gulf Coast
Fishermen's Environmental Defense Fund, the New Jersey
Commercial Fishermen's Council and Lobstermen's
Association, the National Sea Clammers Association, Garden
State Seafood, Inc., the Belford Seafood Cooperative,
Inc., and the Associated Boatmen of New Jersey), and
several former and active politicans (e.g., U.S.
Representatives William J. Hughes, Norman D'Amours, James
J. Howard, Jerome Ambro, and Thomas Evans, Senator Frank
Lautenberg, elected officials in several local govern-
ments in New York and New Jersey, and the New Jersey
Department of the Public Advocate). Its belief system
stresses that (1) ocean dumping severely degrades the
marine environment, (2) ocean dumping poses a great hazard
to public health and safety (Burks 1980), (3) it damages
coastal tourism, commercial and sport fishing industries,
and (4) other disposal alternatives are often less
expensive and less harmful to the environment (U.S.
Congress, House 1982, 1983a, 1983b, 1983c, 1984). It is
noteworthy that the members of both coalitions have
diverse interests and values, and therefore, probably
would not agree on all environmental issues. Their
diversity underscores the significance of shared beliefs
and policy objectives concerning ocean dumping.[1]

As Sabatier notes, "not everyone active in a policy
subsystem will belong to an advocacy coalition or share
one of the major belief schema" (Sabatier 1985: 18).
There will almost certainly be a category of actors whose
dominant concern is with keeping the level of political

conflict within acceptable limits and with reaching some
"reasonable" solution to the problem (Sabatier 1985: 18).
These actors are called "policy brokers."

The policy broker, in this instance, has been the
Environmental Protection Agency (EPA). Initially, in
1971, EPA was clearly committed to the goal of phasing out
sewage sludge dumping, but by 1981, EPA's policy position
represented "a shift in EPA ocean dumping policy toward
making ocean dumping a viable option for waste disposal"
(Spirer 1982: 46). Its brokerage role will be discussed
more fully in the next section.

The strategy of the pro-dumping coalition is (1) to
promote continuation of ocean dumping as a federal policy,
and (2) to oppose redesignation of sewage sludge sites
from 12 miles to 106 miles. The strategy of the
antidumping coalition is (1) to oppose continuation of
ocean dumping as a federal policy, and, if this fails, (2)
to promote redesignation of sewage sludge sites from 12
miles to 106 miles, and (3) to impose user fees on ocean
dumpers to finance research and clean-up activities.

In the next section of this chapter we examine the
degree of influence each advocacy coalition had on U.S.
government policy during 1971-1985.

The Ocean Dumping Government Action Program:
A Policy History

The first concerted effort to control ocean dumping
began in the early 1970s, at a time when many
environmental protection laws were passed (Bakalian 1984:
193). President Nixon, in his February 8, 1971
environmental message to the Congress, announced that the
nation's policy should be "[to ban] unregulated ocean
dumping of all material and [to place] strict limits on
ocean disposal of any materials harmful to the
environment." The EPA transmitted to Congress two days
later a bill that later became the Marine Protection,
Research, and Sanctuaries Act of 1972 (MPRSA). This bill
dictated the strictest possible standards in existence at
the time for any continued dumping. Indeed, the research
program created by MPRSA had the explicit purpose of
"determining means of minimizing or ending all dumping of
materials within five years of the effective date of the
act" (Spirer 1982: 18). In addition, this act established
a permit system under which ocean dumping is regulated
jointly by EPA and the Army Corps of Engineers. EPA sets

criteria for evaluation of all permit applications and
issues permits for dumping of all materials except dredged
spoils; the Army Corps issues permits for dumping of
dredged spoils using EPA's criteria (Lahey 1982: 401).

On October 15, 1973, EPA promulgated its final
regulations and criteria (40 C.F.R. 220-229, 1975) in
which it took a strict, highly restrictive approach toward
applying the criteria embodied in the act (Spirer 1982:
20-21). In these regulations, EPA intended to terminate
all harmful ocean dumping, regardless of whether the
permit applicant could demonstrate that its dumping would
not unreasonably degrade the marine environment (Bakalian
1984: 210). In effect, EPA "established a policy of
phasing out all ocean dumping of sewage sludge" (Lahey
1982: 405). In doing so, EPA assumed a highly protective
approach to ocean dumping.

In 1975, the City of Philadelphia was required to
begin phasing out sewage sludge dumping at the Cape May
site forty miles east of Maryland (Lahey 1982: 406-07),
and to stop dumping there in 1980 (U.S. Congress, House
1984: 234). EPA denied or phased out over 100 dumping
permits from 1973-1979, but this accounted for only about
three percent of the total volume of sewage sludge dumped
in 1978 (Lahey 1982: 410).

On June 28, 1976, EPA issued a proposed revision of
the ocean dumping regulations and criteria (Federal
Register 1976, 41: 26, 644). EPA's new regulations
provided even greater enforcement and phase-out powers
than did its 1973 regulations. A provision was added that
set December 31, 1981 as the date after which all dumping
of environmentally unacceptable sewage sludge had to cease
(Spirer 1982: 26). Congress subsequently wrote this
deadline into MPRSA by amendment in 1977 (91 Stat. 1255,
33 U.S.C. 1412a, Supp. 1985).

When the City of New York applied for a permit to
continue dumping sewage sludge contaminated with toxic
heavy metals, claiming the sludge did not unreasonably
degrade a site twelve miles off the coast in the New York
Bight, EPA on March 13, 1980 refused to permit this
activity after December 31, 1981. The City of New York
brought suit in a federal district court in New York. In
a curious interpretation of statutory language concerning
agency decision-making and rule-making authority--which
some observers have suggested was poorly informed and
poorly reasoned (U.S. Congress, House 1982: 105, 109, 302,
546; Lahey 1982: 407-09, n. 137, 419-22, n. 255)--the
court endorsed arguments advanced by the City of New York

which limited the ability of EPA to terminate ocean
dumping of sewage sludge (City of New York v. EPA).

By the time this decision was issued on April 14,
1981, a new President had taken office who was somewhat
less enthusiastic than his predecessors about
environmental regulation (Hamilton 1986). A significant
change had taken place in the system-wide governing
coalition. However, regulation of ocean dumping was
already under review by EPA in May 1981 (U.S. Congress,
House 1981a: 61).

In the aftermath of City of New York v. EPA, it became
apparent that EPA was shifting its approach toward ocean
dumping. The agency stated that in the future it would be
more "flexible" about dumping and would view the ocean as
a "legitimate" disposal option (Lahey 1982: 422). A draft
of EPA's 1982 revised regulations presented a shift in EPA
ocean dumping policy away from strict protection toward
making ocean dumping a viable option for waste disposal
(Spirer 1982: 46). In effect, the "single-minded
preoccupation with any purported threat to the ocean [gave
way] to a more careful and reasoned balancing of the full
range of environmental, social and fiscal implications of
any ocean disposal policy" (Spirer 1981: 48).

Most recently, EPA announced it would seek to bar New
York City and other municipalities from dumping sewage
sludge in the New York Bight, 12 miles off the New Jersey
coast. Instead, it would designate a dump site 106 miles
at sea off the continental shelf (Blumenthal 1984). On
April 1, 1985, EPA ordered New York City to dump its
sewage sludge at this site, in order to protect beaches
and marine life (Rangel 1985). In reaffirming a tentative
decision made in 1984, EPA was, in effect, making a
concession toward the anti-dumping coalition. Indeed,
"New Jersey officials, commercial fishermen, and
environmentalists who have pressed for years for an end to
ocean disposal of wastes, cheered the decision" (Sullivan
1985). Dumping sewage sludge would be allowed to
continue, but at a location further removed from coastal
populations and fishing enterprises.

In summary, EPA has moved from strict, confrontational
protection of the ocean to a more flexible, accommodating
posture during 1971-1985. To ascertain the reasons for
this shift, we turn to an analysis of factors promoting
policy change.

Factors Affecting Ocean Dumping Policy Change

Sabatier notes that "the extent of policy-oriented learning is contingent upon the feasibility of developing good causal models of the factors affecting a problem" (Sabatier 1985: 10).

One of the major factors influencing policy change by EPA on ocean dumping was the changing status of knowledge: a "growing awareness of the health and environmental risks of alternative disposal methods, and second, a belief that the oceans are less ecologically vulnerable than had previously been thought" (Lahey 1982: 410). During 1975-1981, scientific data accumulated which suggested that ocean dumping posed only modest environmental risks as compared with other threats to the ocean environment (Spirer 1982: 33; Lahey 1982). A growing portion of the scientific community came to believe that "the ocean has a significant self-cleansing ability which enables it to absorb wastes without unacceptable consequences" (Lahey 1982: 417). On the basis of this growing evidence, advisory groups (such as the General Accounting Office, the National Academy of Sciences, and the National Advisory Committee on Oceans and Atmosphere), plus the National Oceanic and Atmospheric Administration, the courts, EPA, and Congress began to reassess ocean dumping regulations (Lahey 1982).

A second major factor influencing policy change was an alteration in fundamental sociocultural attitudes during the late 1970s and early 1980s, as a result of the oil embargo and subsequent energy supply dislocations. Specifically, the "zeal which attended the movement to clean up the environment became tempered by the growing burden of inflation, increased energy consumption, and public discontent with government spending and regulation" (Spirer 1982: 36). This systemic event (i.e., the energy problem) had a profound effect on public, political and media attitudes toward the environment in general and ocean dumping in particular (Spirer 1982: 36).

A third major factor influencing policy change by EPA was a significant change in the systemic governing coalition with the election of Ronald Reagan as President on November 4, 1980, "on a platform which stressed cutting back on environmental and other federal regulations and granting greater autonomy to state and local governments" (Spirer 1982: 38). This administrative change may partially account for EPA movement away from confrontational intergovernmental relations toward a more accommodating federal stance towards municipal sludge dumping, evident perhaps in the agency's decision not to appeal the lower court decision in City of New York v. EPA.

Finally, the most recent factor influencing policy change in ocean dumping may have been a spillover effect from another policy subsystem--that of ocean incineration of hazardous waste. As noted above, EPA recently made a concession to the anti-dumping coalition by moving ocean dumping sites from 12 miles offshore to 106 miles offshore. To some extent, this decision may have been a spillover from pressures brought to bear on the ocean incineration issue by numerous environmental groups. Moreover, Jack E. Ravan, assistant administrator for water at EPA, was a key official with decision-making authority in both policy subsystems during 1983-1985.[2]

All of these factors are essentially outside of the policy subsystem, i.e., they are macropolitical (or systemic) influences upon policy change. According to our hypothesis, such systemic influences must be present for core policy changes to occur. Without such influences, it is doubtful that major policy change will occur. To explore this possibility further, we now turn to an analysis of policy change in at-sea incineration of hazardous wastes.

OCEAN INCINERATION POLICY: TOWARDS GREATER STRINGENCY

The Ocean Incineration Policy Subsystem

The ocean incineration subsystem also contains a large and diverse set of actors. Essentially, two coalitions have developed which we label as "the pro-incineration coalition" and "the anti-incineration coalition." The pro-incineration coalition is dominated by the waste incineration industry including Chemical Waste Management, Inc., (owners of the Vulcanus I and II incineration vessels), At-Sea Incineration, Inc., (owners of Apollo I and II incineration vessels), Precision Conversion and Recovery, Inc., and Sea Burn, Inc.[3] They are joined by the Institute of Chemical Waste Management, the National Wildlife Federation, an environmental group which has developed a split with other environmental groups on this issue, (Technology Review 1984), the State of Florida's Department of Environmental Regulation (DER), and

Congressman John Breaux of Louisiana among others. It has
a belief system which stresses that (1) incineration at
sea is safe and valuable and adds little risk to the
already heavy traffic of hazardous waste chemicals through
American ports (Reinhold 1985: 14); (2) ocean incineration
represents the best liquid chemical waste disposal
technology available at present (Reinhold 1985: 14); and
(3) ocean incineration is a bridge to the future (Piasecki
1985: 10).

The competing anti-incineration coalition is largely
dominated by environmental groups such as Greenpeace, the
Cousteau Society, Friends of the Earth, the Sierra Club,
the National Audubon Society, the Oceanic Society, the
American Littoral Society, the Clean Ocean Action
Coalition, the Grassroots Environmental Association, Clean
Water Action, the Calcasieu League for Environmental
Action Now, the Gulf Coast Fishermen's Environmental
Defense Fund, the Gulf Coast Coalition for Public Health,
the National Campaign Against Toxic Hazards, and the
Environmental Policy Institute among others. However, it
also includes the attorneys general of the states of
Texas, New York, Alabama, and Louisiana, municipal
officials in communities like Lake Charles, Louisiana, the
Texas Shrimp Association, Texas Rural Legal Aid, Texas
Environmental Coalition, the Lower Rio Grande Development
Council, Governor Mark White of Texas, migrant farm
workers, resort owners, representatives of the land-based
incineration industry (e.g. The Hazardous Waste Treatment
Council, ENESCO, SCA Chemical Services, Rollins
Environmental Services, Inc., the Alliance to Save the
Ocean, and the San Francisco Tourism Council), and some
members of the scientific community (Technology Review
1984, Schneider 1984b, Shabecoff 1985a).

The belief system of the anti-incineration coalition
stresses (1) existing ocean incineration technology is old
and remains unproven, i.e., it has not been demonstrated
to be safe (Piasecki 1985); (2) incinerator stack
emissions are toxic and capable of destroying Texas citrus
orchards, cattle ranches, and shellfish grounds (Reinhold
1985: 14); (3) an accidental or operational spill might
devastate the coastal economy, including tourism and the
shellfish industry, (4) EPA is conspiring to create a
waste incineration monopoly, i.e., the ready availability
of incineration ships will discourage more active efforts
to reduce waste production at the source and to promote
recycling and reuse (Piasecki 1985); and (5) at-sea
incineration postpones the growth of a decentralized

approach to toxic waste treatment by concentrating risks
and divorces most of the population from its waste
management responsibilities (Piasecki 1985). Each
coalition has attempted to influence national policy on
this issue through grassroots lobbying efforts and
Congressional lobbying, especially during 1983-1985.

To some extent, EPA has played the role of a policy
broker through its Science Advisory Board (SAB). The
Board issued a report in 1984 that found many unanswered
questions about incineration of toxic substances at sea
and the effect of such burning on the environment and
health. Specifically, the report expressed uncertainties
about measurements and destruction of the wastes.
However, the Board did not advise against the resumption
of incineration activities (Shabecoff 1985b). In general,
EPA has been supportive of ocean incineration of hazardous
waste.

The strategy of the pro-incineration coalition is (1)
to restore public confidence in the efficacy of at-sea
incineration (Piasecki 1985: 9); (2) to get the EPA to
issue permits for both incineration ships and sites for
burning hazardous wastes (Martin 1984: 2-7); and (3) if
EPA disapproves a permit, the ocean incineration companies
plan to litigate (Schneider 1984b: 26).

The strategy of the anti-incineration coalition is (1)
at least to get the EPA to undertake further studies
before approving procedures and/or draft broad regulations
for ocean incineration before granting permits for burning
(Narvaez 1985); (2) at most to prevent the EPA from
issuing permits for sites and ships for burning hazardous
wastes; and (3) ultimately to bring suit against EPA,
challenging the agency's authority to issue final permits
if the regulations are perceived as too lax (Schneider
1984b).

To what extent did either advocacy coalition
successfully exert influence upon the EPA? To answer this
question, we now turn to a discussion of EPA's "action
program" in this area.

The Ocean Incineration Government Action Program:
A Policy History

The Environmental Protection Agency (EPA) has been
involved in ocean incineration research for over ten years
(U.S. Environmental Protection Agency 1985: 1). Starting
in 1974, a series of four research burns were conducted

under EPA permits to gather scientific information about incineration of liquid hazardous wastes at sea and to evaluate ocean incineration as an alternative to land-based disposal options. These research burns were conducted under authority of the Marine Protection, Research, and Sanctuaries Act of 1972, as amended, and the Convention on the Prevention of Marine Pollution by Dumping of Wastes and Other Matter, i.e., the London Dumping Convention (U.S. Environmental Protection Agency 1985: 1).

Between October 1974 and January 1975, 16,800 metric tons of organochlorine wastes from the Shell Chemical Company Deer Park manufacturing complex were incinerated in the Gulf of Mexico. In October 1976, Shell was issued a permit to incinerate up to 50,000 metric tons of mixed wastes at the Gulf Incineration Site. Approximately 29,100 metric tons of wastes were actually incinerated. In 1977, the U.S. Air Force incinerated its stock of herbicide orange at a site 322 kilometers west of Johnston Atoll in the Pacific Ocean. The last series of burns were performed in 1981 and 1982 when liquid PCB wastes were incinerated at the Gulf Incineration Site under a research permit issued to Chemical Waste Management, Inc. and Ocean Combustion Services, B.V. (Federal Register 1985, 50: 8223).

Opposition to ocean incineration coalesced on October 21, 1983, when the EPA published a notice in the Federal Register announcing that Chemical Waste Management had been granted tentative approval to burn 79.7 million gallons of mixed liquid organic chemicals containing PCBs and DDT at a site 170 miles southeast of Brownsville, Texas (Schneider 1984b: 24). A public hearing was held in Brownsville on November 21, 1983, and another hearing was held in Mobile, Alabama during November 22-23, 1983. Over 6,000 people registered at those two public hearings (Federal Register 1985, 50: 8223), some threatening litigation if any permits were issued (Schneider 1984b: 26).

On May 23, 1984, the assistant administrator for water, Jack E. Ravan, issued his decision not to grant the permits to Chemical Waste Management and Ocean Combustion Service. That decision was based on:

(a) The deficiencies in information considered by the Agency in determining the need for incineration-at-sea;

(b) The lack of specific criteria regulating
incineration-at-sea, and;

(c) The fact that the research permits recommended by
the Hearing Officer departed significantly from
the original research permit and thus had never
been the subject of a tentative determination, of
a public hearing or, of public comment.

While the assistant administrator denied the permits,
he did not rule out future ocean incineration. Rather, he
deferred permit issuance until a more deliberative
approach could be developed for ocean incineration. To
that end, he directed his staff to develop a research
strategy that would respond to the needs of the program
and to propose specific regulations for ocean incineration
(Federal Register 1985, 50: 8223).

Thus, EPA is currently developing more stringent
regulations by applying the agency's experience with
land-based incineration facilities and ocean incineration
vessels (U.S. Environmental Protection Agency 1985: 2).
On February 21, 1985, EPA proposed rules that provided a
"regulatory framework" for the ocean incineration program
(Shabecoff 1985a). The proposed rules would modify
provisions in the Ocean Dumping Regulations regarding
issuance of ocean incineration permits and designation and
management of ocean incineration sites (Federal Register
1985, 50: 8222). Specifically, the proposed rules would
require that 99.99 percent of the chemicals burned at sea
be destroyed in the process and, for PCBs and dioxin,
burning efficiency would be required to be 99.9999
percent. In addition, each ship would be required to
carry a full-time EPA employee to monitor compliance with
the conditions of the incineration permits (Federal
Register 1985, 50: 8226-8228). Although these proposed
rules were criticized by various governmental and
environmental groups, they would impose stringent
licensing and operating restrictions on operators of
incinerator ships (Narvaez 1985). By June 28, 1985 (the
deadline for public comments), EPA had received over 4,500
comments and the agency expects to issue final rules by
June 1986. Incineration could begin again about nine
months after that (Reinhold 1985: A14).[4]

Thus, it appears that EPA experienced secondary (or
peripheral) policy-oriented learning by agreeing to
develop a regulatory regime for ocean incineration prior
to the issuance of commercial permits. Core policy

(continuation of ocean incineration), however, appears to be unaffected by the debates between coalitions. To ascertain the reasons for this minor policy revision, we now turn toward an analysis of the resources and constraints of actors involved in this policy subsystem.

Factors Affecting Ocean Incineration Policy Change

Sabatier notes that "while belief schemas will determine the direction in which an advocacy coalition will seek to move government action programs, its ability to do so will be critically dependent upon its resources. These resources include such things as money, legal authority, expertise, number of supporters, etc." (Sabatier 1985: 21).

While the anti-incineration coalition had few monetary resources, they had great strength in terms of number of supporters and available expertise. On November 21, 1983, EPA's "Office of Water officials were met with the largest audience for a public hearing in the agency's history. A total of 6,474 people turned out to register their almost unanimous protest against the burning of hazardous waste" (Martin 1984: 6). EPA's Jack E. Ravan said following this hearing that the outcry was louder than anything he had seen in a decade, and that: "it may be time for us to redefine what our policy is with regard to the ocean" (Martin 1984: 7). EPA officials had not expected the proposed burn to generate so much public outcry, and they responded to the resulting confrontation and threatened litigation by seeking a basis for accommodation of differences, at least temporarily.

This coalition also had strong resources in terms of available expertise. Supporters included Governor Mark White of Texas, Texas Attorney-General Jim Mattox and his Louisiana counterpart, William J. Guste, as well as New Jersey's Essex County Executive, Peter Shapiro and the New Jersey Public Advocate's Office (Schneider 1984b: 26; Narvaez 1985). Additional expertise was provided by several members of the scientific community who testified about health and environmental hazards of ocean incineration (Martin 1984, Schneider 1984b, Connor 1984). Thus, it appears that the anti-incineration coalition was able to mobilize its resources to achieve at least some concession toward its point of view.

As Sabatier notes, among system-wide factors affecting policy change are the basic attributes of the problem

area, the basic distribution of natural resources,
fundamental cultural values and social structure, basic
constitutional structure, changes in socioeconomic
conditions and technology, changes in the systemic
governing coalition, and policy decision and impacts from
other subsystems (Sabatier 1985: 8-14).

Virtually none of these systemic factors favored a
major policy change by EPA in this area. However, the
basic attributes of the problem area--i.e., that the
oceans are a commonly held resource and not protected by
the marketplace--made this problem area a good candidate
for governmental protection (Kamlet 1981: 10). In sum,
the major factors affecting peripheral policy revision in
this area were strong political resources of the
anti-incineration coalition and the pressure for EPA to
play a role as a policy broker. These factors are,
however, subsystemic. This fact suggests that our major
proposition--that drastic policy change will only occur in
the presence of system-wide influences--again appears to
be validated in this case.

CONCLUSIONS: POLICY CHANGE AND POLICY LEARNING

Officials of local, state and national governments
have been active participants in coalitions on both sides
of the issues raised concerning ocean dumping and at-sea
incineration of hazardous materials. Intergovernmental
relations concerning ocean dumping have been
conflict-ridden since the early 1970s, although this
conflict has abated somewhat since 1981, when the national
government abandoned its confrontational stance in
opposition to continued dumping of sewage sludge.
Intergovernmental relations concerning at-sea incineration
were virtually nonexistent until the early 1980s when they
emerged as conflictual amidst the sudden controversy over
introduction of this technology in the United States. At
the present time, it appears that this conflict may
provide some stimulus for minor policy change, but is
probably not sufficient in itself to produce a core policy
change in the area of at-sea incineration.[5]

As Sabatier notes, "policy change within a subsystem
can be understood as the product of two processes: First,
the efforts of advocacy coalitions within each subsystem
to translate . . . their belief schemas into government
action programs and second, the effects of systemic events
. . . on the resources and constraints of subsystem

actors" (Sabatier 1985: 27). More specifically, he hypothesized that "the core (basic attributes) of a governmental action program is unlikely to be changed in the absence of significant perturbations external to the subsystem" (Sabatier 1985: 27).

Our study of policy change in the area of ocean dumping and at-sea incineration of hazardous wastes would seem to support his central proposition. A fundamental change in ocean dumping policy took place during 1971-81, largely as a result of system-wide influences. On the other hand, the core of EPA's policy for at-sea incineration remains the same (i.e., burning will continue), even though secondary aspects of the policy (i.e., a more stringent regulatory regime) may be changed. A major reason for continuation of the core policy is the lack of strong system-wide influences.

In addition, it appears that EPA experienced some degree of policy-oriented learning in both areas. Specifically, in the area of ocean dumping, the EPA "learned" from the findings of the scientific community that the ocean has a greater absorptive capacity than previously believed. Similarly, in the area of ocean incineration of hazardous waste, EPA "learned" from some members of the scientific and environmental community that ocean incineration may not be as safe as previously believed. As we noted above, in the former case, this learning contributed to a fundamental (core) change in policy, while in the latter case, only changes in secondary (peripheral) policy aspects were achieved.

These findings suggest that drastic policy change in either area is unlikely for the foreseeable future. That is, ocean dumping and at-sea incineration will continue, albeit under a more stringent regulatory regime. Changes may occur at the periphery of these policy areas, but core policy changes are unlikely in the absence of system-wide influences.

NOTES

1. These coalitions are not purely "advocacy coalitions"; rather, they are more akin to a "coalition of convenience," i.e, actors with quite different beliefs who happen to find it to their mutual advantage to join hands for a while. In order to form an advocacy coalition, they have to share a set of core policy beliefs.

2. Larry Jensen replaced Jack Ravan at EPA.

3. At-Sea Incineration, Inc. has taken Chapter 11 (bankruptcy) and its future status is uncertain.

4. There is concern that EPA will delay issuing the regulations and continue to permit "research burns."

5. However, the process of policy change in this area is not over yet; the final effect of the anti-incineration coalition on policy may not be known for some time.

REFERENCES

Bakalian, Allan. 1984. Regulation and control of United
States' ocean dumping: a decade of progress, an
appraisal for the future. Harvard Environmental Law
Review, 8:193-256.

Blumenthal, Ralph. March 2, 1984. Policy to change on
ocean dumping. New York Times, p. A1.

Burks, Edward C. April 6, 1980. Eased dumping opposed.
New York Times, p. A1.

Cannon, E. 1985. The National Ocean Policy 'Octagon':
An Economic and Intergovernmental Perspective. Sea
Technology, 26 (January): 47-57.

Congressional Quarterly. 1984. Ocean dumping bill dies.
Congressional Quarterly Almanac, 60: 3.

Connor, M.S. 1984. At-sea incineration: up in smoke.
Oceanus, 27:70-74.

Curlin, James W. 1980. Ocean policy comes of age: the
end of the beginning or the beginning of the end. Sea
Technology, pp. 23-28.

Federal Register. February 28, 1985. Ocean incineration
regulation. Proposed rule. 50: 8222-8280.

Goldberg, E.D. 1981. The oceans and waste space: the
argument. Oceanus, 24.

Hamilton, Michael S. 1986. Deregulation and federal land
management in the 1980s: inducing atrophy in
bureaucracy. In Phillip O. Foss, ed., Federal Lands
Policy. Westport, CT: Greenwood Press.

Heclo, H.L. 1974. Social Policy in Britain and Sweden.
New Haven: Yale University Press.

Kamlet, K.S. 1981. The oceans as waste space: the
rebuttal. Oceanus, 24: 10-17.

Lahey, William R. 1982. Ocean dumping of sewage sludge:
the tide turns from protection to management. Harvard
Environmental Law Review, 6: 395-431.

Martin, Norman. 1984. Texas burns. Texas Shores, 17: 2-7.

Narvaez, Alfonso A. April 19, 1985. Jerseyans criticize plan to burn wastes at sea. New York Times, p. B2.

National Academy of Sciences. 1978. Multimedium management of municipal sludge. Washington, D.C.: National Academy of Sciences.

National Advisory Committee on Oceans and Atmosphere. 1981. The role of the ocean in a waste management strategy. Washington, D.C.: Government Printing Office.

Piasecki, Bruce. 1985. Voyage of the Vulcanus: toxic incineration at sea. The Amicus Journal, 6: 8-10.

Rangel, Jesus. April 2, 1985. U.S. orders halt to sludge dumping near jersey. New York Times, p. A2.

Reinhold, Robert. June 16, 1985. States oppose burning of toxic wastes in gulf. New York Times, p. A14.

Sabatier, Paul. 1985. An advocacy coalition framework of policy change within subsystems: the effects of exogeneous events, strategic interaction, and policy-oriented learning over time. Prepared for the 1985 Annual Meeting of the Western Political Science Association, March.

Schneider, Keith. 1984a. The leper ships: incinerators sent to sea. Oceans, 17:65-69.

Schneider, Keith. 1984b. Ocean incineration: the public fumes while EPA fiddles. Sierra, 69:23-26.

Shabecoff, Phillip. July 6, 1985a. The guerrilla fighter and the lobbyist. New York Times, p. L5.

_____. February 21, 1985b. Rules proposed for ocean burning of wastes. New York Times, p. A12.

Spirer, Julian H. 1982. The ocean dumping deadline: easing the mandate millstone. Fordham Urban Law Journal, 11:1-49.

Sullivan, Joseph F. April 7, 1985. Sludge is being
    pushed out of sight but not out of mind. New York
    Times, p. A6.

Swanson, R.L. and M. Devine. 1982. Ocean dumping policy:
    the pendulum swings again. Environment, 24: 15-20.

Technology Review. 1984. "Burning wastes at sea," Vol.
    87: 85.

U.S. Congress, House. Committee on Science and
    Technology. 1981a. Environmental effects of sewage
    sludge disposal. 97th Cong., 1st sess. Washington,
    D.C.: Government Printing Office.

U.S. Congress, House. Committee on Merchant Marine and
    Fisheries. 1981b. Ocean's assimilative capacity for
    waste and ocean dumping deadline. 97th Cong., 1st
    sess. Washington, D.C.: Government Printing Office.

U.S. Congress, House. Committee on Merchant Marine and
    Fisheries. 1982. Ocean dumping. 97th Cong., 2d
    sess. Serial No. 97-40. Washington, D.C.: Government
    Printing Office.

U.S. Congress, House. Committee on Merchant Marine and
    Fisheries. 1983a. Ocean dumping. 98th Cong., 1st
    sess. Serial No. 98-14. Washington, D.C.: Government
    Printing Office.

U.S. Congress, House. Committee on Merchant Marine and
    Fisheries. 1983b. Ocean pollution. 98th Cong., 1st
    sess. Serial No. 98-26. Washington, D.C.: Government
    Printing Office.

U.S. Congress, House. Committee on Public Works and
    Transportation. 1983c. Ocean dumping of dredged
    material in the New York bight apex. 98th Cong., 1st
    sess. Serial No. 98-8. Washington, D.C.: Government
    Printing Office.

U.S. Congress, House. Committee on Merchant Marine and
    Fisheries. 1984. Ocean dumping--part 2. 98th Cong.,
    2d sess. Serial No. 98-39. Washington, D.C.:
    Government Printing Office.

U.S. Environmental Protection Agency. 1985.
Incineration at-sea: research strategy, February 19,
1985.

8

Building a Federal-State Partnership for U.S. Ocean Resource Management

Marc J. Hershman

I argue that the agenda of state government in the
U.S. should be broadened to include ocean development and
management initiatives. Over the past fifteen years,
state government has spent much of its time seeking to
wrest power away from federal agencies by gaining a
greater voice in federal decision-making. The prevalent
issue used by the state has been the environmental and
economic impact that will result on state and local
populations and resources due to federal decision-making.
The state role of impact identification makes the state a
supplicant to the federal agencies rather than a partner
in fashioning ocean policy.

We are now at a stage in the development of U.S. ocean
policy where the issues should shift away from impact
identification and toward use alternatives. States,
instead of responding in federal arenas, should become
full participants and equal partners in the fashioning of
ocean uses, even in areas far seaward of their borders.
One objective of this paper is to show why a federal-state
partnership is needed and why the state's role must be
enhanced to make the partnership a reality. The second
objective of this paper is to present suggested elements
of state-level ocean initiatives, and to suggest
governmental mechanisms through which the initiatives may
be launched. The paper concludes with a discussion of how
state-level action can help build national ocean policy.

A Federal-State Partnership Is Needed

Ocean management demands of the future are going to
require the efforts of a wide range of players

221

representing different levels of government and diverse interest groups. Reasons for this can be found in recent developments in international law and in writings by students of U.S. federalism.

International law now permits nation-states to exercise broader responsibilities in the ocean area extending 200 nautical miles from the coastline, in an area known as the Exclusive Economic Zone (EEZ). These broader responsibilities are implied from the fact of establishing a common multi-purpose zone which replaces special zones established for particular resource activities. Broader responsibilities stem also from the notion of "sovereign rights" which the coastal nation exercises over all resources. As Cicin-Sain and Knecht (1985: 307) conclude "it appears that the EEZ notion of sovereign rights brings with it the idea of more responsiblity for the common property resources found in the ocean--an increased role of public or common stewardship."

They argue that the "sovereign rights" notion changes the concept of common property from one of freedom to take, with the risk of resource depletion and economic inefficiency, to a concept of higher societal involvement and responsibility. As they put it, this higher societal responsibility can help take the "tragedy" out of the notion of the commons.

But underlying their analysis is the assumption that the community of interests within the nation state is sufficiently bound together through "common traditions and ties" to achieve this higher societal responsibility. The question which their provocative observation raises is what type of common tradition we rely upon to elevate our management responsibilities in the EEZ. Their paper notes how an increase in use and conflict within a newly settled area over time, as occurred in the expansion of the West in the nineteenth century, eventually leads to an areawide allocation scheme, general purpose local government, planning, and zoning controls.

One of the striking features of nineteenth century western expansion policy was the desire to decentralize control, to create territorially based self-government, and to rely on factionalism and competition as a vehicle for encouraging entrepreneurialism and growth. The central government's initial role was limited to exploration, survey, "resettling" the Indians, and subsidizing the railroads, after which it yielded rapidly to state and local government.

Thus, if the analogy to western expansion is apt, one could conclude that one "common tradition" of our system of government is to yield management authority to state and local interests as their stake in resource issues grows. The structure of Congress encourages this, and as Cicin-Sain and Knecht observe, if ocean use and conflict intensify, one can expect pressures for a more sophisticated management system. A move toward sophistication would require a broader and more responsible role for state and local governments as their interest in marine affairs develops.

Principles of U.S. federalism support the notion that a partnership among federal, state and local interests serves the ideals of our democracy. Robert Hutchins (1961) explains that there are "two faces of federalism." The "liberty face" of our system of federalism protects citizens rights by separating governmental power by level and function. The "achievement face" of federalism allows community objectives to be achieved where individual actions are insufficient or unlikely through combined actions of different levels and functions of government. Thus, the form of partnership we create for ocean governance in our federalist system should reflect ideals of liberty as well as achievement. The current structure of ocean management does a more than ample job of protecting our liberties by fractionalizing power. We have fully embraced the arguments eloquently expressed by Bish (1982), Ball (1982), and Cover (1981) that maximum opportunity for individuals to have access to the decision-making process, even at the expense of redundancy and conflict, is healthiest for our system. As will be developed below, the fragmentation of the current ocean management system and the focus on impact problems emphasizes the liberty goal at the expense of the achievement goal.

The achievement goal of federalism is obtained through the "dialectical logic of federalism" (Stewart 1977). In this construct the advantages of both centralized government and noncentralized government may be realized in a single system. For example, noncentralized government can reflect geographic variations and facilitate experimentation while centralized government can take advantage of economies of scale, regulate spillover effects and determine minimum standards. Tribe (1978) takes this idea a step further by noting that

the federal and state governments will have to depend
upon one another in virtually every significant area
of endeavor, and . . . such mutual dependence must
continue to provide the primary assurance that neither
level of government will achieve a threatening
hegemony over all of our public [i]nstitutionalizing
interdependence rather than functional independence .
. . best summarizes the American idea of protecting
liberty by fragmenting power.

Thus, a positive perspective on federalism, viewing it
as a vital dialectical tool for achieving societal
objectives through institutional interdependence, is the
one that must be embraced to deal with the highly complex
issues of ocean management where viewpoints are diverse
and information needs great.

As is true in many aspects of our governmental
affairs, the U.S. has no set pattern for arranging
federal-state relations. The particular roles vary widely
from issue to issue. Fairfax (1982) observes that we are
in an era of "new opportunism" in U.S. federalism. Rather
than characterizing federal-state relations by analogy to
layer cakes, overlapping circles, marble cakes, or
intergovernmental fiscal relations, as many political
scientists have done, she argues that a realistic and
pragmatic approach would be to observe varying
relationships among governmental actors at different
levels, over time, and within a particular policy arena.
She argues that one is likely to see many centralizing and
decentralizing forces at work, resulting in different
levels, branches and players central at different times
and over different issues. She finds comfort in this new
opportunism because it reflects the increasing
sophistication of state, local, and private actors who
forum-shop to achieve their objectives and thus diversify
centers of government authority.

Fairfax's model is borne out in the ocean governance
arena. The many federal ocean statutes contain a wide
array of techniques for state and local involvement. Even
within one statutory arena, there can be a variety of
roles among levels of government, as in the Coastal Zone
Management Act (CZMA) which gives the states a veto over
federal licenses and permits but reserves considerable
federal influence over estuarine sanctuaries. Many of the
statutes contain a checks and balances system (Secretarial
review in CZMA; National Marine Fisheries Service [NMFS]
review of council fishery management plans) further

varying the locus of power on an issue-by-issue basis.
Even more interesting, states or regions can vary greatly
in the relative influence among levels of government in
the exercise of the same management device. For example,
Massachusetts and Alabama responded quite differently in
the consistency review of Corps of Engineers nationwide
permits. (U.S. Department of Commerce 1985: 27).

  There is an inevitability in this diversity of
management strategies because of the sheer size of the
country, varying patterns of use, and wide-ranging values
of coastal populations. However, as will be shown next,
most ocean statutes favor the federal side and fall short
of the dialectical logic and institutional interdependence
which should characterize our federal system.

The State Role Should Be Enhanced

  It is fair to say that state and local involvement in
federal ocean resource decision-making is
institutionalized. The nature of the involvement varies
substantially, ranging from veto power to a mere advisory
role depending on the terms of the federal statute
(Sinclair 1985).

  However, the current system is deficient in two
important ways. First, the decision-making arena is
highly fragmented both according to government level and
according to function. Orr (1985) listed thirteen major
statutes affecting ocean resources in which coastal states
have an interest. Virtually every statute deals with a
single purpose and has procedural and information
requirements that usually do not match those of the other
statutes. A recent Coastal States Organization (1985)
report notes that advance planning for particularly
important regions of the oceans is virtually impossible,
given the functional split that now exists.

  The second deficiency in the system is a more serious
problem and points to the lack of a true partnership
between federal and state interests. The role of the
state in virtually every federal statute analyzed by Orr
(1985) (with the exception of the CZMA) is to provide the
federal decision-maker with advice about environmental
impacts and other costs associated with federal actions
and to argue for mitigation of those impacts and costs.
Depending on the statute, the size of the state's "stick"
to force federal agency compliance with state requests

will vary. For example, in the case of the Deepwater Port Act, a state can veto a proposed federal action.

To be effective in these federal forums, states should be required to go beyond listing potential impacts and arguing for limits or constraints on offshore activities. This approach is negative, and in a sense irresponsible. It is negative because the law calls primarily for identifying ways one can conceive harm occurring from the action. It puts emphasis on ways to anticipate danger. The approach is irresponsible as well because alternative ways to meet multiple ends need not be identified. Thus the commenting state or local governmental unit does not have to face the difficult problem of balancing many demands on resource use. Impact assessment is important, but it should be balanced with a vision of preferred alternatives arrived at through a comprehensive process of goal-setting.

In a partnership, each partner brings something of value to the relationship, shares in the decision-making, and divides the profits or losses in agreed upon proportions. People enter partnerships in order to meet goals they set for themselves. One of the weaknesses in the ocean management system is that most federal statutes do not invite a partnership through collaboration, and hence there has been no incentive on the part of states to struggle to define goals.

However, states should consider developing strategic plans for ocean areas (discussed below) even in the absence of federal statutes encouraging it. Having an agenda for the ocean area offshore from a state would enhance the stature and persuasiveness of state-level participation in federal arenas. The state's role in federal decision-making in the coastal zone was significantly enhanced through the vehicle of federally approved state CZM plans. The same could occur in offshore areas. In effect, the state gains power because it has a set of goals for itself.

Beyond increased bargaining power with federal agencies, there are other important reasons why states should develop ocean plans.

First, ocean decision-making affects ocean use technologies that have both a land and a sea component, with a transportation linkage in between. To understand one component requires an understanding of how the components link together. Whether one is primarily concerned with the ocean element, the shore element, or the transport element, an effective management system must

consider all three. Thus, states cannot make good
decisions about shore-based components without goals that
recognize the other elements. Good coastal planning
requires, therefore, plans and policies for the offshore
area.

Second, state citizens are the participants in ocean
use both offshore and onshore, as well as the recipients
of benefits and impacts. Thus, interest in the general
welfare of state citizens, and exercise of police power
over them when state interests are at stake, is as much
the basis for involvement in ocean issues as is ownership
of the resource or jurisdiction over particular ocean
space. This welfare interest of the state is enhanced as
leisure pursuits of coastal residents bring them in
greater contact with ocean resources (e.g., whalewatching
and cruise ships). And, the recent surge in offshore
exploration resulting in discovery of new life forms,
polymetallic sulfides and seafloor topography will create
stronger bonds between people and the offshore area.
Politicians at the state and local level will respond as
citizen interest in a nearby resource heightens.

Third, and more fundamentally, there is a pressing
need to improve our nation's competitive posture in the
world economy, and the states can play an important role.
The ocean sector of the national economy is small but it
has potential for new technologies, products, and
industries. States can contribute to initiatives in
fields such as marine biotechnology, aquaculture,
fisheries development, minerals, and others. The nature
of that contribution will vary widely, but each state
could build awareness of these activities and encourage
appropriate public support. State-level Sea Grant
programs could be a base on which to build such efforts.

Throughout the history of the U.S., interregional
competition has been a major factor in economic
development. In the ocean sector as well, one could
expect that the competition for jobs and tax-base would
result in local and state governments coming to the aid of
local marine industries and competing for them. Each
state becomes, in effect, a laboratory for experiments in
ocean-related economic development, and a participant in a
race to see who can excel in achievement. A state-level
ocean plan could indirectly spur ocean technology and
development by creating an encouraging environment, if not
direct subsidy.

Elements of a State-Level Ocean Initiative

The enhanced state involvement in ocean issues should proceed in two phases. First, there should be a program of awareness-building about the geography, environment, resources, and uses in the territorial sea and EEZ adjacent to the state. Second, a strategic plan should be devised that identifies the marine strengths of the state and ways those strengths can be mobilized to achieve ocean-related objectives.

The time is ripe for broadening the ocean constituency through specific awareness-building programs. The EEZ Presidential Proclamation of 1983 established a new zone of comprehensive jurisdiction. The zone is 3.9 billion acres in size and has created a new set of stewardship responsibilities on the part of government.

As the National Advisory Commission on Oceans and Atmosphere (NACOA 1984) advised, one of the first tasks is "getting to know the EEZ." Because of their proximity to our diverse EEZ and their close ties with coastal population centers, state and local governments can play a role in "delivering" information about the ocean to people.

Also, public interest in ocean exploration and discovery is high due to dramatic events such as discovery of deep ocean rifts, recovery of gold from shipwrecks, communication among marine mammals, and use of submarine devices to find the Titanic. These major events can be the "hooker" for moving ocean phenomena to the forefront of people's attention. Through these highly visible events, one can then introduce people to other major ocean phenomena and resources: marine biotechnology, air-sea interaction, submarine volcanism, marine minerals, new life forms, and many others.

It is remarkable how ignorant we are of the sea. It is all around us, of immense strategic, economic, and cultural value, and yet the U.S. has invested very little in civilian ocean research and exploration. Only a very few specialists know what the letters EEZ stand for. It took 73 years before the Titanic was located, yet during that same period remarkable scientific and technological breakthroughs have occurred in such fields as communications, biology, and space. Even with the highly dramatic media events sponsored by Jacques Cousteau or the National Geographic, we are at a primitive stage of public awareness and appreciation.

Ocean phenomena occurring in the EEZ immediately
adjacent to a state's boundary can be the subject of
awareness-building and make the oceans more real to
people. For example, the EEZ is a place, a prolongation
of the continent under the sea, and an extension of the
state. It has submarine features and oceanic currents
with names, functions, and discoverers. It has historical
connections with the land mass through submerged ancient
beaches and shipwrecks. It has contemporary connections
because people are exploring and using the area--people
employed by local agencies, universities, and industries.
It has future connections with coastal residents through
potential resource use and marine conservation. Thus, the
EEZ area off the shores of a state can be described
through films, exhibits, and stories in ways that make
them real for people. A visual image of the place can be
created. This is a key first step to building a
consciousness for careful stewardship and an ocean
constituency that can encourage continued exploration,
discovery, and wise development.

Additionally, and more practically, surveys, data
bases, and atlases of the EEZ and its resources are now
being compiled by the National Oceanic and Atmospheric
Administration (NOAA) and Minerals Management Service
(MMS) which will present new information about the zone
(Ehler and Basta 1984; Rowland and McGregor 1984). With
proper translation and interpretation, an important new
public information tool will be available for use by the
states.

The second phase of a state-level ocean initiative
should be the development of a strategic plan. It is
important that state-level efforts in ocean planning
follow the lines of strategic planning rather than master
planning. Strategic plans emphasize self-evaluation about
human and material resources, and require choice among
alternative courses of action in the environment one
chooses to affect. The plan leads to assignment of
responsibility and a reallocation of resources to achieve
the responsibilities through ongoing management activities
(Dowd 1981). It deals with organizing players to move in
particular directions and then checking their progress.
Master plans, on the other hand, identify resources in the
environment, possible uses and impacts and lead often to
identification of zones for preferred uses, or performance
standards for types of use. The master plan too often
becomes an information document rather than a management
tool, and one that can become quickly outdated as new

information is developed, and one that can become unused
because the manager did not develop the plan.

For ocean-related opportunities and impacts, a state
must carefully select where it wishes to apply its
resources. Some issues may be beyond the state's
capabilities or interests, or be minor compared to other
problems. Some issues may be local in nature and best
left to local government. Choices must be made among
development opportunities, conservation practices and
preservation of resources. Such a plan cannot satisfy
everyone and dynamic political leadership is necessary.
However, choices are necessary if states wish to become
assertive in the ocean arena and not rely on ad hoc
responses to EIS's and federal permit applications.

In essence, a call for state-level strategic plans is
a call to shift the orientation of state government toward
goals and their achievement, and away from a preoccupation
with impact amelioration. It is a call to move forward in
a chosen direction, rather than drifting and reacting.
This concept is normally applied to a business
organization sorting its way through a competitive
environment characterized by rapid change and
uncertainty. But it can apply to the executive branch of
government as well. State governors play a lead role in
state policy and in federal-state relations. They must
allocate limited resources among branches of government
and make choices about goals. A governor, similar to a
CEO, must define goals, identify the range of activities
to pursue, shape the kind of human and economic
organization state government will be, and list the type
of contributions the state will make to the community.

Mechanisms for Launching Ocean Initiatives at the State Level

In carrying out awareness-building and strategic
plans, leadership should come from the state's CZM
office. These entities have many years of relevant
experience that can be applied to offshore issues. They
have become advocates for the marine sector because of
policies favoring water dependent uses, public access to
the coast, protection from natural hazards, and coastal
resource protection. They have a strong base of public
support, since many of them grew out of grass-roots public
movements. Their skills in institution building and
policy development for multiple use problems at the

shoreline can be applied to issues offshore. Being at the state level, they can reflect upon and balance a broader range of interests than local governments and yet be closer to political leaders and public constituencies than a federal agency. In short, all the reasons used to assign lead responsibility to the state level of government for coastal management still apply in the case of ocean management.

One of the key strengths in the CZM governmental structure is that the program developers eventually became the program implementers and managers. Thus, the program development efforts were serious and timely because there were strong incentives to move toward implementation, and the process created a cadre of experts who could learn through the dialectical learning process of policy development and implementation feedback. This has been an important strength of the federal CZM program (Matuszeski 1985) and a noted weakness in other regional resource planning efforts (Ackerman 1974).

The linkage of program development and implementation is one of the major challenges of ocean use management because the implementation powers are split between state and federal agencies, and in many cases split among functional agencies within a level of government. This is similar to the problem CZM program managers faced with respect to federal powers in coastal waters. The Corps of Engineers, Coast Guard, EPA, Interior, NOAA, and others have overriding responsibilities in coastal waters because of preemptive federal statutes. CZM programs were developed within this arena with surprising success. States experimented with various forms of cooperative planning, joint procedures, and consistency negotiations. Federal agencies were grateful, in many cases, to have specific policy guidance from authoritative agencies at the state and local level, and respected this local expression of the public interest. Although bumpy at times, a journey toward federal-state collaboration is underway in territorial and internal waters via the CZMA program mechanism.

In ocean areas beyond three miles, federal agencies claim more exclusive authority and in some cases have resisted working collaboratively with the states. In reality, as Ball (1982) has clearly shown, there is a wide range of local, regional, and national interests built into ocean management decisions regardless of the locus of the activity with respect to offshore boundaries. One can expect, therefore, that pressures for a better federal-

state collaborative process will continue to evolve so
long as coastal populations and governments are concerned
with offshore activities. This pressure is especially
strong at present in the arena of outer continental shelf
oil and gas development.

The specific agenda for awareness-building and
strategic ocean plans will vary greatly state to state.
Some possibilities for program development are worth
noting, however. Awareness-building could be linked
closely to the urban waterfront revitalization movement
occurring in virtually every major urban harbor in the
U.S. Literally tens of millions of people come to the
waterfronts for an urban recreation experience. Proximity
to the water and harbor shipping activities is a major
draw and many of these areas include historical, cultural,
and educational facilities such as aquariums and restored
vessels. A unique opportunity is available to describe
the EEZ and ocean use potential as an integral part of
urban waterfronts—a description of what lies beyond the
harbor quay, how the port city is linked to it, the
activities underway or planned, and the need for
stewardship. Since a goal of CZM programs is to support
revitalization, an ocean awareness dimension could be
linked to this program element.

Some initial ocean planning activity by coastal states
is underway, though the scope of these efforts is
limited. The California Coastal Commission (1983)
launched an Ocean Studies Symposium to determine state
action in ocean development and to ensure a role for the
Coastal Commission in marine affairs. No concerted effort
followed the symposium because of a change in executive
leadership resulting in an anti-Coastal Commission
policy. Oregon participates with the MMS in a task force
to gather data concerning sea floor resource potential and
environmental issues. The scope of issues is limited and
does not address a broader need in Oregon—the elaboration
of its marine resources goal in its statewide planning
statute. Washington State is in the early stages of
assessing the status of state policy for the ocean area
and to identify information needs for policy development.

North Carolina has taken specific steps toward ocean
policy development (North Carolina Marine Science Council
1984). A special ocean policy committee of the state's
Marine Science Council evaluated sixteen ocean policy
issues affecting North Carolina's interests. The study
was limited to management issues and excluded the broader
questions of economic development and the problems of

marine research, education or training. The reason given
for the study reflects the frustration of the state with
inaction at the national level:

> In light of the current potential hiatus in
> Congressional activity with respect to a much needed
> update of the nation's ocean policy, we believe it
> behooves the states to pursue their own independent
> analyses of their individual and collective policy
> relationship to ocean and coastal issues, not only for
> their own benefit but also to prepare their
> contributions for future federal-state dialogues.

In March of 1985, North Carolina Governor Jim Martin
directed the appropriate state agencies to begin work on
the nine recommendations presented in the report.
    It is interesting to note that the study was not done
by the state's CZM office, nor are the recommendations
addressed to that office alone. The North Carolina Marine
Science Council is a survivor of the late 1960s era when
many states established marine-related commissions.
Although advisory in nature, these commissions were to
address a wide range of ocean interests of importance to
the states and recommend specific action. The commissions
set up in California, Oregon, and Washington
(respectively, the California Advisory Commission on
Marine and Coastal Resources, the Oregon Coastal
Conservation and Development Commission, and the
Oceanographic Commission of Washington) issued numerous
reports but in each case the coastal environmental issues
dominated. Eventually, when each state established
specific coastal management agencies, the role of the
marine commissions became less clear and they were
eliminated from state government apparatus.
    My preference is to build ocean use policy and
management at the state level upon an established
comprehensive marine program such as CZM. The
fragmentation at the federal level should not be repeated
at the state level. However, a closer study of the marine
advisory commission "movement" of 10 or 15 years ago may
inform discussions about state organization for marine
affairs. What were they set up to accomplish? What kind
of state action did they propose? Did they raise public
awareness, achieve interagency coordination, or recommend
policy alternatives? What did they accomplish? Why were
they abandoned?

Eventually, the CZMA should provide incentives for state-level ocean plans. The mechanism proposed recently in H.R. 2497 (99th Congress) for encouraging special area management plans for estuaries of national significance could be used for ocean plans. Governors nominate areas for special planning. A selection is made by the Secretary of Commerce, based on criteria relating to the importance of the area, the severity of the problems and the likelihood that better planning would solve resource problems. A management conference is convened composed of public officials and private interests which undertakes research, prepares a comprehensive plan, and coordinates implementation. Implementation occurs through existing federal resource management laws, including the CZMA. The Congress would appropriate funds to pay 75% of the costs for a selected number of planning efforts.

Although more study is needed before a specific mechanism is proposed, the approach of H.R. 2497 has positive features that would aid ocean initiatives by states. A selection is made of a critical problem area, thus limiting the number of efforts and the overall costs, and setting a pace appropriate to the pace of ocean development. Initiative comes from the state, but federal, state, and local interests are involved. The parties can adopt a process that is appropriate to the set of problems and interests of a particular area. Finally, existing laws are used for implementation. This highly flexible approach at special area management planning has had success in the coastal zone management arena (Hershman 1983). It may be fruitful, in addition, to expand the federal consistency requirements of the CZMA for ocean areas where plans have been approved. This would provide an incentive for state initiation of planning efforts and an additional implementation device. Since the U.S. Supreme Court has limited the scope of federal consistency in at least one issue area, an appropriate task for Congress may be to expand federal consistency selectively in areas where ocean management plans have been prepared, signed, and approved.

Using State Initiatives to Help Build National Ocean Policy

Given a coastal and marine environment as diverse and far reaching as that of the U.S., the job of policy development for the oceans will be enormously challenging. It makes sense to use decentralized centers

of effort to help tackle part of this job. As explained
above, state governments have already invested in
developing coastal plans and they have a vital stake in
resource development activities off their shores.
Further, states are closest to population centers where
public preferences about use and management are reflected.

In a recent paper, Cannon (1985) makes an eloquent
plea for the development of a more integrated U.S. ocean
policy. He notes that the current system is made up of
policies within functional areas, and that the long-range
ocean planning groups, such as NACOA and the Office of
Science and Technology Policy (OSTP) lack a framework for
reaching consensus on goals. He proposes a logical
progression for such a framework starting with a
specification of economic and defense uses and ending with
a clarification of research needs. Further, he calls for
broad-based participation in policy development by the
major participants in the intergovernmental ocean policy
arena. The eight major participant groups are described
in an "octagon model." One of the eight groups is titled
"state-local" and the list of example members includes
associations tending to have representatives at the state
or local level (e.g., the National Governors Conference
and the American Association of Port Authorities).

His model, in my view, gives inadequate attention to
state and local government interests. He lists them as
equal in stature with such groups as the media, academic
groups, and the judiciary when in fact they can be far
more important. Besides being potent politically and
destined to have much say in ocean policy because of
Congressional influence, state and local arenas can
organize a wide array of input to ocean policy-making.
Established networks of people at the state and regional
levels already work on particular policy problems in
fisheries, marine minerals, etc.

It may be useful to conceive of an ocean policy
development process that starts at a regional or state
level where the national and international interests of
federal agencies are meshed with the more immediate
resource development and conservation problems of concern
to state and local agencies. Such a process might have
mutual educational benefit. Those who have seen ocean
policy as primarily an exercise involving international
relations can be exposed to the issues of importance to
local communities. Conversely, local interests, normally
unconcerned with international ramifications, could learn

of the need for consistency of U.S. action with the LOS
treaty provisions (Belsky 1985).

More importantly, regional approaches to ocean policy
development may be more appropriate at the early stage of
the development of national policy. Many forums produce
social laboratories some of which will be risk-avoiders
and some risk-takers. If there is good communication
among them, both the risk-takers and risk-avoiders
benefit. The risk-taker may risk failure without
disturbing the overall federal stability. The
risk-avoider may wait and benefit from the trial and error
experience of the pioneers. Thus "innovation is more
likely to be tried and correspondingly less likely to be
wholly embraced" (Cover 1981).

It is likely that a decentralized approach to ocean
policy development makes more sense than a centrally
developed one in a country as diverse as the U.S. For the
past ten years the Dutch have been striving to harmonize
all their policies affecting the North Sea (van Hoorn et
al. 1985). It has been a top-down approach including
agency preparatory reports and a major Parliamentary
report, followed by extensive review and reactions from a
wide array of interests. According to van Hoorn and his
co-authors, the results have been modest and the report
met with considerable criticism within the country. They
conclude, however, that "the very existence of the process
of harmonization will prove to be productive for future
developments in North Sea policies." It appears that the
Dutch barely succeeded in making progress and yet they
have only one ocean to deal with, a long and established
set of international relations, a unified parliamentary
system of government, and a long tradition of active
governmental planning and management of physical
resources. U.S. policy-makers might reflect on the Dutch
experience and divide the task of policy development and
harmonization into manageable state-level or regional
segments.

International lawyers have already anticipated the
suggestion that U.S. EEZ policy be developed regionally,
and have responded vigorously. Belsky (1985) argues
against U.S. unilateral action in the EEZ and urges a
"wait and see" attitude accompanied by quiet international
negotiations. He wants to insure that U.S. action
conforms to the Law of the Sea Convention provisions on
the EEZ, thus preserving the Convention rather than
unilateral state action as the basis of international
law. He is specially concerned that regional action be

avoided as it may set a precedent for a "zoning" system
where rights of navigation may vary among regions. But,
it is not reasonable to assume that the EEZ will be
managed uniformly for a nation such as the U.S., whose
shores touch many oceans. Given regional fisheries
management and special navigational rules affecting oil
tankers (e.g., Puget Sound tanker size limitation), great
variation is already occurring. Perhaps minimum national
standards can be determined, but regional variation is
necessary given different physical and resource
characteristics, intensity of activity, sociocultural
values, and historic practices. "Zoning" is inevitable,
in a sense, as soon as you permit a use in one place but
disallow it in another.

Oxman (1984) offers an alternative that is more
attractive than Belsky's "wait and see" suggestion. He
urges that the U.S. accept compulsory dispute settlement
for issues of navigational freedom and pollution
protection in the EEZ. This alternative would allow the
U.S. to act to protect resources and better manage the
EEZ, subject to the review of a neutral international
panel, should that action be challenged by another nation.

It is time to integrate fully the state level of
government into the debate about future U.S. ocean
policy. Resources and their use, even more than defense,
are the driving force behind national ocean policy.
Because of the special regard coastal populations now give
marine resources, whether that regard be based on
esthetic, economic, ecological, technological, or
scientific values, it is essential that government
representatives close to those populations be partners in
determining future directions.

Acknowledgments

Partial support for the preparation of this paper came
from the Washington Sea Grant Program under Grant No.
NA84AA-D- 00011 from NOAA, U.S. Department of Commerce.
The author thanks Miranda Wecker for valuable research
assistance.

238

REFERENCES

Ackerman, B. et al. 1974. The Uncertain Search for Environmental Quality. Free Press.

Ball, M. 1982. Good Old American Permits: Madisonian Federalism on the Territorial Sea and Continental Shelf. Environmental Law, 12:623-628.

Belsky, M. 1985. A Strategy to Avoid Conflicts. Oceanus, 27 (4): 19-22.

Bish, R. 1982. Governing Puget Sound. Washington Sea Grant, Puget Sound Books.

California Coastal Commission. 1983. Ocean Studies Symposium: Proceedings of a Conference held November 7-10, 1982. State of California.

Cannon, E. 1985. The National Ocean Policy 'Octagon': An Economic and Intergovernmental Perspective. Sea Technology, 26 (January): 47-57.

Cicin-Sain, B. and R. Knecht. 1985. The Problem of Governance of U.S. Ocean Resources and the New Exclusive Economic Zone. Ocean Development and International Law, 15 (3/4): 289-320.

Coastal States Organization. 1985. Coastal States and the U.S. Exclusive Economic Zone (Draft Report). June.

Cover, R. 1981. The Uses of Jurisdictional Redundancy: Interest, Ideology, and Innovation. William and Mary Law Review, 22:639-682.

Dowd, 1. 1981. Strategic Management: A Tool for Port Planning. Masters thesis, Univ. of Washington, Institute for Marine Studies.

Ehler, C. and D. Basta. 1984. Strategic Assessment of Multiple-Resource-Use Management in the Exclusive Economic Zone. Exclusive Economic Zone Papers. Marine Technology Society, pp. 1-6.

Fairfax, S. 1982. Old Recipes for New Federalism. Environmental Law, 12:945-980.

Hershman, M. 1983. U.S. Ocean Policy Starts in the Coastal Zone. Paper presented at Coastal Zone '83. Univ. of Washington, Institute for Marine Studies.

Hutchins, R. 1961. Two Faces of Federalism: An Outline of an Argument about Pluralism, Unity and Law. Santa Barbara, CA: Center for the Study of Democratic Institutions.

Matuszeski, W. 1985. Managing the Federal Coastal Program: The Planning Years. Journal of American Planning Association, 51 (3): 266-274.

National Advisory Commission on Oceans and Atmosphere (NACOA). 1984. The Exclusive Economic Zone of the United States: Some Immediate Policy Issues. Washington, D.C.: NACOA.

North Carolina Marine Science Council. 1984. North Carolina and the Sea: An Ocean Policy Analysis. Report of the Ocean Policy Committee.

Orr, W. 1985. The Existing Statutory Roles for Coastal States in Federal Ocean Management Decisions: Identification and Preliminary Evaluation. Unpublished paper, U. of Oregon School of Law.

Oxman, B. 1984. The Balance of the Exclusive Economic Zone: Navigation, Pollution, and Compulsory Dispute Settlement. Exclusive Economic Zone Papers. Marine Technology Society, pp. 116-121.

Rowland, R. and B. McGregor. 1984. Recommendations from the Department of the Interior EEZ Symposium. Exclusive Economic Zone Papers. Marine Technology Society, pp. 50-55.

Sinclair, J. 1985. Characterization of State-Federal Relationships in Existing Federal Maritime Legislation. Unpublished paper, Univ. of Washington, Institute for Marine Studies.

Stewart, R. 1977. Pyramids of Sacrifice? Problems of Federalism in Mandating State Implementation of National Environmental Policy. Yale Law Journal, 86:1196-1272.

240

Tribe, L. 1978. <u>American Constitutional Law</u>, 17. Quoted in M. Ball, <u>Law of the Sea: Federal-State Relations</u>, Univ. of Georgia, Dean Rusk Center, Monograph No. 1: 69).

U.S. Department of Commerce. 1985. Federal Consistency Study - Draft: Executive Summary.

van Hoorn, H. et al. 1985. Harmonizing North Sea Policy in the Netherlands. <u>Marine Policy</u>, 9:53-61.

9

Ocean Resources and Intergovernmental Relations: An Analysis of the Patterns

Biliana Cicin-Sain

This chapter compares state/federal relations in four of the marine policy subsectors which have been discussed elsewhere in this volume: coastal zone management, fisheries management, marine mammal and endangered species protection, and offshore oil development. My observations are based on a longitudinal study, over a ten to fifteen year period, of the Congressional enactment and implementation of the five major ocean laws that provide the governing framework for these policy subsectors: the Coastal Zone Management Act of 1972 (CZMA), the Marine Mammal Protection Act of 1972 (MMPA), the Endangered Species Act of 1973 (ESA), the Magnuson Fishery Conservation and Management Act of 1976 (MFCMA), and the Outer Continental Shelf Lands Act Amendments of 1978 (OCSLAA) (Cicin-Sain and Knecht, in preparation). My comments on implementation are based primarily on observing how these laws are being implemented and are interacting with one another in the context of the Pacific coast, with particular reference to California. Although based on the California experience, the patterns of federalism described in this chapter also echo a number of the hypotheses and conclusions reached about other regions by the authors in this volume.

AN EXPANDED FEDERAL ROLE IN THE 1970s

In a burst of legislative activity vis-a-vis the oceans in the 1970s, Congress moved to establish a strong governmental presence in ocean resources management, often stepping on the toes of the coastal states in the process. A number of the ocean laws enacted by Congress

in the 197Cs represented significant increases in the
scope of government activity—either by expanding existing
governmental roles or by creating essentially new
functions (Cicin-Sain 1982). The Magnuson Act, for
example, created an entire new zone to be managed under
U.S. control—the fishery conservation zone (FCZ),
composing an area of over two million square nautical
miles within which are found 15 to 20 percent of the
world's traditionally harvested marine fishery resources
(U.S. Department of Commerce 1978). Fisheries found in
this area had previously been unmanaged or only partially
managed by the states and by international organizations.
The Coastal Zone Management Act, in effect, added a new
function which had not been performed previously:
planning for coastal areas through federal assistance to
the states. The Endangered Species Act enlarged the scope
of governmental activity in the protection of endangered
species by proclaiming the government's affirmative duty
not only to protect these species, but to restore
endangered species and their habitats to a healthy
condition. In response to energy shortages in the early
seventies, the Outer Continental Shelf Lands Act
Amendments called for more aggressive management of U.S.
outer continental shelf (OCS) resources through a more
elaborate system of planning, increased industry
competition, and tightened environmental controls.

The increased scope of governmental activity brought
about by these Acts involved primarily an enhancement of
the federal role, and a steady centralization at the
national level, although most of these acts also contained
provisions delineating explicit roles for the states. The
Magnuson Act established a new regional management
structure, under federal control, to manage the 200-mile
fishery zone. The Endangered Species Act and the Marine
Mammal Protection Act (the latter in particular) wrested
control away from the states and established federal
supremacy in the protection of marine mammals and
endangered species, engendering intensive
intergovernmental conflict in the process. Although
oriented toward the states, the Coastal Zone Management
Act nevertheless established a strong national presence in
the coastal zone by offering tangible incentives to the
states to implement coastal zone planning goals
established at the federal level. While the OCSLAA
strengthened the role of the states in the oil and gas
leasing process, the basic thrust of these amendments was
to reaffirm and more carefully define the federal

supremacy over OCS resources previously established by the
Outer Continental Shelf Lands Act of 1953.

It is interesting to note that while Congress was
strengthening the federal role in the oceans through these
acts, in other domestic policy areas an opposite trend was
taking place, i.e., devolution of authority to state and
local levels of government. The period that coincides
with the passage of most of these marine acts corresponds
to the period of Nixon's "New Federalism", marked by a
significant reduction of the strong federal presence in
the nation's cities established by the Great Society
programs of the 1960s (Reagan and Sanzone 1981).

DIVERGENT PATTERNS OF STATE/FEDERAL RELATIONS: FROM
COOPERATIVE TO ADVERSARY MODES OF FEDERALISM

When one considers the patterns of state/federal
relations that have evolved since the establishment of
these acts in the early 1970s, one is struck by the fact
that the patterns are very diverse and do not conform to
the notion popularized in the literature on
intergovernmental relations that there is a "dominant"
model of federalism which tends to characterize a
particular time period. In his widely acclaimed book on
intergovernmental relations, for example, Wright (1982)
posits that each different time period contains political
issues, participants' perceptions, and intergovernmental
relations mechanisms which set it apart from the preceding
and following phases. Six major distinctive periods of
phases of intergovernmental relations are identified by
Wright: "Conflictive" in the 1930s and before,
"cooperative" between the 1930s and 1950s,
"concentrated"--1940s to 1960s, "competitive"--1960s to
1970s, and "calculative" in the 1970s and 1980s.

No "dominant" model of federalism can be said to
characterize intergovernmental relations in the marine
policy area. Instead, very different patterns of
state/federal relations prevail in each of the marine
policy subsectors with which we are concerned: coastal
zone management, fisheries management, marine mammal and
endangered species protection, and offshore oil
development.

Figure 1 depicts state/federal relations in each of
these subsectors by mapping the relationship between the
major state and federal agencies that are involved in the
implementation of these acts in California, according to

whether they are predominantly: 1) <u>cooperative</u>, defined
as generally good and amicable relations between the
agencies; 2) <u>conflictive</u>, whereby agencies often take
different positions on issues; 3) or <u>adversary</u>, denoting a
highly conflictual relation, often involving litigation.

"Cooperative federalism" relations can be said to
prevail in the fishery management area--the relationship
between the major federal agency [the National Marine
Fisheries Service (NMFS)] and the state and regional level
agencies (the regional fishery management council and the
California Department of Fish and Game) have generally
been amicable and cooperative, particularly in the
drafting of fishery management plans and in joint research
efforts. Although the Magnuson Act allowed for federal
preemption of state fishery activities in the territorial
sea (the area of state jurisdiction), this authority has
only been used twice in the ten years since the inception
of the act (Rieser 1986).

The case of coastal zone management, in general, also
represents a case of "cooperative federalism." The
relations between the federal Office of Coastal Zone
Management [an arm of the National Oceanic and Atmospheric
Administration (NOAA)] with the relevant state agencies
(the California Coastal Commission and the governor's
office) have generally been quite good--both in terms of
the administration of the planning and implementation
grants authorized under the CZMA as well as the exercise
of the CZMA's "consistency" provision (which gives states
leverage over federal activities within or affecting the
coastal zone by requiring that certain federal actions be
conducted in a manner which is consistent with the
provisions of state coastal zone management plans approved
by the Department of Commerce). More recently, however,
under the more pro-development stance of the Deukmejian
administration in California, the federal OCZM has
occasionally clashed with the governor's office, although
not with the state coastal commission.

"Conflictive federalism" has characterized
state/federal relations in the management of marine
mammals and endangered species, following the preemption
of state management authority over these species
accomplished by the ESA and the MMPA (the latter in
particular) (Cicin-Sain, Grifman and Richards 1982).
While both California and Alaska have attempted to regain
control over these species, neither effort has, to date,
been successful.

Figure 1

State/Federal Relations Within Marine Subsectors

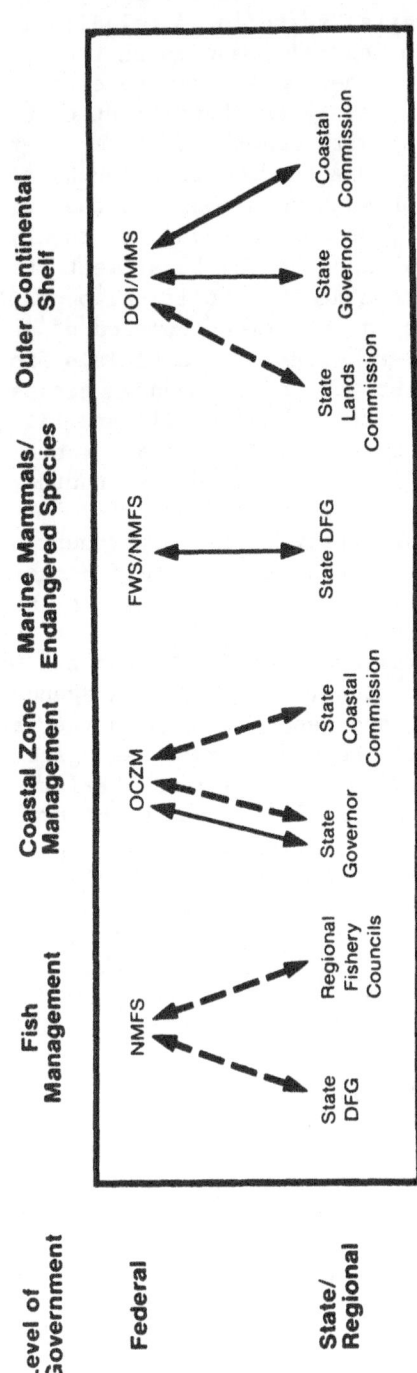

Marine Subsectors

Level of Government	Fish Management	Coastal Zone Management	Marine Mammals/ Endangered Species	Outer Continental Shelf
Federal	NMFS	OCZM	FWS/NMFS	DOI/MMS
State/ Regional	Regional Fishery Councils / State DFG	State Governor / State Coastal Commission	State DFG	State Governor / Coastal Commission / State Lands Commission

Key:

- ⇠ ⇢ Cooperative
- ↑ Conflictive
- ↕ Adversary

Abbreviations:

NMFS = National Marine Fisheries Service
State DFG = State Department of Fish and Game
OCZM = Office of Coastal Zone Management
FWS = Fish and Wildlife Service
DOI = Department of Interior
MMS = Minerals Management Service

"Adversary federalism" relations have, in general, characterized federal/state/local relations, as well as relations between federal agencies in the offshore energy development area. The accelerated development of offshore hydrocarbon resources by the Department of the Interior (DOI) has been met with opposition from other federal agencies (such as NOAA and the Fish and Wildlife Service) through the use of such mechanisms as the "consistency" provision of the CZMA and Section 7 of the ESA.[1] In California, the actions of the Department of the Interior have been met with concerted political opposition and legal challenge by a coalition composed of state government agencies, government officials from local coastal communities, and environmental groups (Kaplan 1982; Cicin-Sain 1986). The hostile and litigious nature of these relations (Bruce 1985) is so pronounced that it is difficult to find ready analogues in other policy arenas.

The relationship between the Department of the Interior--and its bureau, the Minerals Management Service--at the federal level and agencies at the state level, however, is not uniformly poor. As is suggested in Figure 1, the relations between DOI and the California State Lands Commission (the California agency charged with management of oil and gas resources in the territorial sea) have generally been good as these agencies share common pro-development orientations. Relations between DOI and the governor's office, on the other hand, have been depicted as conflictive as the governor's office has often opposed the leasing and development of California OCS lands, with more concerted and vocal opposition taking place during the Jerry Brown regime, however, than under the Deukmejian administration. The relationship between DOI and the California Coastal Commission has been adversarial, marked by periodic bouts of litigation, with the Supreme Court case of <u>California v. Watt</u> as a prime example (Knecht 1984).

EXPLAINING INTERGOVERNMENTAL RELATIONS OUTCOMES

To what are such diverse patterns due? In my view, we can begin to understand how and why different patterns prevail in different policy subsectors by using variables drawn, in part, from the literature on policy implementation success, particularly work by Sabatier and Mazmanian (1981) and Van Meter and Van Horn (1976). Table

1 compares the different policy subsectors on a variety of
variables thought to be important in implementation.
These variables include:

1) <u>Nature of the resources at stake</u>: Here we are
concerned with two aspects: a) The worth of the
resources--how valuable are they? Given the high
value of oil and gas resources, for example, there
will probably always be some level of conflict
associated with their extraction. b) Following
Sabatier and Maxmanian's discussion of tractability of
issues as an important vehicle in determining policy
implementation success, here we are concerned with the
tractability of managing the resources at stake, i.e.,
is the resource/issue area tractable? Or, is it, as
in the case of many fishery resources, inherently
difficult to deal with because of the mobility and
transboundary nature of the resources?

2) <u>History of state/federal relations in the area</u>:
Is there a history of good relations, conflictual
relations, or is there little history of state/federal
interactions?

3) <u>Structure of the Legislation</u>: a) How well
structured is the statute? Are its aims specifically
stated, is the mandate clear and unidirectional or
does it contain multiple and possibly inconsistent
aims? how much discretion does the statute leave to
the implementation process? b) To what extent, if
any, does the statute incorporate the interests of the
other levels of government? If it does, how are these
interests incorporated?

4) <u>Disposition of the implementors</u>: What is the
dispostion of the federal agency implementors toward
the other level of government? To what extent, if
any, are they knowledgeable about and concerned with
the interests of the other level?

5) <u>Nature of the state and federal bureaucracies</u>: To
what extent are the state and federal bureaucracies
similar? Do the agency personnel at each level share
similar training and professional backgrounds? How
much interaction, if any, is there between agency
personnel at both levels? What is the nature of this
interaction?

6) <u>Interest group support</u>: With which level are the
interest groups that participated in the passage of
the statute more involved? With the state or the
federal level? Do informal alliances exist between

TABLE 1

Variables Affecting the Patterns of State/Federal Relations in Marine Subsectors

Marine Subsectors	Nature of Resources a) Worth b) Tractability	History of State/Federal Relations	Structure of Legislation	a) Extent to Which Legislation Incorporates Interests of Other Level b) Through What Means	Disposition of/Action by Implementers
Fish	a) MEDIUM b) Difficult/ Often transboundary	Previous State Control or No Control	- SPECIFIC - Well Structured - Single Purpose	a) GOOD b) State representation on regional councils	- Sensitive to state concerns
Coastal Zone	a) HIGH b) Difficult/ Fragile nature of coastal zone	- Little history/A vacuum - New program	- BROAD/LOOSELY STRUCTURED - incorporating multiple mandates	a) GOOD b) Grants as incentives/ Consistency	- State oriented
Marine Mammals/ Endangered Species	a) INTANGIBLE Difficult to estimate b) Little scientific knowledge	- Previous State Control	- VERY SPECIFIC - Single-purpose	a) POOR b) return of management to states allowed, but has not taken place - cooperation grants do exist, but little state level role	- Mixed old timers pro-state ("hook & bullet" boys) vs. new "environmental mafia"
Outer Continental Shelf	a) VERY HIGH b) Easy/Stationary resources, but high perceived risks	- Traditionally Conflictive - "Dual geographical federalism"	- Incorporated new environmental and intergovernmental reviews	a) FAIR better than before 1978, but still perceived to be inadequate by the states b) state role under OCSLAA consultative only/state role under CZMA consistency unclear	- Antagonistic to states

TABLE 1 Continued

Variables

Marine Subsectors	Nature of the Bureaucracies — Similar or Different?	Interest Groups Supporting the Major Federal Legislation	Patterns of State/Federal Relations
Fish	- Similar and often intertwined - Federal agency often recruits from state ranks	- More pro-state than federal	GENERALLY COOPERATIVE
Coastal Zone	- Similar, as federal CZM in most cases, negotiated with states as to which part of the state government would receive the CZM function	- State oriented - Environmental	GENERALLY COOPERATIVE
Marine Mammals/ Endangered Species	- Very different	- Very pro-federal - Environmental	GENERALLY CONFLICTIVE
Outer Continental Shelf	- MMS and state oil agencies—similar - MMS and other state agencies (coastal commission, Governor's office)—very different	- Pro-state - Environmental	GENERALLY ADVERSARY

the interest groups and either level of government?

Applying these variables to the four policy subsectors in question, we begin the analysis by contrasting the intergovernmental implementation experience in fisheries management and marine mammal management. Although in both of these cases, there was a considerable centralization of authority at the national level in the 1970s, the pattern of state/federal relations has turned out quite differently in these two sectors: generally cooperative in the case of fishery management, generally conflictive in the case of marine mammal management. These differences can be attributed primarily to how the major legislation in each case was structured and implemented, because in terms of the first two variables discussed above—nature of the resources and history—these policy subsectors are quite similar. In both cases, the resources at stake are difficult to deal with—they are often transboundary, and scientific knowledge about their behavior and life cycles is scant. In both cases, too, there was a history of previous strong management control by the states.

In the case of fishery management, however, the interests of the states were incorporated in the provisions of the statute in a number of ways—the states are specifically represented on the regional fishery management councils created under the Magnuson Act and the state bureaucracies play an important role in the formulation and implementation of fishery management plans. At the same time, however, the statute did contain a provision [306(b)(1)] that called for the preemption of state fishery actions if the fishing in a fishery covered by a fishery management plan is "engaged in predominantly within the fishery conservation zone and beyond that zone," and if a state has taken or omitted to take such action, "the results of which will substantially and adversely affect the carrying out of such fishery management plan."

In terms of the disposition of the implementors, the federal bureaucracy, the National Marine Fisheries Service, has traditionally been very sensitive to the interests of state fisheries agencies; it holds periodic meetings to canvass the concerns and opinions of state fishery directors and it consults state policymakers on important fishery policy matters. Moreover, the state and federal bureaucracies tend to be quite similar. The same types of professionals—most prominently, fishery

biologists--populate the agencies at both levels of
government. These are individuals who, because of a
common experience and professional background, understand
one another and speak the same language. In fact,
bureaucrats in the federal agency are often recruited from
among the ranks of state agency personnel.

The interest groups that supported the legislation
(such as, for example, the New England fishermen)
originally had a local or regional power base and were
accustomed to relating to the state fishery agencies.
While the passage of the Magnuson Act served as a catalyst
in promoting the national organization of fishermen and
the creation of national lobby groups such as the National
Federation of Fishermen, the national-level organizational
effort has been rather weak. It is still at the regional
or local level that fishermen's organizations remain most
effective.

The implementation process briefly described above has
resulted in a generally cooperative and amicable pattern
of state/federal relations in fishery management. This
case points to the importance of the characteristics,
disposition, and actions by the implementors in
determining state/federal relations outcomes, because in
this case the statute itself could have been interpreted
and implemented emphasizing a positive approach to state
relations (as it was) or alternatively, emphasizing more
negative interactions with the states through the
application of the 306(b)(1) clause.

In contrast, in the case of marine mammal management,
the statute itself was pro-federal and anti-state--it
wrested control away from the states and established
federal supremacy. Representatives of the states were
thus not surprisingly very opposed to the legislation,
particularly states such as California and Alaska which
had had long (and successful, they thought) experience in
managing marine mammals (Cicin-Sain and Knecht, in
preparation, Ch. 3). Although the statute allowed for the
possibility of returning management authority to the
states and two states (California and Alaska) have made
the requisite applications to regain control, for a
variety of reasons neither one of these petitions has been
successful.

Added to a rather pro-federal oriented statute,
several other factors related to the characteristics of
the implementing agencies and to the manner in which the
statute was implemented, have combined to produce a rather
conflictive pattern of state/federal interactions.

The state and federal bureaucracies that are charged with the management of marine mammals (e.g., the U.S. Fish and Wildlife Service at the federal level and the California Department of Fish and Game at the state level, in the case of California), have become quite different in terms of personnel, agency outlook, and agency constituents. The state departments of fish and game, in general, tend to have a "management" versus a "preservationst" perspective on wildlife resources; that is, they believe that these resources ought to be protected and used for a variety of purposes. This multiple-use orientation is reflected in the wide variety of interest groups with which these agencies typically relate—commercial fishermen, recreational interests, environmental groups.

In the past, federal wildlife agencies such as the Fish and Wildlife Service (FWS) were not substantially different from state fish and game agencies; traditionally, their personnel—the so-called "hook and bullet boys"—were very oriented toward the management of wildlife resources for use purposes. In the 1970s, however, a new breed of young managers, educated in the more environmentally conscious programs of that era, came to positions of authority in the FWS and brought with them novel management approaches stressing the multiple aesthetic, ethical, and ecological values associated with wildlife resources—a view that spurned the use orientation still prevalent among the state agencies. This "environmental mafia" had very close relations with the preservationist interest groups that were responsible for the passage of the MMPA and ESA (Manning 1986). Informal alliances between these sympathetic bureaucrats and the external groups, some think, have served to keep the implementation of the two protective acts faithful to the original legislative intent.

The preservationist interest groups which were responsible for the enactment of the ESA and MMPA and for monitoring the implemenation of these acts—groups such as Friends of the Earth, Defenders of Wildlife, Society for Animal Protective Legislation, Committee for Humane Legislation, Environmental Defense Fund, Friends of the Sea Otter—saw the federal government as the protector of ecological interests and, conversely, the states as the bulwark of the sports and hunting interests. Thus, for example, groups such as the Friends of the Sea Otter in California, in informal alliance with the Fish and Wildlife Service, strenuously fought the California petition to regain management authority over marine mammals (Cicin-Sain et al 1982).

In the case of marine mammal management, then, a federal-oriented statute, added to state and federal implementing agencies with divergent outlooks and orientations, and interest groups clearly supportive of federal control, have conspired to produce a pattern of conflictive state/federal interactions.

With regard to coastal zone management, the resources at stake in this area are of high value and their management is generally difficult. The shoreline represents a fragile and ever-changing area, particularly subject to the destructive forces nature may unleash (such as hurricanes) and to the destructive forces of man who, in his zeal to develop desirable coastal real estate, has often caused irrevocable damage to coastal ecosystems such as wetlands. Notwithstanding the high value of coastal resources, however, prior to the enactment of the Coastal Zone Management Act in 1972, there had been little history of coastal planning and management—either at the national or state levels of government. The CZMA was broadly and loosely structured, incorporating as it did, multiple (and possibly mutually incompatible) goals to conserve, manage and develop the nation's coasts. Its broad language meant that much discretion was left to the implementing agencies to operationalize and further refine the Congressional intent.

Although the legislation represented the most aggressive step yet taken by the federal government into land and water use at the state and local level, the orientation of the act was clearly pro-state. The state level was seen as the appropriate one to take the lead in developing coastal zone management plans; the federal role was seen as one of facilitating this development through the provision of federal grant-in-aids to the states. Moreover, the statute contained a provision, which although initially little noticed, was ultimately to give the states powerful leverage over federal activities in the coastal zone. The "consistency" provision promised the states that if they adopted coastal zone management programs deemed to meet the national interest and other tests found in the act and if they were willing to enforce their programs vis-a-vis other state and local interests, other federal agencies would also be bound by the state plans.

In terms of the implementation of the act, the federal implementors in the new Office of Coastal Zone Management at NOAA were favorably oriented toward the states and worked closely together with agencies in the coastal states to develop a state-level planning and management capability on coastal matters. In fact, the federal bureaucrats were, in many cases, responsible for influencing the selection by the state governors of the state agencies which would take the lead in coastal zone management functions. Over time, as the coastal management effort expanded, both the federal and state agencies came to be populated with personnel sharing similar backgrounds and professional experience--typically young planners with previous experience in allied areas such as urban planning.

Regarding interest group activity, in addition to environmental groups such as the Sierra Club and the Natural Resources Defense Council, the states had played a prominent role in the enactment of the CZMA. Collectively, for example, the National Governors Conference had passed strong resolutions favoring national coastal legislation in its 1969 and 1970 meetings; in 1970, it also authorized the creation of a sub-unit, the Coastal States Organization, for the specific purpose of obtaining national coastal zone management legislation. Individual states, too, which were pioneering coastal zone management efforts (such as California, Oregon, Washington, Rhode Island) became valued participants in the process of debating and shaping the national legislation (Cicin-Sain and Knecht, in preparation, Ch. 3).

In summary, then, in the case of coastal zone management, the federal government embarked upon a national program of coastal planning in the 1970s, taking the lead in an area with little previous intergovernmental history. The broad language contained in the act, the favorable disposition of the implementors toward the states, the fact that the state and federal coastal bureaucracies came to be populated with personnel with similar backgrounds--these are some of the major reasons why patterns of state/federal relations in this policy subsector have been, overall, very amicable and cooperative.

In contrast to the coastal management case where the CZMA filled a vacuum in an area with little history of state/federal interactions, the case of offshore oil development has been marked by a long tradition of state/federal conflict. In the 1930s and 1940s as it became evident that significant oil and gas resources existed offshore the United States, particularly in the

Gulf region and off California, a highly contentious struggle ensued between the states and the federal government over who would own these highly valuable resources (Miller 1984). The issue of jurisdiction was resolved--at least temporarily--in 1953, with the Submerged Lands Act (giving the states jurisdiction over resources in the territorial sea) and the Outer Continental Shelf Lands Act (giving the federal government authority in the area beyond the territorial sea), creating an unusual intergovernmental relations model of "dual geographical federalism" (Miller 1984). Nevertheless, issues related to defining a proper role for the states in decisions affecting the federal outer continental shelf and of sharing the substantial revenues which the federal treasury derives from this area [over 68 billion dollars betwen 1953 and 1983 (Hildreth 1986)] remain contentious.

The move to amend the OCS act in the mid-1970s, which culminated in the passage of the Outer Continental Shelf Lands Act Amendments of 1978, was led by environmental and state interests that wanted to incorporate a more stringent and elaborate environmental review process in the oil leasing, exploration and develoment process, and an enhanced role for the states and the public in oil decision-making. After four years of laborious negotiations, a compromise was hammered out among industry, environmentalists, and the states in the Congressional process that did achieve some of these goals, particularly with regard to the establishment of a much more detailed system of environmental review than existed previously. The gains made by the states in 1978, however, were limited: under sections 18 and 19 of the OCSLAA, the Secretary of the Interior prepares a five year plan for leasing lands on the outer continental shelf and consults with the governors of the affected states on the content of the plan. The consultation with the states required under the act is only that--consultation--with the Secretary of the Interior quite free to override state objections on national interest grounds.

A series of events that have taken place in the last several years demonstrates the inadequacy of this consultation mechanism and the continuing intergovernmental conflict over OCS oil and gas revenues. Annually between 1981 and 1985, Congress passed spending moratoria that set aside huge portions of the California, New England, and Florida coasts through a ban on expenditures for leasing activities (U.S. GAO 1985). The

Congress imposed these moratoria using the backdoor procedure of the appropriations process, thus circumventing the usual congressional committees that deal with energy matters. More recently, in a July 1985 ad hoc negotiation, a handful of California coastal congressmen and the Secretary of the Interior agreed to suspend the California portion of the moratorium and open up approximately 150 tracts for leasing. The new compromise was greeted with opposition by California representatives not involved in the deal, as well as by industry and some environmental groups. The DOI Secretary ultimately reneged on the agreement due to industry pressure, and in February 1986 unveiled his five year leasing plan calling for significant new leasing in California. Extensive opposition to the five year lease plan has been expressed by citizen groups and state and local representatives, and several legal suits are planned (Cicin-Sain 1986). This series of circumventions of the prescribed procedures for oil decision-making is clear evidence of a breakdown in the process, and demonstrates the inadequacy of the intergovernmental consultation mechanisms.

Much of the continuing intergovernmental controversy over OCS oil and gas resources can no doubt be attributed to the first two variables on our list: the great value of the resources at stake and the long tradition of state/federal conflict in this policy subsector. Given these two factors, some level of intergovernmental tension will probably always underlie this area. Nevertheless, factors related to the other variables we have discussed--structure of the statute, disposition of the implementors, nature of the state and federal bureaucracies, interest group orientations--all exacerbate these underlying tensions.

The process of amending the OCSLA, begun in Congress in 1974, was long, protracted and marked by the clashing of two major coalitions: the environmental and conservation groups, joined by national associations representing state and local governments and fishing interests, in favor of reforming the 1953 statute; the large oil companies, their trade associations, other business groups (such as the U.S. Chamber of Commerce), and the Department of the Interior (for much of this time period) opposing changes in the law (Cicin-Sain and Knecht, in preparation, Ch. 3). The final compromise that was achieved in 1978 represented a considerably watered down version of initial proposals calling for a strong state role in federal OCS decisions; as discussed, a rather weak "consultation only" mechanism was enacted. The Department of the Interior, which had vigorously opposed reform of the statute up until 1977, when the Carter administration came into power, was ill-prepared to implement the legislation and initially dragged its feet in producing the requisite federal regulations operationalizing the new requirements set forth by the Congress. Later on, with the advent of the administration of Secretary of the Interior James Watt, the disposition of the implementors could clearly be labelled as anti-state. Watt went about aggressively opening up for leasing, on an unprecedented scale, huge areas of the continental shelf, engendering in the process extensive litigation on the part of both environmental and state interests (Bruce 1984; Chasis 1984).

Added to this aggressive stance on the part of the federal government, the state agencies that represent state interests on ocean matters, such as the California Coastal Commission, have quite different orientations and are responsive to different statutes and constituencies than the largely single-purpose federal Minerals Management Service. The federal agency's major concern is maximizing for the United States the revenues derived from producing oil and gas from the outer continental shelf. In contrast, under both state law and the federal Coastal Zone Management Act, the California Coastal Commission has a multiple-use mandate to balance competing demands for using the ocean and the coastal zone. The interest groups that supported the 1978 amendments, as discussed, are generally in favor of environmental and state interests. These same groups, which were promoting an enhanced role for the states in OCS decisions and improved environmental review procedures in 1978 (such as the Coastal States Organization), are now leading efforts to once again amend the statute.

IMPLICATIONS

What implications does the analysis of these variables pose for the improvement of state/federal relations in these diverse marine policy subsectors? And what implications, if any, do these observations pose for theories on intergovernmental relations?

From the practical perspective of searching for methods for improving intergovernmental relations in marine resources management, several implications are suggested by the above analysis. First, the first two variables discussed—nature of the resources (their worth and tractability), and the existing history of state/federal interactions—are, in effect, constraints or parameters that set the context (positive or negative) of intergovernmental relations in each of the marine policy subsectors. These are variables over which decision-makers have little control. They are, in a way, givens that must be understood, acknowledged, and surmounted in cases where a negative context exists, as they are not very susceptible to change.

The other four variables, on the other hand, are more malleable and subject to change in varying degrees. These variables can potentially be manipulated by decision-makers desiring to improve state/federal relations. The structure of the statute is perhaps the most malleable of these variables. Statutes such as the Magnuson Act, which explicitly incorporate, in a variety of ways, the legitimate interests of the other relevant levels of government, are more likely to result in intergovernmental cooperation. Agency culture is a variable that is more difficult to change or manipulate. At a minimum, however, understanding of the barriers to communication that differences in agency culture, orientation, and type of personnel create, is a prerequisite to breaking down these barriers. The disposition of the implementors is a variable that can be influenced through the selection of appropriate political executives in the federal bureaucracy, a choice in which the Executive Office of the President has considerable say and the Congress has some say. With regard to the last variable, the role of interest groups in the enactment of the legislation and their continued interactions/alliances with either level of government, the political situation created by these interactions must first be understood, and then possibly altered by encouraging the growth of countervailing interest group power at other levels of government.

With regard to relevance to theories on intergovernmental relations, these observations question the wholesale applicability of "dominant" models of federalism to all policy areas. In my view, the notion of a dominant model of intergovernmental relations prevailing during particular time periods is based on a particular set of policy experiences—on the intergovernmental experience in the urban policy and economic policy areas. While these two areas represent a significant part of U.S.

domestic policy, they are certainly not representative of all types of policies. Patterns of federalism prevalent in these policy areas thus cannot be presumed to apply to all other areas.

The original studies and work done on policy implementation, too, had a federal urban/social policy bias, a bias that is now, to a large extent, being overcome as more research work has focused on other policy arenas and as significant attempts have been made to study how implementation processes vary according to the type of policy being implemented (e.g., distributive, regulatory and redistributive policies) (Ripley and Franklin 1986). Possibly in the intergovernmental relations literature, also, the time is ripe for moving beyond "dominant" model analyses to specifying the different forms that intergovernmental relations can take according to such variables as the type of policy involved. In the process of doing this, we can profitably use insights derived from the policy implementation success literature to explain variability in patterns of intergovernmental relations.

NOTES

1. Section 7 of the Endangered Species Act called for other federal agencies and departments to ". . . utilize their authorities in furtherance of the purposes of this Act [the ESA] . . . and to insure that actions authorized, funded or carried out by them do not jeopardize the continued existence of such endangered species and threatened species . . . or result in the destruction of the habitat of such species which is determined . . . to be critical."

260

REFERENCES

Bruce, Edward E. 1985. OCS Lease Sale Litigation: Can
It Be Avoided? In J.D. Nyhart, ed., Coastal Zone and
Continental Shelf Conflict Resolution: Improving
Ocean Use and Resource Dispute Management,
Massachusetts Institute of Technology, MITSG 85-28,
pp. 85-96.

Chasis, Sarah. 1985. Are There Ways to Improve Conflict
Resolution on the Outer Continental Shelf?" in J.D/
Nyhart, ed., Coastal Zone and Continental Shelf
Conflict Resolution: Improving Ocean Use and Resource
Dispute Management, Massachusetts Institute of
Technology, MITSG 85-28, pp. 97-99.

Cicin-Sain, Biliana. 1982. Managing the Ocean Commons:
U.S. Marine Programs in the Seventies and Eighties.
Marine Technology Society Journal, 16, (4): 6-18.

_____. 1986. Offshore Oil Development in
California: Challenges to Governments and to the
Public Interest. Public Affairs Reports, Institute of
Governmental Studies, University of California,
Berkeley, Spring.

Cicin-Sain, Biliana, Phyllis M. Grifman and John B.
Richards, eds. 1982. Social Science Perspectives on
Managing Conflicts Between Marine Mammals and
Fisheries. Santa Barbara, California: Marine Policy
Program, University of California.

Cicin-Sain, Biliana and Robert W. Knecht. In
preparation. Toward a U.S. Ocean Governance Regime:
Evolution and Political Change in Marine Policy in the
Seventies and Eighties.

Hildreth, Richard. 1986. Ocean Resources and
Intergovernmental Relations in the 1980s: Outer
Continental Shelf Hydrocarbons and Minerals. Chapter
6, this volume.

Knecht, Robert. 1984. Coastal Semantics: Offshore Oil
and Coastal Zone Management," The Amicus Journal
(Spring): 4-6.

Kaplan, Elizabeth R. 1982. California: Threatening the Golden Shore. In Joan Goldstein, ed., The Politics of Offshore Oil. New York: Praeger, pp. 3-26.

Manning, Laura L. 1986. The Dispute Processing Model of Public Policy Evolution: The Case of Endangered Species Policy Changes from 1973 to 1983. Doctoral dissertation, Department of Political Science, University of California, Santa Barbara, June.

Miller, Daniel S. 1984. Offshore Federalism: Evolving Federal-State Relations in Offshore Oil and Gas Development. Ecology Law Quarterly, 11 (3): 401-450.

Reagan, Michael D. and John G. Sanzone. 1981. The New Federalism. New York: Oxford University Press.

Rieser, Alison. 1986. Intergovernmental Relations in Marine Fisheries Management. Chapter 4, this volume.

Ripley, Randall B. and Grace A. Franklin. 1986. Policy Implementation and Bureaucracy, second edition. Chicago: The Dorsey Press.

Sabatier, Paul A. and Daniel A. Mazmanian. 1981. The Implementation of Public Policy: A Framework of Analysis. In Daniel A. Mazmanian and Paul A. Sabatier, eds., Effective Policy Implementation. Lexington, MA: D.C. Heath, pp. 3-35.

U.S. Department of Commerce. 1978. U.S. Ocean Policy in the 1970s: Status and Issues. Washington, D.C.: U.S. Government Printing Office.

U.S. General Accounting Office. 1985. Early Assessment of Interior's Area-Wide Program for Leasing Offshore Lands, GAO-RCED-85-66. Washington, D.C.: U.S. Government Printing Office, July 15.

Van Meter, Donald S. and Carl E. Van Horn. 1976. The Implementation of Inter-Governmental Policy. In Charles O. Jones and Robert D. Thomas, eds., Public Policy Making in a Federal System. Beverly Hills, California: Sage Publications.

262

Wright, Deil S. 1982. Understanding Intergovernmental Relations Monterey, California: Brooks/Cole Publishing Company.

10

The Exclusive Economic Zone: A New Opportunity in Federal-State Ocean Relations

Robert W. Knecht

INTRODUCTION

The coastal states of the United States have become increasingly concerned with the present intergovernmental arrangements delineating their role in the management of the resources found in the ocean waters adjacent to their shores. The existing system confines state jurisdiction and authority almost exclusively to the 3-mile band of ocean lying immediately adjacent to the shore--the territorial sea--even though the interests of the citizens of the coastal states are affected by activities located far seaward of this narrow zone. Coastal state interests are also adversely affected by the fragmented approach to ocean management employed in the federally-managed zone beyond 3 miles.

In March of 1983, President Reagan, in an action of great significance to the nation as a whole, proclaimed a new ocean zone fo the U.S.--an exclusive economic zone (EEZ) of 200-miles width. In taking this action, Reagan stated that he was acting consistently with international law which had come to recognize the legitimacy of such zones. Indeed, in the last dozen years or so, more than 50 nations have claimed EEZs of their own.

The coastal states recognized the importance of this development and in 1984 the Coastal States Organization (CSO) applied to the William H. Donner Foundation of New York City for a grant to study more fully the implications of the new EEZ on state-federal relations in ocean management. The states were in particular interested in new ocean activities such as ocean mining and incineration of toxic wastes and how they, the states, could be involved in the governance of the new ocean zone. The CSO EEZ study was begun in January of 1985 and has now proceeded through several stages. It is expected that the individual coastal states will act upon the recommendations coming out of the study at the annual meeting of CSO to be held in December 1986.

For the purpose of this chapter, I have attempted to summarize the general findings of the CSO EEZ study and to highlight some of the main points concerning state-federal relations in the EEZ. The reader will see that the results to date are a blend of the ideal and the pragmatic--a mix of what should be with what can be. The reader should also realize that the ideas presented here, while they eventually may become a part of the CSO policy on the EEZ, so far should be taken as simply the views of the author.

The remainder of the paper is in four parts:
--the nature of the EEZ;
--the responsibilities of government concerning ocean resources;
--some guiding principles for EEZ management;
--options for an improved system of ocean federalism.

THE NATURE OF THE EEZ

The exclusive economic zone, now incorporated into international law, had its origins in an action taken by the U.S. government under President Truman in 1945. By the end of World War II it was clear that there were likely to be substantial amounts of oil and gas underlying the continental shelves of the United States. In September of 1945, Truman issued a proclamation claiming the resources of the continental shelf for the United States. This was the first serious effort by any nation to extend its jurisdiction over resources beyond the narrow territorial sea--typically three or four miles in breadth. With this proclamation, the U.S. laid claim to an ocean area that extended out as far as 200 miles or more from its shores, depending on the width of the geological shelf.

This move by the United States represented a fundamental change in the ocean jurisdictional situation and it triggered similar actions by a number of other nations over the next two decades. Nations without continental shelves invented other pretexts to support extensions of their jurisdiction, for example, the protection of important fisheries stocks. Latin American nations in particular found support in the U.S. move for their earlier notion of "patrimonial seas" and were quick to proclaim their own 200-miles zones, capturing valuable offshore tuna resources in the process.

Nation after nation followed suit and by the time that the Third United Nations Conference on the Law of the Sea (UNCLOS III) convened in the mid-70s, it was well accepted that coastal nations could claim the resources in a relatively broad belt of sea adjacent to their territorial seas. This principle was codified and elaborated in the EEZ articles of the LOS Convention and is now firmly a part of international law.

In March of 1983, President Reagan, perhaps as part of an effort to show a positive ocean policy following U.S. rejection of the LOS Convention, proclaimed an exclusive economic zone of 200-miles width around the entire U.S. shoreline. This action more than doubled the amount of area, land and ocean, over which the United States now has resource jurisdiction.

Many observers, including this one, feel that the U.S. adoption of an EEZ is a very significant action with important long term implications. For the first time, an offshore closing line has been established which encompasses almost all U.S. marine jurisdiction. Up to this point, we have had a series of resource or activity-specific laws which had varying types of rights, each with its own implied or specific seaward geographic limit. But in this action, the President established a zone of uniform width within which a set of uniform legal rights--sovereign rights--apply.

The existence of this new zone--the EEZ--offers a splendid opportunity to reexamine the manner in which we have been managing ocean resources and particularly to look at the issue of the state and federal roles in ocean management. This is because (1) management arrangements in the new zone are likely to be examined by Congress sometime in the near future; (2) a number of coastal states are experiencing growing frustration with the present state-federal arrangements and the degree of conflict generated seems to be increasing; and (3) recent changes in international ocean law could affect federal and state roles in ocean governance.

The next section outlines present governmental responsibilities/duties with respect to the conservation and development of ocean resources. An attempt is made to

determine the extent to which the federal or state levels
of government must assume certain of these
responsibilities.

THE RESPONSIBILITIES OF GOVERNMENT CONCERNING OCEAN RESOURCES

Before discussing the principles that ought to define
possible new intergovernmental arrangements in the EEZ, it
is useful to examine the role of government in general and
the range and variety of its responsibilities with regard
to the conservation and development of ocean resources.
Some of the complications, complexities, and tensions
associated with ocean management undoubtedly arise because
of the multiple and sometimes conflicting purposes of
government with regard to the oceans.

Listed in Table 1 are six broad purposes that
government serves in the ocean. Those at the top of the
list are clearly "national" in nature and would most
likely be carried out by agencies of the federal
government, whereas the final two roles arguably could be
performed by either the federal or state level of
government.

Coastal state governments have strong interests in how
these governmental roles are performed in the EEZ since
major segments of their coastal populations can be
affected. Four specific "interests" of the coastal states
in the management of EEZ resources can be singled out:

1. Coastal states are "home" to most users of the
EEZ; hence coastal states and their citizens have major
economic interests in the conservation and rational
development of the EEZ.

2. Coastal states have important "public trust"
responsibilities and economic interests within their own
jurisdictions to protect; hence they have to be concerned
with "spillovers" and other adverse environmental effects
emanating from poorly regulated uses in the adjacent EEZ
that could damage state resources.

3. New EEZ-related activities compete with other
ocean activities of economic interest to the coastal
states and their communities for access to valuable and
limited coastal space for necessary shoreside facilities
(ports, processing plants, etc.) resources, often at the
expense of the traditional users.

4. Coastal states are "owners" (proprietors) of the ocean resources lying immediately adjacent (landward) of the EEZ and hence are concerned with "drainage" of state oil and gas fields and other actions that could reduce the value of state resources.

Table 1

GOVERNMENTAL ROLES IN THE OCEAN

Role	Function
1. INTERNATIONAL RELATIONS	– insure consistency with foreign policy goals
2. NATIONAL SECURITY	– maintain the national defense
3. INTERSTATE COMMERCE	– protect free commerce between the states
4. PROPRIETARIAL	– as resource owner, secure maximum earnings for the public
5. PUBLIC TRUST	– conserve renewable resources for future generations
6. REGULATORY	– protect the public welfare, prevent conflict

Given these four interests, the coastal states necessarily have to be concerned with many of the actions of federal agencies taken in connection with the governmental purposes set out in Table 1. The degree and magnitude of coastal state interest will depend upon the nature of the demands and risks placed upon state and local resources (including the shoreland) as well as the risks to EEZ resources of major economic interest to the adjacent coastal state (for example, fisheries).

As a step in developing its EEZ policy position, CSO is formulating a set of guiding principles that it feels are fundamental to rational resources management in the EEZ. These principles deal with the issues of equity (in decision-making, in sharing of benefits), the characteristics of a rational management system, and our obligations to future generations, and are summarized in the next section.

SOME GUIDING PRINCIPLES FOR EEZ MANAGEMENT

While the resources of the EEZ are legally owned by the nation as a whole, the impacts of development of those resources, both positive and negative, fall disproportionately on the citizens of the adjacent coastal states. The challenge, therefore, is to devise a new kind of ocean federalism, one that recognizes the need to balance fairly the benefits to be derived by the nation from particular EEZ developments with the costs to be borne by others having legitimate but different interests in the EEZ.

As mentioned above, to be fully equitable, such a scheme should accommodate four (often competing) sets of interests:
   --the interests of the nation as a whole;
   --the interests of competing ocean users;
   --the interests of affected coastal states;
   --the interests of future generations of Americans.
[Examination of our present system of ocean management in federal waters shows, I believe, major shortcomings in accommodating three out of four of these interests; only the national interest seems to be adequately handled.]

As one stage in the formulation of an EEZ policy, the coastal states are setting down the principles that they believe are important in guiding the development of a new EEZ management system. Those most relevant to the intergovernmental aspects of ocean management are listed below.

1. Given the riches of the oceans adjacent to the United States, the recent proclamation of a U.S. 200-mile EEZ offers the promise of great benefits to the American people. To obtain these benefits, early national attention should be given to the creation of an appropriate management regime for the conservation and development of the resources of the EEZ.

2. Given their proximity to the sea and the extent to
which activities in the adjacent ocean affect the economy
and environment of coastal areas, coastal states have
substantial additional interests beyond those of the
inland states in the rational management of the EEZ.

3. It is neither feasible nor desirable for the
national government to attempt to represent all of the
public interests in ocean activities beyond the
territorial sea. As general purpose governments with
existing coastal and ocean competence, the coastal states
are best equipped to act on behalf of the ocean interests
of their citizens.

4. The overall goal of EEZ resources management
should be to provide sustained long term benefits to the
people of the nation as a whole while ensuring that the
impacts on the citizens of the coastal states are
equitably handled.

5. The extension of ownership over the resources of
the EEZ by the United States carries with it an inherent
public trust duty to conserve renewable resources and
ensure access to those resources for future generations.
Since the present and future citizens of the coastal
states are those most likely to be affected by the
discharge of this duty (or the failure to do so), coastal
state governments have a special responsibility to ensure
that this public trust duty is fully incorporated into EEZ
resource decisions.

6. The present dividing line between state and
federal jurisdiction in the ocean--the seaward limit of
the 3-mile territorial sea--measures only the presently
legislated division in the ownership of ocean resources.
Very substantial economic and environmental interests of
the coastal states exist well beyond this arbitrary line.

7. Recent changes in international law as it applies
to the oceans--specifically, the formal recognition of a
200-mile zone (the EEZ) within which coastal nations have
essentially total control over resources--opens the way
for a reconsideration of the roles played by the federal
and state governments in the management of ocean
resources. Resource exploitation in the U.S. EEZ has now
effectively become a domestic issue and as such,
principally the concern of the state and federal
governments of the United States. It is no longer the
legitimate interest of other nations. Resource-related
exploratory and development activities in the EEZ can and
should be viewed as separate and distinguishable from
other ocean uses of an international character (e.g.,

navigation).

8. Long term commitments of fixed ocean and shoreside space to a given activity should be considered major ocean use decisions and should require the mutual consent of the federal government and the affected coastal state. Coastal states and communities which are full participants in such major ocean use activities should receive an appropriate share of the governmental revenues from such activities.

9. The economic and social benefits of the EEZ will be more quickly and efficiently realized if an orderly and stable regulatory framework is in place. Predictability comes with the establishment of a fully equitable system—one in which all affected parties are effectively represented in the established decision-making process and hence do not have to rely on delay tactics, such as legal action, to have their concerns properly addressed.

10. The interconnected and dynamic character of the physical and biological systems in the ocean places certain demands on the planning and management process. In particular, the process must be an integrated one with a workable decision-making capacity to deal with various kinds of resources and uses. The single-purpose approach to ocean management now in use will become increasingly inefficient in handling multiple uses in the EEZ.

11. An efficient EEZ management system will be one that has the capacity to accommodate advance planning for important ocean areas, to facilitate informed trade-offs among various uses, and to bring about the early and equitable resolution of conflicts between competing ocean uses or users. Effective EEZ management will result in multiple use to the maximum extent permitted by conservation considerations, in maximum benefits to the public, in the predictability needed for private sector decision-making, and will provide the stewardship needed on behalf of future generations.

OPTIONS FOR AN IMPROVED SYSTEM OF OCEAN FEDERALISM

As they reach the final stages of their EEZ study, the coastal states are considering how best to obtain an EEZ management scheme that is consistent with the guiding principles listed above. Five rather different approaches have been studied:

I. <u>Voluntary (using the discretion available under existing ocean legislation)</u>: In this approach, federal agencies would agree (after considerable discussion, no doubt) to recognize and incorporate additional "interests" into their EEZ decision-making. Existing mechanisms for coordination and cooperation would be expanded, especially at the regional level, to provide timely coastal state (and other) input to federal managers. Memoranda of Understanding would be employed to record these new arrangements.

II. <u>Presidential Executive Order</u>: Basically the same as I above, except that an Executive Order signed by the President would be used to put in place the modified EEZ decision-making scheme. Federal ocean managers would be required to take account of coastal state input within the limits set out in the Executive Order. Existing ocean legislation would be unaffected since the new rules would be within the discretion already contained in the legislation.

III. <u>Legislative Overlay</u>: Here, new legislation would be drafted which would define "major ocean use decisions" (or a similar concept) and would require concurrent decision-making by the affected coastal state and the federal government before such projects could go ahead. Hence, shared decision-making would be required on large offshore oil projects, ocean mining activities, and in connection with the approval of certain kinds of ocean disposal sites.

IV. <u>Ocean Policy Commission</u>: The approach here would be for coastal states to support pending proposals calling for the creation of a high level national ocean policy commission. The coastal states would urge that such a commission be established as soon as possible, and make recommendations for a second generation U.S. ocean management system capable of adequately handling our increasing use of the oceans. The states would also encourage study of possible new regional entities to manage ocean resources and study of the ways in which a broadened U.S. territorial sea might affect state-federal interests in ocean management.

V. Ocean Awareness, Education, and Planning:
Slightly different than the other approaches, this
option calls for an increased coastal state role in
making the public aware of the oceans and their
potential benefits. Coastal states would also take
the initiative in the formulation of strategic plans
for the conservation and development of the EEZ lying
adjacent to their shores.

It is not the purpose of this chapter to attempt to
forecast the position that the coastal states will adopt
concerning the EEZ in December of 1986. Rather, the
purpose is to describe the process being followed by this
group as it attempts to reconfigure ocean federalism to
better suit its needs and the changing situation.

Regardless of the specific positions and actions
decided upon by the coastal states and any responses to
them by the Congress and/or the administration, particular
emerging ocean problems will almost certainly force their
way onto the national agenda, thus ensuring that
state-federal relations in ocean matters will continue as
a prominent national topic over the next several years.
Three of these problems are listed below.

--EEZ ocean mining legislation: A consensus has
developed that a new legislative framework is needed
to establish an appropriate regulatory regime for
ocean mining in the EEZ. Use of the oil/gas
legislation to govern ocean mining is felt to be
inappropriate. This new legislation will force
consideration of state and federal roles in ocean
management.

--Ocean incineration of toxic wastes: EPA will
continue to attempt to authorize research burns off
the East and Gulf coasts and the affected coastal
states will continue to object until a more
satisfactory state-federal decision-making process is
put into place.

--Ocean disposal of radioactive wastes: The member
nations of the London Dumping Convention recently put
in place a moratorium on the ocean dumping of low
level nuclear waste. Representatives of the U.S.
government were against the moratorium but were
outvoted. Given this and the fact that the United
States continues to study the oceans as a disposal

site for high level nuclear wastes, the whole issue of
the oceans and radioactive waste will surely soon
arise domestically. At that time, part of the debate
will necessarily focus on the role and standing of
adjacent coastal states with regard to the use of the
oceans for such activities.

Making predictions about the future is risky business
in any field. It is especially so in a field as volatile
as ocean management. Nonetheless, I feel that several
trends in intergovernmental relations regarding the oceans
are reasonably likely:

i. The federal government will continue to reduce its
effort and its financial support for coastal state
programs in the areas of coastal planning and
management, and since the problems continue, the
coastal states will pick up an increasing share of the
support for this work.

ii. The coastal states will be seen increasingly as
important contributors to national ocean policy,
filling the void being left by the federal government.

iii. Negotiation and bargaining between federal
agencies and affected coastal states will be used more
and more to settle ocean disputes. Eventually, these
ad hoc approaches will be replaced by national EEZ
management legislation which embraces the principles
hammered out in the individual settlements.

iv. A national ocean policy commission will be
created by legislation and will (eventually) recommend
a fundamentally restructured ocean management program,
one in which the state and federal roles are made
consistent with new demands, realities, and
competence. The recommendations of the commission
will pave the way for expansion of the U.S.
territorial sea to 12 miles and will set the stage for
a new and more equitable division of resource
ownership in the expanded zone. In this way, the
coastal states will acquire not only additional
planning and management responsibility, but also the
resources and incentives necessary to do the job.

About the Authors

THOMAS J. ANTON

Professor Anton came to Brown from the University of
Michigan in 1983 to become the founder and director of
Brown's new A. Alfred Taubman Center for Public Policy
and American Institutions. He has been a Fulbright
Fellow, a Guggenheim Fellow and holder of the John F.
Kennedy Fellowship from the government of Sweden in
addition to being the recipient of numerous grants
from foundations and government agencies. His recent
books include Moving Money: An Empirical Analysis of
Federal Expenditure Patterns and Federal Aid to
Detroit, and he is currently working on a book on
federalism to be published by Random House. In
addition to his activities at Brown, Professor Anton
is a member of the Technical Review Panel for the
United States Treasury Department's "Studies of
Federal, State and Local Fiscal Relations." Locally,
he was recently appointed a commissioner of the
Providence Housing Authority.

DOROTHA M. BRADLEY

Dr. Bradley is a graduate of Mills College and
recently received her Ph.D. in Political Science from
the University of Arizona. Her research interests are
in the fields of public environmental and natural
resource policy and American institutions. Most
recently her work has concentrated on the relationship
of federalism to public lands and water policy.

BILIANA CICIN-SAIN

A marine policy specialist, Dr. Cicin-Sain is an
Associate Professor of Political Science at the

275

University of California at Santa Barbara. She has
written articles on implementation of U.S. ocean laws,
on resolution of conflicts among multiple ocean users,
on comparative marine policy, and on fisheries
management policy. Her previous background includes
service as a policy analyst in the National Oceanic
and Atmospheric Administration and the Department of
Housing and Urban Development in Washington, D.C., and
visiting research appointments at the Marine Policy
and Ocean Management Center of the Woods Hole
Oceanographic Institution, Harvard University and the
University of Southern California.

MICHAEL S. HAMILTON

Assistant Professor of Political Science at the
University of Southern Maine, specializing in natural
resources/environmental politics and administration.
He is the author of articles in Policy Studies
Journal, Natural Resources Journal, and the Journal of
Energy Policy and Law. His recent interests concern
coastal growth management; impacts of retrenchment
practices on bureaucracy and administration, the
search for the public interest in official
decision-making, and state policies for regulation of
power plant siting.

MARC J. HERSHMAN

Professor Marine Studies, Adjunct Professor of Law,
and Acting Director of the Institute for Marine
Studies (1986-87), University of Washington, Seattle.
His expertise in law and public affairs has been
applied to a wide range of coastal zone and marine
resource management problems, including shoreline
industrial siting, port development, environmental
protection, fish and wildlife mitigation, urban
waterfront revitalization, and national marine
policy. He directs a Sea Grant research and advisory
services program within the Institute and is the
author of a textbook on coastal management. He is
also editor-in-chief of the Coastal Zone Management
Journal and has been President of The Coastal Society.

RICHARD HILDRETH

Professor of Law and Co-Director of the Ocean and
Coastal Law Center at the University of Oregon's
School of Law. His first professional involvement
with the coast was during the early 1970s in southern

California where extensive condominium development was
leading to serious beach erosion. To gain an
international perspective on coastal management he
took a Fulbright grant in 1973 to study the subject in
Sweden, augmenting that experience with a recent
sabbatical year in Australia and New Zealand. As his
recent role in reviewing and recommending changes for
Oregon's coastal zone legal regimes would suggest,
Hildreth strives to put his expertise into practice.
The text, Ocean and Coastal Law, he has coauthored
with Ralph Johnson, is considered the definitive
treatment of that subject to date.

HELEN M. INGRAM

Professor of Political Science and Adjunct Professor
of Law, University of Arizona. Dr. Ingram received
her undergraduate degree from Oberlin College and her
Ph.D. in public law and government from Columbia
University. Her areas of expertise include water and
natural resource policy. She is current president of
the Policy Studies Organization and is the treasurer
of the American Political Science Association. She is
the author of many books in the area of public policy,
especially water policy. Among her publications is
the co-authored book, Saving Water in a Desert City.

STEPHEN R. KELLERT

Associate Professor, School of Forestry and
Environmental Studies, Yale University. Dr. Kellert
has conducted extensive research on the socioeconomic
aspects of wildlife conservation and management. His
current research includes a study of Japanese
attitudes towards the environment.

LAURISTON KING

Deputy Director of the Texas A&M Sea Grant College
Program and Adjunct Professor of Political Science at
Texas A&M. He has written on the politics of higher
education, various issues in marine policy, and has
contributed chapters to books and articles to journals
including Polity, Ocean Development and International
Law, Marine Technology Society Journal, and Oceanus.
He is currently engaged in a study of the role of
Congress in ocean policy.

ROBERT W. KNECHT
Adjunct Senior Lecturer in the Political Science and
Environmental Studies Departments at the University of
California at Santa Barbara. He also consults in the
fields of ocean and coastal management. Between 1981
and 1984, Knecht was a Senior Fellow in the Marine
Policy Center of the Woods Hole Oceanographic
Institution specializing in ocean policy advice to
developing countries including Colombia and Ecuador.
Earlier he served in a variety of positions with the
National Oceanic and Atmospheric Administration
including Assistant Administrator for Coastal Zone
Management and Director of the Office of Ocean
Minerals and Energy. Since 1984, Knecht has made his
home in Santa Barbara, California with his wife, Dr.
Biliana Cicin-Sain, who is also active in political
science and marine policy fields.

JAMES P. LESTER
Associate Professor of Political Science at Colorado
State University, where he specializes in state/local
politics and public policy analysis (especially
environmental policy). He is the co-editor of The
Politics of Hazardous Waste Management (Duke
University Press, 1983) and author of several articles
in Western Political Quarterly, Policy Studies
Journal, Publius, Ocean Development and International
Law, and State and Local Government Review. His
current interest is concerned with the impact of
President Reagan's "New Federalism" on state
environmental policy.

ALISON RIESER
Director of the Marine Law Institute, University of
Southern Maine, and Lecturer in Ocean and Coastal Law,
University of Maine School of Law, is a lawyer (J.D.,
The George Washington University) and marine policy
analyst with ten years experience in government and
policy research. Formerly with the U.S. Environmental
Protection Agency and NOAA, she was an
Attorney-Advisor for Fisheries in the NOAA Office of
General Counsel during the first year of
implementation of the MFCMA. She subsequently served
as a consultant to the New England Fishery Management
Council. She was a Research Fellow at the Marine
Policy and Ocean Management Center at the Woods Hole

Oceanographic Institution. She is editor of the
quarterly newsletter, Territorial Sea.

MAYNARD SILVA

Dr. Silva holds a Ph.D. in Political Science from the
University of California, Santa Barbara. He is
currently a Research Specialist with the Marine Policy
and Ocean Management Center of the Woods Hole
Oceanographic Institution. His research has included
analysis of marine resources management in the United
States, Colombia, Ecuador, Mexico, and Canada. He has
published articles on marine policy in Ocean
Development and International Law and Coastal Zone
Management Journal. He is currently editing a
symposium issue, entitled "The Ocean and Public
Policy," for Policy Studies Journal.